INTANGIBLES

Also by Joan Ryan

Molina (with Bengie Molina)

The Water Giver

Shooting From the Outside (with Tara VanDerveer)

Little Girls in Pretty Boxes

INTANGIBLES

UNLOCKING THE SCIENCE AND SOUL OF TEAM CHEMISTRY

JOAN RYAN

HarperCollins*Publishers*

HarperCollins*Publishers*
1 London Bridge Street
London SE1 9GF

www.harpercollins.co.uk

First published in the US by Little, Brown and Company,
a division of Hachette Book Group, Inc. 2020
First published in the UK by HarperCollins*Publishers* 2020

1 3 5 7 9 10 8 6 4 2

A catalogue record of this book is
available from the British Library

ISBN 978-0-00-824111-7

Printed and bound in Great Britain by
CPI Group (UK) Ltd, Croydon

MIX
Paper from
responsible sources
FSC™ C007454

This book is produced from independently certified FSC™ paper
to ensure responsible forest management.

For more information visit: www.harpercollins.co.uk/green

To Mike Krukow

CONTENTS

INTANGIBLES

INTRODUCTION

"The contribution of team chemistry to winning is easily the biggest hype in sports."

—Richard Lally in
The Enlightened Bracketologist

"Every once in a while you hear an expert that says team chemistry is overrated. You just write that person off."
—Hall of Fame baseball manager Tony La Russa

When my mother died suddenly at the age of seventy-six, she and my father had been married fifty-five years. My father, who was seventy-nine at the time of her death, had minor back problems and occasional memory lapses but otherwise was pretty healthy. Soon, however, his appetite waned, and his mental acuity deteriorated. While doctors struggled to find anything wrong, his once-broad shoulders became a wire hanger beneath his shirt. He was flummoxed by the telephone and remote control. And then, nine months after we buried my mother, he died. The cause of death was the puzzling "failure to thrive."

I knew the term only in connection to babies, having remembered learning about "sterile" orphanages in Europe at the turn of the century. To stop the spread of germs and disease, nurses were instructed to hang sterilized sheets between the cribs and to refrain from touching the babies except to feed, clothe, and bathe them. Soon the babies were sicker than ever. They ate less. They were more lethargic. Many contracted the very diseases the sterile practices were meant to prevent. Death rates soared to 75 percent at some orphanages. At one institution, every baby died. Similarly, hospitalized children cut off from their parents for long stretches of time often withered and died.[1] Doctors were stumped.

Not until the 1940s, when Austrian-American psychiatrist René Spitz began to study the case, did a theory begin to emerge: Babies need physical and social interaction to flourish. To test his hypothesis, he found two groups of babies to compare.[2]

One was being raised in an orphanage, the other in a women's prison. The orphans were essentially isolated in their cribs, with a lone nurse tasked with caring for seven babies. The second group lived in the prison nursery where their mothers cared for them every day. These babies also interacted with other babies and the nursery staff. After a year, Spitz compared the two groups. In motor skills and cognitive performance, the orphans severely lagged behind their prison counterparts. After two years, 37 percent of the orphans had died but none of the prisoners' babies. By the third year, the prison infants walked and talked at levels comparable to those of children raised in family settings. At the orphanage, only two of the twenty-six children could walk and articulate a few words.

American psychologist Harry Harlow built on Spitz's research. Anyone who has taken an intro to psychology class probably remembers Harlow's disturbing experiments on rhesus monkeys in the 1950s.[3] Baby rhesus monkeys were taken from their mothers soon after birth and put in cages with two inanimate surrogate "mothers." One was a bare-wire figure with a square plastic head; it offered 24-hour access to milk. The other figure was layered with soft terrycloth and had a round face with big eyes and a smile. But it offered no food. The monkeys spent nearly all their time cuddling and embracing the terrycloth surrogate. They left it only to feed quickly at the bare-wire mother. The researchers then took the terrycloth mother away for up to nine months. The babies eventually lost interest in eating. They behaved erratically. They curled up in a ball. Vital body rhythms—heart, respiration, sleep—were disrupted. Like the orphanage babies and my widowed father, they died from "failure to thrive."

The results of these studies clearly show that babies need more than just caretaking to develop normally. They need to meet another's gaze, to be held close, to hear the lilt of a voice and the beat of a heart. Like all primates, humans are pack animals. We all have our tribes, whether family, congregation, friends, workplace, or team. We need connection today as much as we did when our ancestors lived in caves. And it's not just infants, of course. Like the case of my own parents, long marriages that end with a spouse passing can often catalyze the death of the widow or widower. My mother's presence provided something more essential to my father than food, water, or sleep.

On a July afternoon in 2009, a few years before my parents died, I found myself in a large white tent outside of what was then called AT&T Park in San Francisco. There, a group of middle-aged former baseball players were gathered for a reunion. Some were businessmen now. Some still made their living in baseball. There were a few jowls. A smattering of beer bellies. Two or three looked like they could still leg out a slow grounder. Bursts of laughter punctuated the conversations. The familiar give-and-take. And something else. I could hear it in their voices and see it on their faces, exactly as I remembered: They still loved each other.

Twenty years earlier, these men had drenched each other with champagne as 1989 National League champions. I was a youngish sports columnist for the *San Francisco Examiner* at the time, but that season and those players have stayed with me throughout my career. As with every romance in my life, I fell first for their story. They were a junk-drawer jumble of a team, rife with factions that had the potential to split the clubhouse: hard-drinking carousers and born-again Christians, African-Americans and Southern whites, Latinos from three different countries, college guys and functional illiterates, ambitious youngsters jockeying for roster spots and fading veterans trying to hold on. I never knew exactly what I'd find when I pushed open the clubhouse door back then. Maybe it would be the portly ace pitcher perched on the exercise bike with a Parliament in one hand and the *Chronicle*'s crossword puzzle in the other; or the kid from New Orleans with the lopsided grin tossing insults in his happy, high-pitched screech; or the six-feet-six-inch snarl of a man whom teammates called Buffy (to his great irritation) barking again at the beat writers for some obscure slight. At least one of the Christian players—God Squadders, we called them—would have his head in his Bible, perhaps reciting a prayer for whichever teammate thought it'd be funny to slip a pornographic photo into Leviticus. I'd surely see the hairy, funny veteran everyone called Caveman hobbling toward the trainer's room for treatment on his scarred, patched, curbside-couch of a body. Their unlikely star that year was a gold-toothed former gangbanger who had been traded twice in seven months, nearly quit the game, and then found redemption among these men in the dank concrete clubhouse in the bowels of old Candlestick Park.

The ringleader, den mother, and raconteur of that team was a cop's son named Mike Krukow, a pitcher whose arm was so shredded by '89 that he couldn't raise it high enough to comb his hair. But he still loved the game like a kid and seemed to know exactly what a teammate needed and when he needed it. Those '89 players fought and judged, competed and goaded, and loved each other openly and without reservation. They bridged every fissure that season. It was a Peter Gent novel: raucous, funny, tender, heartbreaking, and ending not with a Disney triumph but with the literal fissure and fracture of a 6.9 earthquake in the middle of the World Series.

Two decades later, almost every one of them showed up for the reunion, flying in from Horseheads, New York, and Pittsburgh, Pennsylvania, and Lake Havasu, Arizona. As I made my way through the party tent, catching up with everyone, two words kept popping up: team chemistry. It's a term you hear a lot in sports. The triumph of the scraggly, big-hearted team has been a story-telling trope since at least as far back as Gideon's overmatched army in the Old Testament. From *Braveheart* to *The Bad News Bears,* from *The Magnificent Seven* to *Hoosiers,* Hollywood has served up the formula in a million different ways. I love all of them. I'm a total sucker. Show me Gene Hackman's underdog high schoolers from Hickory, Indiana, slow clapping in the locker room, and I'm reaching for the Kleenex.

While, in real life, team chemistry is often dismissed as a throwaway explanation for every over-achieving, fun-loving team (Look! We all have beards!), those '89 Giants sure seemed to have *something* going on that defied traditional explanations. I'd seen glimmers of the phenomenon on other teams, too, of course, during the twenty-five years I've worked as a journalist in sports— fifteen as a sports columnist and more than a decade as a media consultant with the San Francisco Giants. On those teams, the players seemed to make each other better. I had experienced it myself in my first job out of college, in the *Orlando Sentinel's* sports department. We were a tight-knit staff of a few rookies like me and a slate of veterans who deleted our adverbs and introduced us to scotch. We'd go out for burgers and beer around midnight after we put the paper to bed. Every July, we'd gather at dawn at Bill Baker's apartment to watch the finals of Wimbledon and knock a tennis ball around afterward. Looking back, I'm struck by how easily we organized ourselves as a tribe, with roles to play and inside jokes and a vague sense that who we were in that group was different from who we were with anyone else. We liked each other, helped each other, and took enormous pride in what we produced every day. The sports section was better because of it.

If *some* human beings possess the ability to have such a profound physiological impact on each other, as spouses and caretakers of babies do, it stands to reason that all human beings have the ability, at least to some extent, to influence the performance and productivity of those around them. Could the success of the '89 Giants be a foundational example of the power of team chemistry?

With that question in mind, I began reading research papers and books on group dynamics, psychology, emotion, linguistics, love, the military, neuroscience, gender, leadership, evolutionary biology, mirror neurons, and a variety of sports. Really, just about anything I could get my hands on that might provide some insight into how we perform better or worse based on who we are around.

I came across a story in the *New York Times* with the headline "The 'Love Hormone' As Sports Enhancer" about a neuropeptide called oxytocin. This is the stuff that is produced in the brain and released in our bloodstream when, for example, we fall in love or when women go through labor or breastfeed, fostering strong feelings of trust and connection. It can also be triggered by meaningful touch.

Aha! Suddenly a lot of things I had seen in sports began to make total sense. Male athletes are so much more physically affectionate with one another than men in general (at least American men). They *always* seem to be touching each other—hugging, high-fiving, slinging their arms around one another, holding hands at courtside as the final seconds tick down in a close basketball game. In the Giants' clubhouse, I've seen guys on the couch draped over each other like puppies as they watched TV. I watched a player in the dugout rubbing the top of a teammate's head for good luck through an entire inning. Teammates embrace with full-bodied gusto, not with the shoulder bump that passes for a hug in the outside male world.

Now I know the scientific explanation for all that touching. Oxytocin helps them to bond and to operate as a close-knit tribe. A gesture of trust, such as a reassuring arm around a teammate's shoulders, triggers the release of oxytocin in the recipient's bloodstream, creating a reciprocal feeling of trust and connection. Evolutionary psychologists theorize this is why oxytocin developed in humans (and lower primates). We needed a trustworthy pack with whom to hunt, gather food, and fend off enemies. The human brain had to figure out a way to create bonds so strong that members would sacrifice themselves for the survival of the group.

What's particularly fascinating about touch and the release of oxytocin is that, through a network of "mirror neurons," the feelings of trust and bonding that they trigger are contagious. Mirror neurons were first observed during experiments with macaque monkeys in the early 1990s. Italian researchers had monkeys pick up objects and then observe fellow monkeys picking up objects. The same set of brain cells leapt into action whether they were carrying out the action or simply watching it. These brain cells came to be known as mirror neurons.[4]

Through brain imaging, we know that humans have mirror neurons, too. Neuroscientist and psychologist Christian Keysers, now at the University of Amsterdam, tested the phenomenon in an experiment similar to the macaque-monkey research.[5] He split a group of fourteen participants into two groups. One group was lightly touched on the leg with a feather duster. The other group simply watched a video of someone being touched on the same spot. The same area of the somatosensory cortex was active whether the person felt the feather or simply watched someone else being touched by the feather.

In other experiments, people were monitored as they watched videos of happy faces and angry faces. The cheek muscles we use for smiling were activated in people watching happy faces, and the brow muscles we use when we're angry were activated in people watching angry faces. Marco Iacoboni, a UCLA neurologist and neuroscience professor who wrote the book *Mirroring People: The Science of Empathy and How We Connect with Others,* believes this phenomenon is what helps us to feel empathy. We mirror other people in order to identify the emotion they're feeling. One study tested this theory by having subjects hold a pencil between their teeth, thus severely restricting their ability to mimic. They performed much worse in detecting emotional changes in other people's facial expressions. (This raises interesting questions about the connection between the flat affect common to those on the autism spectrum and their poor ability to read other people's emotions.)

Iacoboni's research has found that the more people like each other, the more they seem to mimic. "Couples have a higher facial similarity after twenty-five years of marriage," he wrote. "The higher the quality of the marriage, the higher the facial similarity. The spouses become a second self."

The impact of mirror neurons is a major factor in explaining how team chemistry may work on a biological level. A locker room is an enclosed environment where everyone sees everything. So is a dugout, a bus, or a plane. Let's say Buster Posey drapes his arm around a rookie and tells him his perfect throw from right field that nailed a base runner saved the game. The rookie's bloodstream floods with oxytocin. He's feeling happy and confident and connected to the superstar veteran in a way he hadn't felt before. Now let's imagine another rookie is watching this interaction from across the clubhouse. The mirror neurons in his brain "feel" Buster's touch as if it's happening to himself. His somatosensory cortex lets loose a hit of oxytocin, and this rookie feels happier and more connected to Buster Posey, too. Amazing.

Of all the sports I could choose to illustrate team chemistry, baseball might seem the least likely. Basketball, football, soccer, hockey, and almost any other would seem more relevant: In those sports, players have to cooperate on every play—passing balls or pucks to each other, blocking, screening. Yes, baseball players throw the ball to each other, but that's about it for cooperative interaction on the field. The batter, pitcher, and fielder stand alone. With rare exceptions—such as double-play combos and pitcher-catcher conferences—no player can help a teammate complete his assigned task. In that way, team chemistry would seem to apply least to baseball.

Which is exactly *why* I chose to focus largely on baseball. America's "national pastime" is more like a regular workplace than any other sport. In most offices, employees are alone in a cubicle performing an individual task. The employee's task is integral to the common goal, whether manufacturing cell phones, designing software, or putting out a newspaper. Understanding how team chemistry works in a baseball clubhouse, consequently, helps us understand how it works in any group with a shared purpose.

Michael Lewis's book *Moneyball* had come out a few years before I attended the Giants' reunion. The book famously pitted the intuition and wisdom of old-school baseball scouts against the statistical analysis of a new generation. Baseball analyst Bill James coined the word "sabermetrics" back in 1980 to describe this growing field of baseball analytics, a nod to the Society for American Baseball Research (SABR). Of course, even before Lewis's bestseller, most major-league teams already were using analytics to evaluate players. But after *Moneyball*, every front office suddenly had bunkers of young Ivy Leaguers churning out proprietary algorithms and new statistical categories with ever-longer acronyms (PECOTA, BABIP, LIPS, VORP).*

Relying on hard data to gauge a player's value or understand how a team succeeded or failed obviously makes sense. Our own minds are spectacularly biased and thus unreliable observers. We're wired more for stories than mathematics. Our ancestors explained the movement of the sun with tales of gods hauling it across the sky in flying chariots. Aren't we doing the same thing, the SABR folks ask, by explaining wins and losses with stories of an unmeasurable, undefined phenomenon called team chemistry?

To that point, in the years following the Giants' reunion in 2009, I couldn't help noticing that every World Series champion was said to have great chemistry. Every single one, from the 2009 New York Yankees to the 2019 Washington Nationals. "Proof" of team chemistry included one or more of the following: matching hairstyles (face or scalp), celebratory rituals (e.g., pie in the face), elaborate handshakes or dance moves, clubhouse pranks, humorous nicknames, hand gestures (e.g., the 2010 Texas Rangers' claw and antlers), catchphrases, big team dinners paid for by a magnanimous superstar, and a manager who "lets his players be themselves."

If team chemistry does exist, and it has such a profound impact, how could it be as simple as all that? Come up with a few gimmicks and start sizing the rings?

I wondered about the acrimonious Oakland A's and New York Yankees during the 1970s, the "twenty-five-players, twenty-five-

---

* These acronyms stand for "player empirical comparison and optimization test algorithm," "batting average on balls in play," "late-inning pressure situation," and "value over replacement player."

cabs" teams. They could barely get through a road trip without a fistfight, yet they won championship after championship. Why didn't the lack of chemistry matter for them?

Conversely, what about good-chemistry teams that *don't* win? The 2007 Washington Nationals come to mind. Spring-training stories gushed about their fun team dinners and how they brought back the old-school kangaroo court to foster camaraderie. That team finished sixteen games out of first place. They didn't have the talent. The satirical *Onion* once ran a headline that captured this perfectly: "Great Team Chemistry No Match for Great Team Biology."

Hall of Fame baseball manager Jim Leyland falls in the talent-is-everything camp. We talked one spring afternoon in 2010 inside the visiting clubhouse in the Oakland Coliseum. He was managing the Detroit Tigers at the time, the fourth and final team in a storied career that earned him three Manager of the Year Awards and a bronze plaque in Cooperstown. He waved me into the cramped manager's office, stubbing a Marlboro out in a paper cup on his desk. He had the leathery face of an old baseball man and the curmudgeonly demeanor, too, which is to say he gives the impression of being, at all times, one scotch away from taking a swing at someone.

"To me chemistry was a subject you took in school," he said, and he tapped another cigarette from the pack.

"I had teams that'd go to chapel together every Sunday, couldn't win a game. So that don't mean shit to me. Forget chemistry out here. Don't worry about it. Don't think about it. It's so over-used in sports. It's the first thing normally some journalist who doesn't know what he's talking about brings up. Whenever some-body's losing, you hear they have bad chemistry. There's 'problems in the clubhouse.' There's a problem here, there's a problem there. All it does is get managers fired, whether it's true or not. It gets players traded.

"Listen, it all begins and ends with talent. If you have a horseshit team, they can all go out to dinner together, but they're not going to win a lot of games. That's why I'm all about talent. That's what this is all about. Now whatever you get beyond that—everybody likes each other, that's all bonus. That makes your season more enjoyable. It doesn't necessarily make it more successful."

As ten minutes with Leyland stretched to forty, however, the manager began to change his tune, sort of. He agreed that "personality and people skills create the electricity" and that players need to trust that "each guy is not on his own agenda." He got worked up about the impact of veteran players in the clubhouse.

"Let me tell you this," he said. "Good veteran players are the best tonic your team could have. The younger players see that if the veteran players believe in the program, they'll follow suit. But if you get veteran players that are pissed off they can't play anymore, that's the worst scenario you can have."

Wasn't he saying that factors beyond talent can affect how a team performs?

Tony La Russa, another Hall of Fame manager, would give a resounding yes. La Russa was still coaching the St. Louis Cardinals in April of 2010 when we talked in the visitor's dugout at AT&T Park. He had won two World Series championships by then and would notch a third in 2011, his final season as a manager. Intense and declarative about most things and particularly so about team chemistry, La Russa has been honing his understanding of the concept since his first managerial job in 1979.

"If you think players can be around each other every day for eight months and it doesn't matter what the vibes are between them, you're foolish," he said.

Get him going about team chemistry and he's like Elmer Gantry delivering a TED Talk, preaching its power in detailed themes and sub-themes with examples and supporting evidence. In short, he said, chemistry can be distilled to three values: respect, trust, and caring. He drills those values into his players. He recruits and mentors team leaders to model and evangelize them in the clubhouse.

"The larger that leadership group, the better it is for the team and each individual. [Former manager] Chuck Tanner said if you have good chemistry, it's like you traded for a superstar, and I believe it."

That same season I spoke with La Russa, the San Francisco Giants were beginning to emerge as what some might call a case study in chemistry. Manager Bruce Bochy referred to his 2010 club as "a band of misfits" and "the Dirty Dozen." No one predicted these cast-off veterans and unproven youngsters would end up on a cool Wednesday in November riding trolley cars up Market Street through a shower of confetti. However, despite having witnessed this unlikely championship season firsthand, I was no closer to understanding the dynamics of team chemistry than I was driving home from the '89 team reunion a year earlier.

That December, I went to Orlando for Major League Baseball's winter meetings, the annual gathering of managers, general managers, executives, and media (plus out-of-work baseball people looking for jobs). I was learning a ton about clubhouse behavior and relationships, and how folks inside baseball perceived chemistry. But I still had a thousand questions.

How do we know team chemistry actually exists? If it exists, what is it? Is it similar to romantic chemistry, some magical connection that happens among and between certain human beings? And how does it affect performance? After all, why even talk about team chemistry if it doesn't affect performance?

My search for answers split into two strands that curled around each other like a double helix. One revolved around the friend-ships, resentments, humor, fights, ego, and humility in the club-house, the other around the science of how and why such things matter to performance.

Both, however, start in the only place they can: the human brain.

CHAPTER ONE

YOU COMPLETE ME

Two doors down from the No Name Bar in Sausalito, California, sandwiched so tightly between two tourist shops I almost miss the entrance, is the office of UC San Francisco psychiatrist and psychotherapist Thomas Lewis. He's the principal author of *A General Theory of Love,** a beautiful mindblower of a book that includes this sentence:

"[No human] is a functioning whole on his own; each has open loops that only somebody else can complete."

As we know from the orphanage studies and cases like my father's, the human brain, for all its power and complexity, does not come preprogrammed with everything necessary to live. But that's not the open loop Thomas Lewis is talking about.

Mammals need other mammals to *flourish*, and humans most of all. I remembered enough from high-school science to know that early humans evolved into one of the most social, cooperative species on earth because, of course, they needed each other to stay alive. They weren't fast enough or strong enough to battle mammoths alone. Coordination required communication. Before

---

* Coauthors Dr. Fari Amini and Dr. Richard Lannon, both psychiatrists, were professors at UC San Francisco when Lewis was in his psychiatric training residency there.

language in our little hominid tribes, we still managed to let each other know where food could be found, which berries made you sick, and how to bring down a bison ten times your size.

Walking upright elongated our vocal tract, which produced a broader and increasingly nuanced range of sounds. With our face no longer covered in hair, facial muscles became visible. We learned to "read" the messages embedded in the variety of muscle combinations, particularly around the eyes: worry, joy, fear, confusion, surprise. We could now see the blush of embarrassment and the flush of love. Our largely hairless body, with eighteen square feet of exposed skin, became a soft keyboard for the language of touch: I trust you, It's OK, Stop that. Our eyes changed from almost completely brown—like the eyes of other primates—to having bright white sclera around our corneas, allowing us to convey immediately where we were looking—Pay attention to that snake over there!—and also enabling others to get a glimpse of our intent: deceit, kindness, malevolence. The big, jutting primate brow disappeared, clearing the way for our eyes to be more easily observed. Over the course of three million years, our brain quadrupled in size. This was an unusual development.

Brain size generally corresponds to body size. Elephants have enormous brains; squirrels, small ones. Ours are way bigger than our bodies would dictate. In fact, we have the largest brain relative to our body size of any animal. Anthropologist Robin Dunbar concluded that our brain grew so large not so much to house our intellect but to accommodate our massive amount of social wiring.[1]

The modern human brain holds around one hundred billion neurons, which are like the brain's motherboard, ceaselessly downloading info from everything in our vicinity and routing it to the appropriate departments for processing. Our brain gathers signals from everyone around us—tone of voice, body language, odor, behavior—a "veritable dictionary of mood and intention," as biologist E. O. Wilson puts it. Our face continually sends signals we don't even know we're sending. We have muscles in our chin, the bridge of our nose, and our forehead that most of us cannot consciously control. For example, if you asked people to pull down the corners of their lips without moving their chin muscles, only about 10 percent could do it. But almost everyone does it automatically when they're profoundly sad. These hardwired expressions are almost always fleeting, disappearing behind the expression we want the world to see.

We pick up on the signals and react not only by altering our own mood and body language, but our heart rate, hormones, and metabolism—a thousand tiny recalibrations every moment. This is the dance of human tribes, each of us forever influencing one another with such speed and subtlety that we barely notice.

Thomas Lewis's book never mentions team chemistry, but on page after page that's what he describes.

"I know almost nothing about sports," Lewis said as he sank into a black armchair and crossed his ankles on the ottoman. "I have patients come in and talk about sports, so I've heard about it, but I didn't get that gene."

Short stacks of paper formed a ragged semicircle on the floor around his chair. Floor-to-ceiling bookshelves gave way to a picture window that opened to a view of the Sausalito Ferry and Richardson Bay.

Lewis had the soft and calming voice you'd expect from a psychiatry professor, but his husky build and Saturday-afternoon-at-Costco loose pullover brought to mind a hockey dad. The small table on his right was a clutter of three soft-drink cans, a crumpled coffee cup, and a half-empty bottle of mineral water.

Lewis told me about giving a lecture one day when a woman asked a question about heaven. He doesn't remember the specifics. What he does remember is being struck for the first time by the near universality of people's concept of heaven: a reunion with the people we love. Hell, on the other hand, is banishment. I thought about Tom Hanks's character in *Cast Away*, who survives in part by turning a volleyball into a companion named Wilson. The success of the film depended on the audience buying into Hanks's emotional connection to the ball. We did, even if we didn't know exactly why.

"Relationships are ultimately *the* central thing for human beings," Lewis said. So much so, he said, that we are often literally in sync with those closest to us. The heart rhythm (not heart rate) of a mother and baby, for example, will synchronize to within a second of each other. "And it's specific to that mother and infant," Lewis said. A woman's heart rhythm doesn't synchronize with a baby that isn't hers. Similarly, the respiratory rates between people in a conversation, if they have a close relationship, will synchronize.

I understood the open-loop system in the extremes, namely abandoned children and lonely, isolated adults. But what about the rest of us in everyday life? What do other people supply to us that we can't generate on our own?

"There are a lot of aspects of life that are hard to observe, I think, if you're not a psychiatrist. I wonder sometimes, how do people get along?" Lewis said, smiling.

In a clinical session, he said, he is so attentive to everything about his patient that he notices how he is changed from hour to hour, depending on the client. "Everything about another person is contagious," he said. "You can tell that a part of who *you* are in the moment comes from who the *other person* is. You're not the same person. Not radically different, but different enough that it's noticeable."

I wondered what kinds of things he noticed.

"You just feel like: Oh, I'm funny with this person," Lewis said. "Or I'm smart, or have more ideas, or can't think of anything to say. You get changed. And that's because part of who you are is determined by other people."

I knew exactly. I also felt particularly funny with certain people. I asked Lewis if I was mimicking my friends' funniness or were they tapping something in me I already had?

"There really isn't a 'you' in the way you think there is," he said. "There *is* a you that is unchanging. But a part of you is always supplied by other people."

I had to wrap my brain around that. But the more I thought about it, the more I knew there was something to it. Who I am with my sisters and brothers in Florida is different from who I am with my friends in San Francisco. Who I am with my husband is different from who I ever was with boyfriends before him. Who I am with my son is totally different, for good or ill, from who I am with anyone else on the planet.

The chatter of tourists drifted up from the street. I told Lewis that there are people in sports who reject the suggestion that anything other than talent, training, and preparation account for an athlete's performance. Lewis arched his eyebrows, which qualified in his range of measured emotions as flabbergasted shock. .

"That," he said evenly, "is very surprising to me."

In early 2017, I was asked to interview Michael Lewis onstage for a Bay Area speaker series. His book *Moneyball* popularized the notion in baseball that if you couldn't count it, time it, or measure it, it didn't matter to performance. In other words, chemistry was as relevant as lucky underwear. He had just published *The Undoing Project: A Friendship That Changed Our Minds*. It's about the extraordinary relationship between Israeli psychologists Daniel Kahneman and Amos Tversky, who summoned from each other such profound work on behavioral economics that it earned Kahneman the Nobel Prize. (Tversky had died by then, and Nobels are awarded only to the living.) Each was brilliant in his own right. But together they changed how we think about thinking. Lewis's book describes how they supplied new facets to one another's personality. The men could hardly be more different: Tversky was funny, self-assured, and sharply critical; Kahneman was quiet and, as Michael Lewis put it, "a welter of doubt." But in Tversky's company, Kahneman felt funny and confident, something he'd never experienced. With Kahneman, Tversky was agreeable and uncritical. Their relationship was about who and what the two of them became in each other's presence.

In the green room before the onstage interview, I hoped to ask Lewis how and why these two men were able to influence each other to such a significant degree. I wanted to know if writing *The Undoing Project* had altered his thinking on team chemistry fourteen years after *Moneyball*. First, though, to break the ice I mentioned to Lewis I had been meeting with his good friend, a UC Berkeley social psychologist named Dacher Keltner, to whom Lewis had dedicated *The Undoing Project*. I told him that Keltner might collaborate on a study for my book.

"What's your book about?" he asked.

"Team chemistry."

"Doesn't exist," he said.

And that was that. I found this puzzling. If Tversky and Kahneman could change so markedly in each other's company and elevate the quality of each other's work, wasn't it possible that any two human brains could do the same? Even two athletes' brains? Perhaps the stumbling block for him was applying the phenomenon to groups. Yet history is rife with examples.

The "Lost Generation" of writers and artists in Paris after World War I—Ernest Hemingway, F. Scott Fitzgerald, Gertrude

Stein, Ezra Pound, Man Ray, Pablo Picasso—inspired each other to take risks in their work, to be bold and audacious. The result was groundbreaking literature and art. The same was true for an earlier group of French painters whose cross-pollination of ideas and energy created Impressionism; and for Sigmund Freud and his psychoanalytic colleagues in Vienna; and for Charles Darwin and his network of biologists, geologists, and ornithologists in London and Cambridge who drew out the best in each other to hone a theory of natural selection.

By sharing knowledge, energy, motivation—and enjoying the discovery process together—the artists and scientists produced something more exciting than each could have produced alone.

I watched it happen with the Giants in 2010, my third year as the team's media consultant. I didn't exactly *see* it. I didn't know enough yet to read the signals—embedded in voice, touch, facial expression, words, humor, nicknames, eye contact, a thousand things—crisscrossing the clubhouse like neurons in one big brain. I couldn't see how this web of connections and recalibrations, this complex interplay of relationships, was coalescing into something all its own—a culture. And how this culture became like a gravitational force, bending everyone toward each other and a common goal.

For fifteen years at the Giants, prickly home-run king Barry Bonds was the bright, scorching sun around which the rest of the organization orbited. Three years after he left, a new dynamic took its place, turning two unlikely men into team leaders and a band of misfits, castoffs, and youngsters into World Series champions.

CHAPTER TWO

THE ARROWLEAF

"Trust doesn't mean that you trust that someone won't
screw up. It means you trust them even when they do
screw up."

—Ed Catmull, former president of Pixar
and Walt Disney Animation Studios

Not everyone sees the thin layer of paranoia that coats certain
clubhouses, but Aubrey Huff did, and right away. His history and
personality had conditioned him to expect it. He reflexively scru-
tinized teammates' words and tone of voice for the subtle derision,
the hidden agendas. He was still in many ways the uneasy, awkward kid in Mineral Wells, Texas, whose father had been shot and
killed at the apartment complex where he worked as an electri-
cian. Aubrey was six years old. On weekend nights during high
school, he preferred the batting cage behind his mobile home to
the minefield of teenage social life, swinging the bat beneath the
floodlights long after his mother, grandmother, and sister had
gone to bed. He was the most valuable player at the three-
thousand-student Vernon College in north Texas before transfer-
ring to the super-competitive baseball program at the University

of Miami. He felt like a sheltered hick among the brash, frat-boy athletes. He adopted an arrogant, hard-partying, sarcastic alter ego he called Huffdaddy.

That's the person I met when he arrived at the Giants' spring training facility in January of 2010.

The Tampa Bay Rays had drafted him in the fifth round in 1998, and he reached the big leagues just two years later. In Huff's five and a half years there, the Rays finished in last place five times. They lost more than a hundred games three times. Traded to the Houston Astros in 2006, Huff experienced half a season of winning baseball, though just barely: The Astros finished 82–80. Huff was twenty-nine. Then it was on to the awful Baltimore Orioles for two and a half more seasons of last-place finishes.

Over the years, Huff had become indifferent both to winning and to the team concept. He was not known for logging hours in the gym. He tended to show up at the ballpark right before stretching and was in his car by the time the stadium emptied. *Go to the field, get your ass kicked, go home.* At the start of each season, he'd hang a new calendar in his rental house and count down the days until he could pack up for the winter. This isn't to say he didn't play hard. He did. He played in all 162 games in 2002 and led the Rays in home runs for most of his years there. Good stats, every ballplayer knows, secured you a good contract. But by 2010, those days were over for Huff. He was thirty-three years old. He had never played in a postseason game. One could argue he had never played in a meaningful game, when the team's fate hung in the balance. In short, he wasn't a winner, on or off the field. In the midst of his three-year, $20-million contract with the Orioles, he went on a local radio station after downing nine Bud Lights and called Baltimore "a horseshit town." He was traded the following season and finished out 2009 with the second-place Detroit Tigers. After being benched for poor play, he responded by pouting and stewing in the dugout.

"In all honesty, going into the off-season, I was thinking if nobody calls, thank god. I'm done. Just ride off in the sunset, and before you know it nobody will remember me. I was just totally over it," Huff told me during a long phone conversation years later. He barely picked up a bat or lifted a weight that winter, before the 2010 season. He lurched from the strip clubs to the casinos and back home to his wife on a roller coaster of alcohol and Adderall. His marriage was falling apart.

As spring training drew near, the Giants had struck out twice on signing a left-handed first baseman who had some pop in his bat, and Huff became their best option. They offered just one year at $3 million—a lot of money for most of us, but a comedown for the ten-year veteran. Huff took it.

Only six of ESPN's thirty-six baseball commentators predicted the Giants would reach the playoffs in 2010. No one at *Baseball Prospectus* did. The team had no slugger with the power of past Giants greats like Willie Mays, Willie McCovey, Will Clark, or Barry Bonds. In the pitching rotation was a twenty-year-old country boy named Madison Bumgarner, just two years removed from high school. Their ace, Tim Lincecum, a long-haired, pot-smoking, waifish introvert, looked like a bat boy but threw like Sandy Koufax. In his three years in the major leagues, he had already won two Cy Young Awards as the best pitcher in baseball. Their up-and-coming catcher was a crew-cut rookie out of Georgia with the Old West name of Buster Posey.

With Barry Bonds gone, the hierarchy within the team flattened. No emperor meant no minions, no one walking on eggshells, afraid of drawing the star's criticism. The judgment fell away. Lincecum was a rock star in San Francisco, mobbed by fans, hounded by reporters, wooed by sponsors. He could have been a diva. Instead he was one of the guys, having a great time. Same thing for the other young players and the smattering of aging veterans, who understood how short a career is. They all wanted to win—and have fun while doing it.

What happened that season reminded me of E. O. Wilson's description of an arrowleaf plant. When one grows on land, its leaves are shaped like arrowheads. In shallow water, they look like lily pads. Underwater, they're long, seaweedy ribbons. The environment awakens something in the plant, freeing it to transform into the shape best suited to its surroundings.

I happened to be in the hallway when Huff arrived at the Giants' Scottsdale, Arizona, ballpark for his first day of spring training. He strutted toward the clubhouse like John Travolta in *Saturday Night Fever:* shoulders back, chin up, grin wide, as if crowds might part to make way. This was Huffdaddy, the swaggery guy with armor around his insecurities. He was girding himself for a fourth new clubhouse in five years. He stuck his head into a side room where coaches were drinking coffee around a conference table. "Aubrey Huff," he announced to each man, circling the table and shaking hands like a seasoned salesman.

In the clubhouse, a few other early-arriving players were changing out of their street clothes. Huff knew they'd be well aware of his reputation as a shitty teammate. He set down his equipment bag at his locker and braced for the chore of introducing himself to men who might be less than excited to have him on the team. He was stashing deodorant and shaving cream when pitcher Matt Cain appeared with his hand out, welcoming him to the squad. Then Tim Lincecum came by. One by one, players greeted him. "There was an aura in the air, the way everybody talked to each other," Huff said later. "The way everybody looked at each other. It just felt so much different than anything I've been a part of."

Later, he watched as players from all different backgrounds squeezed shoulder to shoulder around a table in the middle of the clubhouse, slapping down cards in high-stakes games of booray and hearts. Huff remembers liking the eccentric closer—a twenty-fourth-round draft pick named Brian Wilson—with his black nail polish, Mohawk, and a black beard that would spawn half a dozen Twitter accounts. He also took to the sunny Dominican veteran Juan Uribe—plucked from the free-agent scrap heap a year earlier—who called everyone "Papi."

"Uribe, what's my name?" Huff asked one day, later in the season.

"Papi, you know I know your name," Uribe said.

"No, what's my name?"

"Shut up, I *got* you."

Huff laughed when he told the story later. "He had no fucking idea what my name was. And it was perfectly OK with me." Huff had his own quirks. He once ambled toward the clubhouse bathroom buck naked, asking if anyone had seen his toothbrush. It was protruding from his rear, a sight that broke up his teammates as intended. ("Now, the bristles weren't in my butthole," Huff made sure to tell me.) Later he began wearing a red thong under his uniform pants to rally the team out of a losing streak.

By the end of spring training, Huff was periodically joining the card games and lobbing sarcastic Huffdaddy remarks across the room. But he kept a safe distance. He knew he was just a replacement part and operated as he always had, like an independent contractor loyal only to himself.

Early in the season, however, that changed. The Giants were playing the Pittsburgh Pirates in San Francisco. Huff crushed a pitch to the right-field wall. As the ball caromed past the fielder, he rounded first and made for second. Already gasping for air, Huff tapped second and headed to third. His eyes bulged at the sight of the coach leaping wildly and waving him home. He chugged down the line and slid across the plate with the grace of a sandbag, completing one of the most entertaining and least likely inside-the-park home runs in history.

Teammates swarmed Huff in the dugout, roaring with laughter and slapping high fives. Huff sank onto the bench, red-faced and heaving, but also laughing. Someone handed him a cup of Gatorade. Young third baseman Pablo Sandoval fanned him with a towel. In the clubhouse after the game, the barbs and howls erupted all over again each time the TV showed replays of Huff's runaway-beer-truck trip around the bags. The funniest digs came from Huff himself.

"That's when I felt finally that I was really part of a team," Huff said later. "I finally felt part of the guys."

From a physiology standpoint, the warm, exultant reception from teammates almost certainly set in motion the production of oxytocin in Huff's brain. He experienced the *physical* sensation of acceptance. Huff's heart rate slowed. A rush of serotonin and dopamine—piggy-backing on the oxytocin—lifted his mood and his energy.

Over time, he began to feel an ease he hadn't known since, well, maybe ever. He became more open to the everyday signals of trust and became more trusting, more accepting, and less self-centered in return. His life outside of baseball was a mess—he was still drinking and popping Adderall, and his marriage was still crumbling—but with his teammates he could be the person his teammates seemed to think he was. He began arriving at the park early and leaving late. He rediscovered his power at the plate and led the team in doubles, triples, and home runs. Most surprising, he found teammates gravitating to him for advice or a laugh, as if he were a leader.

"They'd ask me about things," he said, "and that had never happened to me in my life."

Paul Zak picked me up at my hotel in Ontario, California, on an August morning in 2016 in a black Mercedes with a vanity plate that read *OXYTOSN*. He was trim, tanned, and sported a stylish touch of gray at the temples. He dressed like a hip politician: crisp blue dress shirt with the cuffs turned up at the wrist, a leather braided bracelet, pleated slacks. I had seen his TED Talk, so I knew the hug was coming. He hugs everyone he meets. Hugs are known to release oxytocin.

Zak is an economics professor and the founder and director of the Center for Neuroeconomics Studies at Claremont Graduate University. His economics studies had piqued his interest in the nature of trust. The most prosperous countries had the most trusting cultures; only when people trust that banks, governments, and businesses are behaving fairly and honestly can economies flourish. Zak got to wondering what made one person trust another. Was there a biological mechanism of trust?

By chance one day in 2000, on an airport shuttle in Nevada, Zak found himself next to anthropologist Helen Fisher, well-known for her studies on the biology of love. In discussing their respective work, she asked Zak if he had ever studied the connection between trust and oxytocin. At that point, he had never heard of oxytocin, the so-called love hormone.

He learned that oxytocin is produced deep inside the brain in a hormone-regulating region called the hypothalamus. The hypothalamus then dispatches oxytocin to the tiny, almond-shaped amygdala, which has a high concentration of oxytocin receptors. The amygdala is essentially the brain's emotional scanner, interpreting every sight, sound, smell, taste, or touch for its emotional meaning. The amygdala tells us a friend's curt tone, for instance, means she's not happy. In animals, oxytocin fosters nurturing in rodents, monogamy in prairie voles, and social bonding in almost every species tested. When Animal A nuzzled, played with, or otherwise signaled to Animal B he was safe to approach, Animal B's brain released oxytocin and was friendly in return.

To Zak, that looked a lot like trust. Was oxytocin the biological underpinning he was hunting for? With two colleagues at Claremont, Zak recruited students to participate in a well-known exercise called "the trust game."*

They sat the students in cubicles and, at random, assigned them partners, who never saw each other or communicated directly. A computer screen in each cubicle told the partners they each had ten dollars in an account. It was theirs to keep just for showing up. But they also had an opportunity to increase the amount.

The first student was asked if she wanted to give some of her ten dollars to her anonymous partner and told that whatever amount she transferred would be tripled. If she gave five dollars, the partner would see his account balance increase by fifteen to twenty-five dollars. The anonymous partner now had the option of sending money back. If he sent ten dollars, for example, they'd both end up with fifteen, boosting their initial take-away by five. Of course, he could pocket the entire twenty-five dollars and call it a day. His partner would never know his identity. There would be no repercussions.

Zak found that 98 percent of the partners *did* send money back. The question was why.

He took blood samples from each student before and immediately after they made their decisions to send money. He measured the levels of ten different chemicals. Only oxytocin showed a before-and-

---

* The two colleagues were former University of Pennsylvania professor Robert Kurzban and graduate student William Matzner.

after change—and only in the recipients, not the initial senders. In other words, receiving money raised the students' levels of oxytocin. The more money they received, the higher their oxytocin level. Zak and his team were pretty sure at this point that one partner's gesture of trust triggered the release of oxytocin in the other. But they couldn't be sure. Maybe the chemical was released simply because of the mini-thrill of receiving money and had nothing to do with trust.

They pulled in more students for more rounds of the trust game. This time, the students didn't decide for themselves how much to transfer to their anonymous partner. Instead, they picked a Ping-Pong ball from a bucket. On the ball was a number from one through ten, which determined how much the student transferred. The recipients knew the transfer amount had been determined randomly. The results were startling. The oxytocin levels of the recipients were significantly lower than those of students in the earlier rounds, and the amounts they sent back were significantly less generous.

Zak also studied distrust and found that its effect was just as powerful as trust—though only in men. In general, when male students received three dollars or less in a transfer, they were angry and sent back next to nothing. No surprise that their blood showed a spike in a high-octane testosterone called dihydrotestosterone (DHT). The more distrust the men felt, the more distrusting they were with others, with a correlating boost in DHT. On the other hand, when women received a transfer of three dollars or less, Zak found, their testosterone didn't spike. They felt hurt, disappointed, and sometimes angry, but they almost always sent back a comparable amount no matter how small the initial transfer.

But Zak still couldn't be certain that oxytocin, and not some other factor, was responsible for increasing the students' generosity in the trust game. Via a nasal spray, he delivered synthetic oxytocin to half the participants and a placebo to the rest. The oxytocin groups sent back more than twice as much money as the placebo groups.

The conclusion: When people show trust in us, our brains release a surge of oxytocin, which primes us to be trusting and generous in return. Trust begets trust.

The evidence of oxytocin's impact on bonding and trust, while not yet conclusive, became compelling enough to catch the attention of the US Department of Defense.

The military has long operated on the premise that bonding and trust are essential to performance. This is a big reason for boot camp: hardship fosters bonding. It's also why soldiers still march during training. Marching into battle is an absurd strategy in modern war, as antiquated as muskets and bayonets. But it is still a staple on military bases around the world because marching in unison, like synchronous chanting and singing in religious rituals, facilitates connection and cooperation.[1] Similarly, the ritual of sports teams warming up before practices and games with synchronous stretches strengthens their bonds as it loosens their muscles.

At the core of team chemistry is the profound impact we have on each other, psychologically and physiologically, and research on the military continues to pile up the evidence. Studies have found that emotional connections not only foster selflessness and sacrifice on the battlefield but also help mitigate post-traumatic stress disorder (PTSD). UCLA did an astounding study on this, using the pension rolls from the Civil War.[2] Detailed medical records were kept on more than 90 percent of the thirty-five thousand soldiers in the Union Army's pension program. This treasure trove of data allowed researchers an unprecedented look at the arc of the soldiers' lives, from the actual units in which they served through old age and death.

Many units in the Union Army were made up of men from the same town. Because the pension rolls included the hometowns of every soldier, researchers knew which men fought alongside friends and neighbors and which men didn't. Men in these connected units were less likely later in life to develop physical ailments like cardiovascular disorders, which are sometimes indicative of undiagnosed psychiatric conditions. In other words, being in a more tightly bonded company reduced the likelihood of suffering from what we now call PTSD.

The invention of synthetic oxytocin got the Department of Defense wondering if it could help accelerate the bonding process, thus producing high-performing units faster and protecting soldiers against wartime stress more effectively. In 2016, the Pentagon turned to a UC San Francisco researcher named Josh Woolley.

His lab—the Bonding and Attunement in Neuropsychiatric Disorders Laboratory, or BAND Lab—occupies a squat prefab building on the sprawling campus of the San Francisco VA Medical Center. It sits at the end of a narrow drive below the main parking lot, tucked out of sight like a toolshed on a grand estate. I visited him one rainy afternoon, passing a dusty artificial ficus tree in the entryway, the only nod to hominess in an expanse of filing cabinets and gray cubicles with nameplates like "C14 Thrive Lab" and "C15 BAND Lab (MD/Post-Doc Cubicle)." But I heard young voices and laughter and caught glimpses of researchers in jeans and sneakers under their white lab coats.

Woolley said his office is too much of a mess for me to see, so we sat in a small room usually reserved for behavioral experiments, which is why there were high-definition cameras mounted in three corners and, on a table, a dozen or so "Biopac" systems that measure sweat, heart rate, cardiac impedance, and other automatic physical responses. Woolley has an MD in psychiatry and a PhD in neuroscience. At forty years old, he still looked like a grad student: glasses, short hair, plaid shirt, black jeans, running shoes, and bright, striped socks. He has long been driven to understand the

35

psychological and physiological power of social connection. For him, the research is not an academic exercise. He still sees patients one day a week, mostly military vets, and is awestruck by what they were willing to sacrifice for their comrades.

He choked up telling me about the Vietnam radio operator who, under pounding artillery fire, risked his life remaining at the radio by himself to get help for his embattled unit.

"People were getting killed, and he stayed; he kept doing it, alone, even though he was in danger and people were dying," Woolley said. "It was very moving. I was telling him it was amazing, and he was like, no. He was actually embarrassed by it. You read these stories about heroism and people that win the Medal of Honor and things like that—they often say it wasn't heroic what they did. They just didn't think about it that way. They thought, 'My friends—what else was I going to do?'"

Woolley's experiments with synthetic oxytocin, along with the work of several colleagues, landed them a Department of Defense grant for a three-year study on the neuropeptide's impact on team cohesion among ROTC recruits.* Their goals were to better understand the psychobiological mechanism of cohesion; to develop a way to measure the cohesion of a team; to see if, and how, synthetic oxytocin could enhance it; and to determine any correlation to performance.

Woolley warned that the experiment might accomplish none of those things. He is critical of scientists who jump to sweeping conclusions that make interesting headlines in the *New York Times* science section but whose results, it often turns out, cannot be replicated. So he couched his own postulations with "We don't know yet," "That's what I'm thinking now," "This is just a first step."

---

* Woolley worked with coinvestigators Sophia Vinogradov, MD, Thomas Neylan, MD, and Wendy Mendes, PhD, at UC San Francisco and collaborators Michael Kraus, PhD, at Yale and Dean Carson, PhD, at Stanford University.

Woolley's research targeted exactly what I was trying to under-stand about team chemistry—the scientific underpinnings of bonding's impact on performance. The initial experiments in his double-blind study, which involved three strangers collaborating on a task, were conducted at UC Berkeley with student volunteers and, later, cadets. The work was arduous. From video of the test-ing sessions, researchers had to code the participants' gestures and facial expressions—every nod, smile, and furrowed brow; every instance of eye contact and eye aversion. They had to note who took charge, who noticed a fellow participant's confusion and stepped in to help, who offered the choice of snacks to her fellow volunteers. Every snippet of conversation went through a language-analysis program. Physiological data from body monitors were analyzed to see if heart rates, breathing, or other autonomous responses became synchronous and how the body responded dur-ing social interaction and task performance.

With a large enough sample size, Woolley said, the data could show a significant relationship between oxytocin and cohesion, and between cohesion and performance. Or not.

The results would be ready in two years, he said. Or not.

I checked back in two years. The results weren't ready. As one researcher reminded me more than once, "Joan, science is slow." It's not that I expected team chemistry to pop out one day from behind a research paper or a clubhouse door and explain itself to me. But as my research mounted and my interviews multiplied, I started to feel like I was trying to solve a puzzle by picking through a mountain of random pieces.

Pat Burrell had been Huff's larger-than-life teammate at the Uni-versity of Miami. He had been the quarterback on his high-school football team and the star slugger on the baseball team. As a junior at Miami, he was named the best college baseball player in the country. That June, he was the first player picked in the MLB draft, by the Philadelphia Phillies. Philly fans expected Burrell to be the next Mike Schmidt, and though he had several outstanding seasons, he fell short of the hype. During the 2008 World Series against the Tampa Bay Rays, Burrell had just one hit, but it was a doozy: a double in Game 5 that would clinch the championship. Afterward, Burrell was a hot commodity, and the Rays laid out more than $16 million to secure his services for 2009 and 2010.

But Burrell, a golden boy all his life, played so abysmally and clashed so sharply with manager Joe Maddon that just twenty-four games into the 2010 season, with $8 million still owed on his contract, the Rays dumped him. "How bad do you have to be performing to be cut by a team that counts every penny more closely than Ebenezer Scrooge?" one Tampa Bay sportswriter wrote.[3]

Burrell was on the downside of thirty-three. He went home to Arizona and sat by the phone. Weeks passed. No offers.

In the meantime, Huff was lobbying the Giants' brass to sign his old college buddy. He knows how to win, Huff told anyone who would listen. He's the slugger we need in the lineup, a student of the game, a hero of the 2008 World Series! He was the Giants' kind of player, Huff pushed: hard-nosed, old school, big bat. And he was from the Bay Area, a nice local connection. Because the Rays were paying his salary, the Giants could pick him up for almost nothing. They signed him to a minor-league contract in late May and by early June, he was in the Giants lineup.

Burrell arrived in the clubhouse seeming not a bit humbled by his failure in Tampa Bay. Broad-shouldered and square-jawed, he commanded the attention of every room he entered. His good looks and regal bearing brought to mind the prince in *Beauty and the Beast*, though he was princely in few other ways. Like Huff, he had a vulgar bent that stood out even by baseball standards. But he had a reputation for playing hard and smart, for being a winner.

He blossomed in his new environment, just as Huff had. He rediscovered his passion and energy. He radiated confidence. And the clubhouse, like the superorganism it is, absorbed that passion, energy, and confidence and became something new. Not radically so. More of a shift, the way a dinner party changes when a particularly charismatic guest arrives. Burrell would round up teammates for pregame stretching with an old-fashioned *"C'mon, boys!"* When the team lost, he let no one hang his head: "We'll get 'em tomorrow." He slung an arm around the bench players about to pinch-hit in a tight game. "You got this," he'd say matter-of-factly, more reminder than exhortation. He pushed the players to look out for each other. After a Giants pitcher struggled through a long inning, wearing himself out throwing way too many pitches, Burrell barked at upcoming Giants hitters, "You have to take pitches! Give our guy time to catch his breath!"

Like Huff's, Burrell's performance on the field reflected his ease and sense of purpose in the clubhouse. He led the team in slugging percentage (total bases per at-bat) and was second only to Huff in on-base plus slugging percentage (OPS). His batting average soared from .218 during his tenure in Tampa to .266 in San Francisco. He hit eighteen home runs.

No one was affected by Burrell's presence more than Huff. "It was almost like a long-lost brother had come home," he said. Huff felt more capable and confident. He couldn't let go completely of Huffdaddy—he was still loud and swaggery—but he cared about the men at the other lockers. It mattered what they thought of him. He could never be a leader on his own, but he could with Burrell, almost as if—in line with our open-loop nature—Burrell completed him. "I was not used to being the guy who people are looking to for answers," Huff said, laughing, when we spoke on the phone. "I was the guy that kind of took it light in the clubhouse, and all of a sudden I felt this responsibility to be the guy that the media would go to after games, and I'm like, 'Holy shit, I'm not used to this.'"

One day in the clubhouse at the end of August, Burrell found Huff and together they ushered Lincecum into the small office. The superstar pitcher had lost all five of his starts that month. The Giants had slipped six games out of first place. Lincecum didn't seem to be listening to his coaches or manager Bruce Bochy, and he balked at suggestions that he improve his workout routine. He had been so spectacularly successful his entire life that he seemed paralyzed by failure.

"Timmy, man, I know you're struggling, bro," Burrell said, leaning forward in his chair, locking eyes with the young pitcher. "I know this is hard for you. But we need you, Bud, we need you."

Huff mostly listened. Burrell was pointed but loving. "Look, Timmy, you're our rock. If we don't have you, we're dead. We're dead."

"As I'm watching Timmy," Huff told me later, "his head starts coming up, the chin's coming up, the chest is coming out a little bit more. You could see in his facial expression, in his eyes, *that somebody had belief in him.* He's 0 and 5. He's getting bad press. Everybody's on him. And then something was triggered inside of him. You could *see* it. I'm sitting there in awe watching and listening to this. And no shit, the very next start against Colorado, on September first, he shoved it up Colorado's ass."

What I had learned about the brain from Zak, Woolley, and others seemed to be playing out in the relationships and dynamics of these men. Huff and Burrell felt trusted and valued, triggering the release of oxytocin and dopamine and creating a newfound sense of commitment and connection to their teammates. They, in turn, showed trust in Lincecum, revving his own brain chemicals to shift how he believed in himself. This contagion of beliefs and emotions, the very core of team chemistry, changed the course of the Giants' season. Lincecum went eight innings that day against the Colorado Rockies, striking out nine in the 2–1 victory. He went on to win five of his six starts in September. With seven days left in the regular season, the Giants climbed into first place and held on to win the division.

Something kept nagging at me. Where was testosterone in this sea of feel-good brain chemicals? Here we had a team of twenty-five highly competitive young athletes coursing with testosterone. You could see it in their nose-to-nose arguments with umpires and explosions at opponents whose home-run trots were too slow (Disrespectful!) or bat flips too theatrical (Showing up our pitcher!). Testosterone is one reason home fields give teams an advantage. Researchers have found that athletes' testosterone levels are higher before home games than before road games, perhaps a vestige of ancestral tribes protecting their territory against outsiders. You would think that inside the clubhouse big, bad testosterone would counteract kind, generous oxytocin. But that wasn't happening with the 2010 Giants. Oxytocin was winning. Nobody, including macho-men Huff and Burrell, was overtly jockeying for power. Nobody was commandeering the clubhouse sound system to foist his playlist on everyone else. Nobody was calling team meetings to mark his territory as leader. Why weren't these calling cards of testosterone showing up in the players' behavior?

Because testosterone has an engaging, social side.

Lab experiments found that in a group of strangers, high-testosterone people were the most highly regarded by the other members.[4] They didn't gain such status by overpowering the

41

group, as you might expect from this somewhat misunderstood, macho hormone. Quite the opposite. They did it by fitting in, listening, helping out.

The researchers found that high testosterone fuels a *drive* for stature. This drive makes us adjust our mindset and behavior to whatever the group values most, thus allowing us to win over its members. In this way, testosterone is an arrowleaf. On the climb up the social ladder, the environment influences how testosterone expresses itself.

But the research also showed stark anomalies. Some high-testosterone athletes weren't leaders at all. In fact, some were among the lowest-status players. What was going on? Scientists found that another hormone, cortisol, was altering testosterone's impact.[5] Though cortisol is commonly known as the stress hormone, its actual purpose is to counteract stress. The more stress you feel, the more cortisol your body produces to get you back to equilibrium. Thus, high levels of cortisol indicate high stress.

"Here's what I think is happening based on research and intuitive leaps and my experience as an athlete in team sports," said Kathleen Casto, a biopsychologist who has conducted substantial research on testosterone's and cortisol's connection to leadership, most recently with the 2016 women's Olympic field hockey team.[6] "If you have high testosterone, then you're motivated for status among teammates. If you have high cortisol, maybe you're an anxious person, stressed out. You don't realize your [negative] impact on teammates. That results in low status. In other words, you want status, but you're not good at achieving it."

This suggests a physiological explanation for Huff's transformation. He finally found himself on a team where he was accepted and valued. This would surely relieve the stress of proving himself, of defending himself against naysayers, including the one in his own head. Perhaps his cortisol level dropped during the 2010 season with the Giants, his behavior changed, and his teammates were drawn to him as a leader.

As recently as 2007, the Giants' clubhouse had been as cliquey and snipey as a middle-school cafeteria. Many of the veterans were on the downside of their careers and kept to themselves except, it seemed, to cut rookies down to size for talking to the media too much, playing music too loud, celebrating a home run too exuberantly. I remembered what Jim Leyland had told me:

"When you get the veterans to buy into the program, that is a treat for a manager. When the veterans don't buy into the program, and they can't really play anymore, and you have to start replacing them with younger players, you got fucking chaos on your hands. Trust me."

By 2010, with the veteran cliques gone, a new openness settled over the clubhouse. "It's given all the younger guys a chance to be themselves," Lincecum said that year. "They're not just in their lockers staring at the wall or sitting at the table not talking." Players seemed to feel a sense of belonging and trust that allowed for lots of joking and honest conversation. They looked forward to coming to the park every day. They knew they'd have fun. And they were winning.

As I write this, I can almost hear the talk-radio voices leap an octave. *"They aren't winning because they're having fun! They're having fun because they're winning!"*

Yes, of course, winning is more conducive to having fun than not winning. The converse is also true: Having fun is more conducive to winning than not having fun. In that 2010 clubhouse, players ragged on each other with insults that, to me, would be knives in soft flesh but drew howls of laughter, even from the target. Nothing seemed off-limits. No one ever seemed wounded.

Little did I imagine that this humor, as juvenile and crude as it was, showed how much they trusted each other. Successful teasing requires mutual trust. You trust that the target understands the goodwill you feel toward him. The target trusts that your teasing means he's part of the tribe.

"Joking cultures are trusting cultures," said social psychologist Gary Alan Fine, who has been writing about and studying humor since the 1970s.[7] "You can't have a teasing relationship with people you don't really care about."

Teams, like most work groups, are not made up of equals. Some have more authority, money, and tenure. But to function successfully as a team, everyone needs to operate as if they're equals. Humor, especially teasing, allows stars and coaches to show they're one of the guys or gals. "One way for a high-status person to be effective is to be willing not just to be the giver of humor, but the target as well," Fine said. "In effect, he's saying, 'I'm a leader, but I'm not different from you. I can take a joke.'"

Fine points out the words *target* and *take*. They suggest incoming fire. When we good-naturedly suffer the slings and arrows of outrageous insult, we show commitment to the tribe. It's a form of hazing. The teasing asks: Do you trust us, and can we trust you?

How does this help performance?

In a truly trusting culture, trust is as taken for granted as gravity. We are oblivious to its pull, to its effect on our mindset and thus our performance. Consider a high-stress scenario. You're pinch-hitting in the bottom of the ninth in a tie game. Or you're making an important presentation in front of your organization. As soon as our brain registers the stressful situation, our heart begins to pump faster. Our mindset determines what happens next.

If we trust that our colleagues and bosses believe in us, that they'll stand by us even if we fail, we perceive stress as a challenge instead of a threat. Our brain releases hormones that cause our blood vessels to open up, delivering the extra blood into our brain and muscles to fortify us. Our body is primed for action. We feel emboldened to take risks that can push our performance to the next level. We don't have to play it so safe because we know, no matter what the outcome, our tribe will be there.

The opposite of a trusting culture is organized paranoia. "You start over-processing everything, scrutinizing everything everybody says, looking for unfairness and criticism," said Rod Kramer, a professor of organizational behavior at the Stanford Graduate School of Business. "It's a productivity killer."

Instead of nervous excitement, we face stress with nervous fear. We perceive the situation as a threat. Our blood vessels constrict instead of expand, limiting the flow of blood and oxygen to our brain and muscles. Our body goes into a virtual crouch, preparing for the blows of failure. "The physiology of positive emotion is the antithesis of the physiology of stress," said UC Berkeley psychology professor Dacher Keltner. "Stress wears you down. It makes you cautious. It tightens you up. You choke."

By season's end, Huff had more home runs (twenty-six) and more runs batted in (eighty-six) than anyone else on the team. The Giants advanced through the Division Series, the National League Championship Series, and on to the team's first World Series championship in fifty-six years, their first ever in San Francisco. Anchored by Lincecum, young pitchers carried the Giants, but it was Huff who anchored the offense. He had become a fan favorite, a go-to guy for reporters, and an honest-to-god team leader. *Aubrey Huff.*

But he never played as well or had such impact again. The following year, with a new two-year contract from the Giants, his performance and influence eroded to the point of irrelevance. He had become a star, at least in San Francisco, with the indulgences and scrutiny that came with it. His addiction to Adderall escalated, as did his drinking. He had panic attacks—one so severe he left the team without notice and was gone a week. His wife had filed for divorce several months earlier, though they ended up staying together, at least for a few more years. (They divorced in 2018.)

When the Giants returned to the World Series in 2012, Huff was on the bench. He had just one hit in ten plate appearances. Then his career was over.

But for that one season in 2010, in that particular clubhouse among those particular men, he was a leader. His was an ungainly, stumbling kind of transformation, but in some ways as elegant and awesome as the arrowleaf's.

The sun was beginning to disappear behind the trees at Claremont Graduate University. Paul Zak and I had walked to a small campus café, and we returned to the question of defining team chemistry.

"I think chemistry is a real thing," he said. "We have a shared chemistry, and oxytocin is part of that. Baseball's insane because of the number of games they play, right? It's hard because you're tired and exhausted, and what do you have at the end of the day? You got a team. They need you, and you better recognize that you need them.

"That's the 'I got your back' thing. I want to know that when the shit hits the fan in the game, you'll break a leg. That's what I really want to know. If that's the case, that says *I* need to be that kind of person, too. Otherwise I'm not a member of the team."

He took a sip of coffee, gathering his thoughts.

"I would say that—maybe you're going to laugh at this—but I think it's that you really have to love the people that you are on a team with. In a really fundamental sense. From a neurologic sense, for sure. Also behaviorally. You have to take that three a.m. phone call when his wife kicks him out of the house. You got to be fully in as a human being, not just as a player, I think. Because it's too hard otherwise."

Every now and then, a player who is the embodiment of chemistry itself arrives on a team. These players carry much more than their fair share of the chemistry load, seeming to lift whatever team they join. I call these men and women Super-Carriers.

CHAPTER THREE

SUPER-CARRIERS, OR THE CURIOUS CASE OF JONNY GOMES

"Give me one guy who makes five guys better."
—Don Wakamatsu, former baseball manager

The Society for American Baseball Research held its second annual analytics conference at Arizona State University in March 2013. A lanky, square-jawed pitcher named Brandon McCarthy settled into a chair onstage for a panel discussion. McCarthy had participated at the inaugural conference the previous year, too. He was a rarity among major league players at the time. He completely embraced analytics. He had begun reading Bill James's sabermetrics books for fun, mostly to win baseball arguments on social media. He soon was following the daily stream of statistical analyses on websites like sabr.org and FanGraphs.com. He liked the black-and-white clarity of analytics. He had improved his own performance by applying what he learned. In short, he was both aficionado and practitioner and could hold his own with the mathematicians and baseball geeks in the Arizona State University auditorium.

Halfway through the discussion, the moderator brought up the squishy, anti-analytic notion of "clubhouse guys" whose presence supposedly somehow makes a team better. What was McCarthy's take?

The pitcher paused. He rubbed his face, knowing his answer might come as a surprise, and maybe a disappointment, to the acronym-and-algorithm crowd.

"I think they're really important," he said. "And the reason I say that now—much more than I have in the past—is just being part of the A's team last year."

By which he meant he had spent a season with Jonny Gomes.

I had never crossed paths with this player. But I knew if I was going to understand team chemistry, I needed to understand Jonny Gomes.

You go one of two ways when you're a nomad. No place is home, or every place is.

Gomes bounced around the major leagues for eleven years. He was an eighteenth-round draft pick for Tampa, where he played a few years before moving on to Cincinnati, Washington, DC, Oakland, Boston, back to Oakland, and finally Kansas City. His longest contract was two years. Gomes arrived at new teams barely knowing anyone, having to ask for directions to everything from the trainer's room to the commode. No matter. He would glide into the clubhouse as if walking through his own front door. He never considered the possibility he might not fit in. The team was already family simply by virtue of being his team. In that way, baseball was simpler for Gomes than for most players. Not simpler to play—he was a journeyman outfielder. Baseball was simpler because he operated according to a single directive: Do whatever the team needs, on and off the field. He can't remember when he didn't think this way. It traces back to a small neighborhood baseball diamond in Petaluma on the momentous day he received his first uniform.

Petaluma is a sprawling town forty miles north of San Francisco where old Victorians and stately oaks give way to working-class neighborhoods and then rolling hills dotted with egg and dairy farms and cattle pastures. In a middle-class and upper-middle-class community, Gomes and his brother Joey, older by a year, rotated the same few T-shirts and pants every day. They each had one pair of generic sneakers. Their clothes seemed to mark them as different, which, Gomes soon realized, they were. Jonny, Joey, and their mom moved constantly—about twenty-five times by the time the boys finished high school. Dad lived with his second family and, as Jonny and Joey got older, didn't see them much. Mom cut hair, dealt cards at Artichoke Joe's, cashiered at a gas station, waited tables, answered phones at offices. Thanksgiving dinner arrived most years in a box from the food bank. Five chairs held the extended family for the holidays: Mom, Joey, Jonny, and Grandma and Grandpa, themselves long ago divorced. No aunts or uncles or cousins. No Christmas tree most years. Mundane catastrophes, like worn brake pads, meant another eviction soon enough. The boys knew that within thirty days of the notice they'd be stripping their beds and tossing their belongings into trash bags. Sometimes they'd log a night in the car, but almost always by the time school let out in the afternoon, their bags and mattresses would be on a different floor in a different bedroom, sometimes across town, other times down the block. Mom handed out new keys. For Gomes, every house and apartment was more or less the same. None was home.

One day on that small field in Petaluma when Gomes was seven years old, he sat cross-legged with a dozen other boys he knew from school. Gomes pulled on his first uniform, a black shirt with *Plumbers* across the front in white letters and a matching black cap. He looked around at the other boys. They all looked the same. All Plumbers. It no longer mattered who had designer jeans and who had knockoffs. He couldn't articulate it at the time, but at the ball field he wasn't different from anyone else. He belonged completely. Every boy on the team cheered for every other boy. After games, they ran around the concession stand and under the bleachers together. Gomes loved being part of the pack. At some point, he noticed that pumping up a teammate could change the kid's mood for the rest of the game and that the kid's energy seemed to spread to other teammates. "OK," he thought. "All right." For Gomes, baseball came to feel "like Thanksgiving and Christmas all at once with all your cousins running around."

The feeling never left him, and as he climbed through the ranks, he played full-throttle every day, as if he felt death's breath on his neck. The truth was he *had* felt death's breath. The first time he was sixteen years old. He was with his friend and baseball teammate Adam Westcott in the back of a car heading down a mountain road. Gomes was in the seat behind the driver. The car fishtailed, swerved to the right, and slammed into a telephone pole. The two girls in the front seats were barely hurt. Same with Gomes. But Adam had been crushed and died two days later.

The second time Gomes was twenty-two. The minor-league season was over, and Gomes was back in Petaluma. He felt a pain in his chest but rode it out for more than a day before going to the emergency room, where doctors realized he was having a heart attack. He was rushed to the operating room, where surgeons performed angioplasty on a pinched valve. Had he waited much longer, he learned, the heart attack likely would have killed him. (There has been no recurrence of heart problems.)

When Gomes arrived as a rookie in 2005, Tampa Bay had finished last in six of their first seven years as an expansion team and was known as a listless, every-man-for-himself team. From Little

League through high school, college, and the minor leagues, Gomes had never been among teammates that cared so much about their own stats and so little about winning. (Aubrey Huff was the first baseman on that team.) One day, Gomes was sitting in the dugout next to a veteran player who was correctly predicting every pitch their own pitcher threw. Gomes asked how he knew. "He's tipping pitches," the player said. That means he was unwittingly signaling—by, for example, tilting his glove a certain way before fastballs—what pitch was coming, thus giving the batter a great advantage. Gomes was excited. "You have to tell him," he said. But the player refused. "I might have to face him next season," he said.

Gomes tried not to let the team's selfishness bother him. Families behaved poorly sometimes, but they were still family. Besides, he had a highly developed knack for finding a kinsman wherever he happened to be. In Tampa, Gomes found Toby Hall, a fellow Northern Californian and veteran catcher who took the rookie under his wing. The two talked constantly to one another, in the clubhouse, in the dugout, in restaurants and bars. Hall taught Gomes how to use his time on the bench to study pitchers and hitters, how to get his mind right after a bad game. Even as the Rays stumbled through another one-hundred-loss season, Hall rooted his ass off for Gomes, and Gomes did the same for Hall. Gomes woke up every morning wanting to make Hall proud. Then one day in 2006, the Rays traded Hall to the Dodgers. Though Gomes had known Hall for less than two years, his departure "was like a death," Gomes said.

His reaction was, by any measure, extreme. Pro baseball is a business. Players come and go. Hall was a teammate, not an actual brother. Gomes knew this but couldn't help how he felt. Teams were family; clubhouses were home. He didn't go onto a team and *create* a home and family for himself. He unearthed them.

This, it turned out, was Gomes's true baseball talent. Yes, he could play a solid left field, hit some balls out of the park, steal some bases. But Gomes's singular gift was that he genuinely, deeply, actively cared. Over time in Gomes's nomadic baseball life, a pattern began to take shape: His teams won.

His Tampa Bay Rays reached the World Series in 2008 for the first time in franchise history after a decade of mostly last-place finishes. His 2010 Cincinnati Reds reached the playoffs for the first time in fifteen years. His 2012 Oakland A's, predicted to lose one hundred games, shocked the baseball world by winning ninety-four games and the American League West. His 2013 Boston Red Sox and 2015 Kansas City Royals won the World Series. This all could be coincidence. Maybe he was baseball's Forrest Gump, a guy with the extraordinarily good fortune to stumble into the right situations. After all, he spent most of his career as a part-time outfielder. His lifetime batting average was a weak .242. Hardly anyone's definition of a linchpin or beating heart.

Brandon McCarthy and Jonny Gomes were both in their second year in the big leagues when they met at an Arizona gym where a number of major leaguers trained during the off-season. McCarthy kept a low profile as would be expected of a newbie. But Gomes dove right in, ragging on guys, telling jokes. McCarthy had never seen anyone like him. He changed the vibe of the workout group as soon as he blew through the door every morning. "He had kind of a power over everyone," McCarthy told me.

The two didn't interact again until six years later when Gomes arrived in Oakland in 2012. McCarthy had been with the A's a year by then. His old workout buddy hadn't changed. Shaved head, red beard, tattoos, a bulge of chew. Still loud and funny. He would at least enliven the team, which it sorely needed after 2011's eighty-eight losses. Most prognosticators predicted more of the same, or worse, for 2012. But before spring training had ended, McCarthy knew the experts were wrong. Something was happening. These guys believed they could win. When they lost nine games in a row early in the season, they shrugged. What team didn't spend a little time in the mud? Then they *did* start to win. McCarthy had no statistical proof and wasn't sure yet if he believed it himself, but he had begun to consider the possibility that Jonny Gomes had something to do with it.

On a breezy October afternoon in 2016, Gomes answered his door in a gray T-shirt and basketball shorts. His red beard was shorter than it once had been, but his head was still shaved, and the tattoos on his thick arms had only multiplied. He lived in a sprawling enclave of enormous homes—four-car garages, waterpark pools, guesthouses, outdoor kitchens—on the northernmost end of Scottsdale, Arizona, out where the desert rises toward the McDowell Mountains. Stately front doors were festooned with cornstalks and pumpkins. So was Gomes's. But his house was easy to spot. It was the only one with a two-and-a-half-ton, camouflage-green, monster-tire M35 military truck in the driveway.

I had formed an image of Gomes in my head from all the research I had done on the guy. I had a thick, three-ring binder full of it, the largest assemblage of material I had on any single person for this book. I hadn't intended to collect so much. But stories and interviews were easy to come by. Major-league players call you back when your message says you're writing about Gomes. Washington Nationals' All-Star outfielder Jayson Werth called on his way to physical therapy. Gomes had joined the Nationals halfway through the 2011 season.

"When Jonny came in, the whole culture shifted—to the

point where I went to [manager] Davey Johnson and said, 'Hey, we really need Jonny Gomes next year. We really need him,'" he said. The Nationals didn't keep him. "As a player you get a sense of chemistry and the effect that people have on it—good or bad. A lot of times the front office, coaches, managers, they're not really part of the clubhouse. So unfortunately, the team chemistry thing doesn't always make a whole lot of sense to them."

Cy Young winner Jake Peavy from the 2013 World Series champion Red Sox told me, "Jonny Gomes is the best team-chemistry guy I ever played with. He was a huge part of what made us go."

"Even on the day he doesn't play, Jonny's impacting the game, and you can't say that about a lot of major leaguers," said All-Star Dustin Pedroia, also a Red Sox teammate. "He sees the game in a different way than a lot of players. Even coaches, they don't see the game like he does. And he brings an element of toughness, and that's what the Red Sox are about. They're blue collar. You got to get in the fight to win. That's what the city and the fans want. I knew Jonny would be a perfect fit for the Red Sox. And it just so happened he was a free agent [in 2013]."

In my head Gomes was a rough-edged Seth Rogen: gregarious, chatty, funny. But the guy who opened the door was quiet and reserved, almost cool. We had exchanged a dozen or so texts over several months, and he had sounded completely on board with the interview. Enthusiastic even. Now I was wondering if he was having second thoughts. I followed him through a high-ceilinged living room and dining room and into an enormous kitchen warmed by Halloween decorations and cookbooks and fresh flowers. In the corner was a small table loaded with bins of crayons, paints, and construction paper. We sat in the breakfast nook. Gomes tucked a pinch of chewing tobacco inside his bottom lip.

"You still do that, huh?" I said in a teasing way, trying to connect.

"Keeps me close to the game," he said, and I remembered: For the first time since he was seven years old, Gomes had no team.

After winning the World Series with the Royals in 2015, he signed in 2016 with the only organization that made him an offer, the Tohoku Rakuten Golden Eagles in Japan. He didn't speak their language or understand their culture. Most days he sat by himself in the clubhouse and dugout. Nothing about it was home or family. He left after playing in just eighteen games (and performing poorly). He had been home now for five months, and I wondered if for him losing baseball—the clubhouse, the teammates, the shared purpose—is a version of what psychiatrist Thomas Lewis had told me about losing a longtime partner, that it literally felt like losing a limb.

We had fallen into awkward small talk when a tiny girl in a sparkly princess costume skipped into the kitchen on bare feet and climbed onto Gomes's lap. She burrowed into the crook of his arm and breathlessly reported the latest plot twists of the My Little Pony video she was watching in the other room. Capri was three years old and the youngest of Gomes's three children. Their names appear in Old English script on Gomes's right forearm below an older tattoo that says, "Tough Times Go Away... Tough People Don't."

Gomes made a little show of gasping at Capri's stories about Pinkie Pie and Twilight Sparkle. "No way!" he said. Her mission complete, Capri started wriggling off her father's lap, and he set her bare feet back on the floor. Off she skipped with a wave. "Bye, Daddy!"

Gomes worried that his children were growing up with so much abundance and ease that they were missing out on the experiences that shaped him and his brother. Will they work hard? Will they have the same appreciation for things? "I never lost a damn thing. I wouldn't lose a hat, I wouldn't lose a glove, I wouldn't lose a shirt. I knew where my baseball uniform was, because I'd do the laundry."

"Scarcity teaches you to waste nothing," I said. I suggested that seems true for the game itself, at least for him. He could take nothing for granted. I wondered if he consciously set out to make the greatest impact he could in whatever time he had. Yes, he said. And I wondered if he knew the impact would be unmeasurable and, in many quarters, unacknowledged. *Yes.* The lightbulb went on, he said, when he was playing for the Cincinnati Reds in 2009, and the team's biggest star, Jay Bruce, asked him a question about hitting strategy.

"I'm like, 'Me? You think I have that answer?' It was a question I would be asking of someone else," Gomes said. "I learned something important: Even the best player on the team is still searching for a strategy." The exchange knocked down the wall between him and the big stars, the way the Plumbers uniforms did between him and the rich kids that first season of Little League.

More guys began to seek his advice. They seemed to think that because he had been to the World Series the previous season with the Rays, he was imbued with some sort of special wisdom. He was, though not necessarily from his World Series experience. Gomes seemed to smell what guys needed. He knew when to joke, inspire, push, teach. He found ways to nurture their confidence. For example, a struggling young player might wake one morning to read Gomes's quotes bragging about him in a story. Another might be reassured with a well-timed lie from Gomes that the manager wasn't mad at him at all but in fact thought the world of him. He might go watch a video of a slumping teammate's at-bats and quietly share what he saw.

"In the big leagues, it's all about a race to adjustments," Gomes said, "and whoever can make the adjustments fastest. So to make an adjustment a majority of the time it has to be from input from someone else." The guy could accept or reject the feedback. Gomes said he never took it personally. The actual information was only part of his message. He was also communicating to his teammate, "Look, we've got to care about each other. We're all in this together."

That's what chemistry is, Gomes told me. "It's players really caring about each other, and that's why teams play better when they have it." His voice was picking up. He shifted in his seat so he was now almost facing me.

"I hate comparing our game to war, you know, but if you had to pick one guy to go with you into the foxhole, would you pick the best shot? Or would you pick the guy who would jump in front of you? It's like picking teams for a sandlot game. You don't pick the best player. You pick your best friend because he'll play like hell for you whether you're behind by one run or ten runs.

"It's no different in the majors. When I'm in the outfield, and my buddy's on the mound, I'm not letting that ball fall. I'm going all out. When I'm on second and my buddy's at the plate, I'm scoring for him."

Conversely, if your teammate is a total jackass, "it just turns your fight down," he said. "That's the human element. We're not race cars. It's impossible to not have feelings about teammates and to not have those feelings affect how you play sometimes."

These are the dynamics Brandon McCarthy observed in 2012 that changed how he thought about chemistry.

McCarthy had accepted as common sense that selfless, cohesive teams had an easier time winning than fractured, ego-driven ones. He had also accepted as common sense that winning fostered this selflessness and cohesion, not the other way around. Winning feels awesome, so of course you want to *keep* winning.

Guys start focusing less on individual outcomes and more on team outcomes. They lay down a bunt here and there. They take the walk, break up the double play, dive for the sinking line drive, pass along advice. They rack up wins. Everyone's in a better mood. Guys are joining in on the card games. They're grabbing dinner together on the road. And finally, inevitably, they're attributing their success to chemistry when all along it was always about the winning.

McCarthy had certainly known teams like that. But on the 2012 A's he saw something different. The cohesion and selflessness— the chemistry—preceded the winning. He saw it as early as spring training. There were so many new faces and tons of young ones. McCarthy watched Gomes work the clubhouse like a conductor directing an orchestra. He kicked up the seriousness at the right time and dialed it back just as easily. He boosted egos, soothed tempers, held people accountable for weak effort and poor behavior without being an ass. He was particularly skilled with the rookies, whose swaggers couldn't mask the smell of fear and doubt. Gomes made them feel safe. McCarthy watched over the course of the season the impact that had on their performance. A twenty-five-year-old rookie named Chris Carter, for example, had barely gotten on base during his brief debut in the big leagues in 2011. He was a different player in 2012, posting one of the highest on-base percentages and on-base plus slugging percentages on the team.

"If you feel more comfortable and you're having more fun, I think better parts of you come out," McCarthy said. "In no way could I quantify that, but I feel like there has to be a sort of trickle-down effect. You don't feel you're uptight. You don't feel like you'll let people down. It makes it a little easier to perform."

Ever the analyst, McCarthy broke down the trickle-down effect into two general categories: atmosphere and information. Atmosphere is what he referenced above: A relaxed and accepting environment that lifts anxiety and unleashes a player's full potential. The second category—sharing information—seems straightforward and obvious. The more information a player has, the better he's likely to perform. But in a baseball clubhouse—perhaps in any competitive group—the impact of information depends as much on a teammate's feeling about the messenger as on the content of the information.

"Let's say a teammate gives you a piece of advice," McCarthy explained. "Because you trust him, you accept his advice. Let's say over the next two months, the advice saves you from giving up three runs. Three runs aren't much, but they might be the difference in [winning] a couple of games. And that's a result of me trusting that player. If there are thirty or forty of those interactions among players on a team over the course of a season, it might be a nonquantifiable thing, but it's a very, very real thing.

"The flip side is you don't like that guy. He could tell you something and your brain goes, 'Don't care.' [Now the] advice gets lost. And all of a sudden those three runs that I would have saved, now I've given up. And the team is worse for it."

Because Gomes earned everybody's respect, McCarthy said, "he can say things other people can't say, and guys are going to buy into it."

Josh Donaldson was a case in point.

Donaldson was a flamboyant first-round pick who struck more than a few teammates as arrogant and show-offy. During batting practice one afternoon, Gomes saw some guys roll their eyes when the young third baseman launched a pitch over the scoreboard. "*You* do that," Gomes told them, shutting down the snark. Gomes saw the kid was incredibly gifted but had a lot of growing up to do if he was going to help the team win. One day, with the A's ahead by eight runs late in a game, Donaldson slammed his bat and helmet in the dugout after striking out.

Gomes got in his face. "Whoa! We're about to win a game here. What are you mad about?"

"I can't be mad that I struck out right there?" Donaldson snapped.

"No," Gomes told him, "you can't. You got to bottle that up. Go home and smash a coffee cup or something. But you can't do that on the field."

Gomes wanted to add, "Because it's selfish. Because the only performance that matters is the collective one. Because the only stat that matters is wins." But he didn't. He knew when guys were ready to listen and seized on later openings with Donaldson, teaching him in a million small ways that talent alone wasn't going to carry him to the heights of major-league baseball. Donaldson listened. He began to flourish, and, three years later, he beat out superstar Mike Trout for the American League's Most Valuable Player Award.

After a ragged beginning, the A's won nineteen of twenty-four games in July. They became kings of the comeback, winning one walk-off after another—finishing games with leaping, helmet-flipping, kids-on-a-sandlot pileups at home plate. Rituals had developed—the handshakes, inside jokes, nicknames. They took to cranking up the "Weekend at Bernie's" rap song and dancing the extremely geeky "Bernie Lean." (Check it out on YouTube.) They slapped shaving-cream pies in each other's faces during postgame interviews. No team seemed to be having more fun than the Oakland A's. Unheralded players emerged, as they always do on such teams. Brandon Moss was a twenty-eight-year-old journeyman who had spent most of his eleven-year career bouncing around the minor leagues. He landed with the A's in 2012 on a minor-league contract. Days before the contract was going to expire in mid-June — Moss had already planned to play in Japan and then join the fire department back home in Loganville, Georgia — the A's suddenly called him to the big leagues to platoon at first base. Gomes was platooning, too, so Moss sat with him in the dugout just as Gomes had sat with Toby Hall in Tampa. They talked about strategy and approach, about what Gomes saw in Moss's at-bats, how he might try this or that. Baseball talk gave way to conversations about childhood, family, fear, failure, pain. Moss was surprised.

"We're very guarded," he said of ballplayers. "We don't let people in very often. As a man, especially as a competitive man, when you open up and let your guard down, you're seen as a little bit weak. But Gomes is not afraid to be vulnerable. You can talk to him about anything. What it's like to get released. What it's like to play badly. He's a real person. That doesn't come along as much as you would think in a locker room."

I was talking to Moss in 2017 inside the visitors' clubhouse at AT&T Park. He was two and a half months into his first season with the Kansas City Royals, with whom Gomes had won his second World Series championship two years earlier.

"I've only been here half a year, but I already heard the story a number of times about Gomes with Christian Colon," Moss said. Colon was a bench player who, in Game 5 of the 2015 World Series, hadn't been up to bat for six weeks when he drove in the go-ahead run in the twelfth inning to clinch the championship. In the post-game interview on television, he credited Gomes with taking him under his wing and keeping him ready.

"Jonny Gomes doesn't steal bases. He doesn't run," Moss said. "But here's Gomes sitting down with a guy and showing him something that might help them win a World Series game — and it does. He didn't have any idea that situation would come. He's getting this guy ready for the opportunity that he may have, and Gomes wasn't even on the postseason roster. He could have been the guy that said, 'Fuck this. They screwed me.' "

At the A's, Moss blossomed. He hit nine home runs in his first twenty games and kept hitting.*

The A's took over second place by winning thirteen of their last fifteen games in August. Nipping at the heels of the first-place Texas Rangers through September, the A's caught them with just one game left in the season. Each team had ninety-three wins and sixty-eight losses. After three hours and sixteen minutes on a Wednesday afternoon in early October, in front of 36,067 screaming A's fans, the A's beat the reigning American League Champions, 12–5, to clinch the division title.

"In their underdog role," a reporter for the *New York Times* wrote, "the A's pulled off one of baseball's great surprises in recent decades."

Most everyone on the team pointed to Jonny Gomes as the difference-maker. This reportedly included general manager Billy Beane, according to an A's insider.† But if Beane believed Gomes played a critical role in the A's success, he didn't believe it enough to bring him back in 2013.

No one sets out to be a Super-Carrier of chemistry. You'd rather be the guy with the multimillion, multiyear contract. Super-Carriers often emerge from that stratum of players hired to fill a gap in the lineup, to step in when the starter pulls a hamstring.

---

* He made the All-Star team two years later with the A's and then played in Cleveland, St. Louis, and Kansas City and went back to the A's in 2018. As of this writing, he has yet to swing a bat in Japan or fight fires in Loganville.
† Beane, whose embrace of analytics and dismissal of chemistry were famously detailed in Michael Lewis's book *Moneyball*, politely declined requests to be interviewed for this book.

They're skilled enough to play in the big leagues, but not necessarily to excel. Like freelancers of every ilk, they're usually short-timers, lurching from contract to contract. They're attractive to teams because they make up in grit and personality what they lack in physical talent.

Everyday or situational carriers of chemistry can be anyone, including superstars like Derek Jeter and Trevor Hoffman. All-Star slugger Keith Hernandez said superstar Pete Rose was a carrier. "He was the most infectious player I ever came across. He made everybody feel great," he said. Few superstars are also Super-Carriers, though they exist. One is legendary point guard Sue Bird. Though just five feet, ten inches tall, she has managed to win nearly everywhere she plays: two state high-school championships, two NCAA championships with the University of Connecticut, four Olympic gold medals, and, at last count, three WNBA championships. "When I put my team first, all the good things happen," she told Sam Walker of the *Wall Street Journal*. "I function well as a basketball player when my team is functioning well—that's when my game shines. I try to be as smart and selfless as I can, and in the end I get a lot more in return."[1]

Some stars become Super-Carriers only as their careers begin to fade. For the Cleveland Indians in 2013, it was a forty-two-year-old faded star named Jason Giambi. He was brought in that year to create what manager Terry Francona called "atmosphere." The Indians won ninety-two games. Giambi played in fewer than half, during which he compiled a sickly .183 batting average. Yet when the Indians reached the postseason, Francona called Giambi the team's most valuable player. "I don't think we'd be here without G," he told reporters.

Legendary UCLA basketball coach John Wooden always tried to find a carrier to be his "perfect sixth man" (though he didn't use the term *carrier*). This player possessed "just the right dynamic qualities—a highly emotional individual who gets instant adrenaline flowing as soon as you call his name." Statistics, Wooden said, "never reflected the true value of such a player."[2]

Super-Carriers possess a complex combination of characteristics not generally associated with conventional sports heroes. Instead of glory and status, they chase connection and purpose. They are empathic, caring, and communicative. Having accepted their own failures and shortcomings, they can allow themselves to be vulnerable. They're self-deprecatingly funny, happy to be the butt of their own—and everyone else's—jokes.

They are charismatic though almost never clubhouse preachers. The clubhouse preacher—the rousing-speech guy—often wears thin over time, whereas the Super-Carrier's influence is enduring. Super-Carriers draw teammates to them and keep everyone from spinning off into orbits of their own. Pam Kerwin, one of the early executives at Pixar, once told me how she defined talent: Talent is delivering what the team needs. In this way, Super-Carriers are among the most talented people on any team, whether in sports, business, or anything else.

Eric Hinske was that guy on the 2013 Arizona Diamondbacks (D-Backs). Brandon McCarthy happened to land with the Diamondbacks that season, hard on the heels of playing with Jonny Gomes on the 2012 A's. Hinske, like Gomes, wasn't a star. He was an infielder at the end of his career. The first week of the season, the D-Backs played a five-and-a-half-hour sixteen-inning game in St. Louis, flew to Milwaukee in the dead of night, landed at six a.m., and then got stuck in traffic on the way to the hotel. Everyone was exhausted and cranky and desperate to get a few hours' sleep before playing the Milwaukee Brewers later that day.

"It turned out to be my favorite bus drive of my career," McCarthy said. "Hinske was on the mike the whole time at the front of the bus, and I just remember thinking I'm going to die of laughter. The whole bus was the same. Just uproarious. It was incredible how funny he was in this awful situation. A lot of his jokes and comments carried with us the next few months. They became running jokes."

The Diamondbacks released Hinske less than three months later, in late June. The first-place D-Backs lost five games in a row, their longest losing streak of the season. Three weeks later, they fell out of first place and never recovered, finishing eleven games behind the Dodgers. I'm not saying the D-Backs' season hinged on a thirty-six-year-old backup first baseman. My point is that inside the clubhouse, his absence was felt.

"We were just not as good," McCarthy said. "He had created something, whether consciously or just by instinct. But once you take him out of that, the inside jokes die, those little connection points go away. There's just a gap there and there's nothing there to fill it."

Like Gomes, Hinske had a tendency to land on championship squads. He played in three World Series in three years with three different teams: the 2007 Red Sox, the 2008 Rays, and the 2009 Yankees. "It was past the point where it was an anomaly," McCarthy said. "It's like 'OK, I think he's got something to do with this.'"

But how can we know? If there is a way to measure the impact of a Super-Carrier, I haven't found it. Neither the number of World Series appearances on a player's résumé nor the number of testimonials from teammates is proof he improved his team. But can science make a compelling case for the Jonny Gomes effect?

We know humans are programmed to continually pick up signals from one another. Those signals change our own brain and body, altering everything from our mood to our heart rate. Are there people whose signals are stronger than most people's? Yes, of course. Actors, for example. The average person simply talking on-screen is boring. Without a word, a good actor's face can be riveting. It can move us to tears. The actor is transmitting signals that affect us psychologically and physically. Maybe Super-Carriers, like actors, are super-signal-senders. But was there neurological evidence for Gomes's impact on his teammates?

I had asked Josh Woolley, the neuroscientist at UC San Francisco, about this when we met. He had clamped his hands to the arms of his chair and leaned back.

"I guess I find that question confusing. If I say I feel connected to this person, and I *don't* feel connected to *that* person, and my behavior with this person is different than my behavior with *that* person, what other evidence could there be?"

Well, I said, *scientific* evidence.

He emitted a sound I took as a harrumph. He said it made no sense that we continually question the truth of our own experience, the truth of what we see with our own eyes. "People say, 'Well, therapy might make people better, but unless we find a biomarker, then it's not real,'" he said.

Consider a kid learning new things in school, he said. She takes a test. She gets the answers right. We know something real transpired in the student's brain because we witnessed the impact: She summoned the correct answers. When we see that happen over and over, we can safely deduce that her interactions with her teacher were directly related to her ability to answer the test questions.

"Learning, social connection, feelings—all of these things *are in the brain*," Woolley said. "They're not magic."

So here's a scientist saying I don't need "scientific" evidence to prove that Gomes's impact on his teammates was real. The players' experiences—what they saw, heard, did, felt—*are* the evidence. But, I said, how could I be sure the players' reports of their experiences are factual? Maybe they just *believed* Jonny Gomes had an effect.

Woolley began to look slightly exasperated. He asked if I had ever watched *Dumbo*. Did I remember the feather? Dumbo's ears give him the ability to fly, but he doesn't believe it. Then he is given a "magic" feather that he is told can make him fly. And he flies.

"It's not the feather, of course," Woolley said. "It's his ears. What I'm saying is it's not surprising to me that a team would have a person they would think of as a totem or a good-luck charm. And that doesn't mean it doesn't work."

This is called the placebo effect. In medicine, when a patient is led to believe that a pill will ease her pain, it often does, no matter what is actually in the pill. We often think of it as a trick, that the phenomenon is purely psychological. Research, however, has found that placebos trigger very real physiological responses. Our expectation of pain relief, for example, can awaken the pain-relief system in our brain, allowing our body to respond as if it is processing a real pain medication, Woolley said.

"One of my mentors," he continued, "said, 'People come to me after seeing several people for pain. I'm the expert, and I give them a prescription that evidence suggests will work. But I also really sell it. Because they're going to respond.' There's also a thing called the nocebo effect. If you tell people about all the bad [side effects] that can happen, more than likely they'll have the bad things."

Everything in our environment affects our brain, so why wouldn't our own beliefs? I thought about the *yips*, a word first used to describe the psychological brain freeze that renders golfers unable to sink an easy putt. In baseball, fielders suddenly can't make routine throws to first base, and pitchers can't get the ball over the plate. Generally, there is nothing physically wrong with them.* Their minds seem to have taken hold of a belief, and their bodies have gone along with it.

Yet some of the same people who recognize the yips as real don't believe the reverse is true: that belief can elevate performance. Maybe the Jonny Gomes effect is simply a projection of his teammates' beliefs. They *think* he's making them better, so their performance improves. Their bodies deliver on what their minds expect.

"This is a real phenomenon," Woolley said. "It's really in the brain. It's a real thing. It happens. It affects performance."

Gomes is coy about what really happened before Game 4 of the 2013 World Series between Boston and St. Louis.

It was hours before the first pitch at Busch Stadium on October 27, 2013. The St. Louis Cardinals were up two games to one in the series. Red Sox manager John Farrell posted his lineup. As always, it immediately went out to every media outlet in the country. Daniel Nava was starting in left field, which was expected. Nava and Gomes had platooned in left all season: left-handed Nava played against right-handed pitchers, and right-handed Gomes played against lefties. The Cardinals had right-hander Lance Lynn on the mound in Game 4, so Nava was in the lineup.

The Red Sox clubhouse leaders—Dustin Pedroia, David "Big Papi" Ortiz, Jon Lester, and half a dozen others—convened, made a decision, and went as a group into Farrell's office.

"Jonny Gomes is playing," Big Papi said.

Farrell balked at what seemed like a ridiculous request. The lineup was already posted and distributed. Managers don't sud-

---

* According to the Mayo Clinic, some people have the yips due to a neurological condition that affects specific muscles.

denly change the lineup, especially during a World Series, without an extremely good reason like a last-minute injury. Daniel Nava was having a great year. He had batted .303 during the regular season, a career best, compared to Gomes's .247.

More important, Gomes had yet to get a hit in the series. He'd been awful, even against lefties. He had no hits as a starter in Games 1 and 2 and none as a pinch hitter in Game 3.

But his teammates wouldn't budge. The Red Sox had lost Games 2 and 3. If they didn't win Game 4, they'd be down three games to one. They'd be one game away from losing the series. The leaders on the team believed they played better with Gomes out there with them.

"Gomes became such a huge part of what made us go that it didn't matter if it was a right-handed starter," said a former Red Sox player who requested anonymity. The episode has never been made public. "Having Gomes on the field, the way everybody on that team felt about him—he pulled such a weight that was unexplainable."

Faced with what amounted to a mutiny, Farrell changed the lineup. He put Gomes in left, moved Nava to right, and scratched the usual right fielder, Shane Victorino. The Red Sox announced Victorino had developed lower-back tightness.

Gomes said he was taking batting practice with the last group of batters (players not in the lineup are the last to take their swings). "Someone tapped me on the shoulder and said I was play-ing," he said. He didn't ask any questions.

Fast-forward to the bottom of the sixth inning. The game was tied 1–1 with two outs.

Dustin Pedroia reached base on a single. Boston's All-Star slugger, Big Papi, stepped into the box. Every person at Busch Sta-dium knew the Cardinals were going to walk him. Why? Gomes was up next, and he was zero-for-the-series. The Cardinals brought in a fresh arm to face him, a rookie reliever named Seth Maness, a right-hander Gomes had never faced. Ordinarily, while an unfamiliar reliever is warming up, Gomes would pop into the dugout to check out the scouting report. Instead, Gomes not only drifted as far away from the dugout as possible, but he also avoided all eye contact with Farrell. "If I go to the dugout or catch his eye," Gomes said, "there's a chance he's going to pull me for a pinch hitter."

Gomes knew one thing about Maness: he's a big sinker-ball guy, and a righty's sinker breaks down and in on a right-handed hitter like Gomes. It is a bitch to hit. First pitch—whoosh!—down and in for a ball. Gomes stepped out and asked himself, Who does this guy remind me of? He suddenly thought of San Diego Padres pitcher Luke Gregerson. Gomes had faced him in 2012. Same arm slot and movement on the ball. He stepped back in. Maness worked Gomes to a 2–2 count. Gomes knew the sinker was coming. He had to get in front of the pitch, catch it before it breaks.

He did. The ball sailed 387 feet over the left-field fence, a spectacular three-run homer that put the Red Sox ahead for good. They won, 4–2, tying the series at two games apiece. Boston went on to win the next two games, clinching the championship. Gomes started both.

The numbers would show that, besides the one home run, Gomes had a miserable postseason. In three rounds of the playoffs—the American League Division Series, the American League Championship Series, and the World Series—Gomes managed just seven hits in forty-two plate appearances for a dismal .143 average.

His teammates, however, would show you a different number: The Sox were 10–1 in the games Jonny Gomes started.

"Everybody on that team believed when you get to that point

in the season, matchups don't matter," Pedroia told me. "You win with the people. You win with your guys. It's like anything. If you're going to lose at something, you want to lose your way. That's how we all felt. If that team would have lost that year in the World Series, and we had run our guys out there, there's not one guy who would have said, 'We should have done something different.' We wanted to make sure we left it all out there, and we had our guys in. We just felt: We need him in there. That was it. We've all sacrificed so much to get to this point. Let's do it our way."

I asked Pedroia *why* he and his teammates believed they needed Gomes.

"I don't know. Baseball is baseball. Numbers in baseball at that time of the year are irrelevant. That's always been my mindset. Do I want Jonny Gomes up with the game on the line? Every time. I don't care if he doesn't have a batting average. You know you're going to get a good at-bat every time. He gives us a chance. You know he's never going to lack confidence, and he's never going to quit. I'll take my chances every time."

I have to insert in here what happened the following season. In the middle of the 2014 season, the Oakland A's traded their Warrior, Yoenis Céspedes, to the Red Sox. Arriving from the Red Sox in that trade was Jonny Gomes. He had flourished in Oakland two years earlier on one of the best team-chemistry squads he'd ever played on. He was excited about returning, especially with the A's in first place by a huge margin and poised to make a run at the World Series.

"But I walk into the clubhouse," Gomes said, "and everyone's head's down. You look around like, whoa, why are your heads down? I tried everything I could [to turn it around], but it didn't matter." The A's players, already tightly knit, closed ranks after the shock of Céspedes's departure. They were not enthusiastic about outsiders in their circle. To Gomes's great frustration, he became just another veteran player on a disintegrating team, underscoring the situational nature of archetypes and team chemistry, even for Super-Carriers.

Past the pool and the children's play structure in Gomes's backyard stands a beautiful rustic guesthouse that he built with his World Series bonus check. This is where he keeps his memorabilia. It's all wood and stone with high ceilings and a granite-top bar that stretches almost wall-to-wall below a sign that reads, "THE OUTHOUSE." Wine bottles in refrigerated display cases cover one wall. Behind the bar, enormous wood doors slide open to a theater. Shadow boxes of bats, gloves, and spikes hang alongside loads of framed photos and magazine clippings. One is the April 23, 2013, cover of *Sports Illustrated,* published two weeks after bombers killed three people and injured hundreds at the Boston Marathon. The cover features a photo of Gomes standing on second base with his arms flexed like a bodybuilder's, the BOSTON on his jersey just above STRONG in huge red type. Beside it, behind glass, are the spikes Gomes wore in that World Series and, next to that, a poster of his Red Sox teammates leaping on one another in celebration. Gomes stood in the theater, taking it all in. He said it still seemed a bit unreal to him.

"I didn't really have a lot of knowledge about the history of the game, you know?" Gomes said. "When I get to Cincinnati, one of the oldest organizations in pretty much all of sports, and seeing the pictures of the Big Red Machine [the Cincinnati Reds of the 1970s], and seeing the [championship] flags, that's really where it clicked for me: Winning, in our game, is the only anniversary. You know? We don't celebrate any of our five Triple Crown winners. We don't celebrate Andruw Jones winning his tenth Gold Glove.

We don't celebrate Ted Williams hitting .406. It was a big eye-opener. You want to be remembered in this game? It's not about being great. It's about winning."

Here among his baseball memorabilia, immersed in his base-ball life, Gomes was looser and warmer. He was smiling more and had more eye contact. I felt like I was getting at least a glimpse of the person everyone had been telling me about. Maybe he was that person only with his teammates. This room held their pres-ence. Only they could summon his one superpower.

A year or so later, I thought about Gomes during a conversa-tion about team chemistry at the famed Chicago improv theater The Second City. When I described Super-Carriers, a director named Matt Hovde lit up. Yes, he said, improv groups definitely had them.

"You might have someone in an ensemble who individually isn't the most talented, but if you replaced them with a funnier person, that show wouldn't necessarily be demonstratively better," he said. "Because sometimes that person is serving a purpose that you can't discern from the outside. It's the utility improviser who always makes choices that bring out the best in other people's choices. They're great set-up people. You can't just have all Mel Brooks and Tim Conways. You need Harvey Korman, too."

I like that: Jonny Gomes, the Harvey Korman of baseball.

If Super-Carriers of chemistry exist, it seems reasonable that Super-Disruptors do, too. In sports, these types of players are called "cancers." I had little doubt that a single player could ruin a team as surely as a single player could lift it. And I had little doubt which player was the super-est of baseball Super-Disruptors, the starkest example of a team cancer.

I was wrong on both counts.

CHAPTER FOUR

SUPER-DISRUPTORS, OR THE CURIOUSER CASE OF BARRY BONDS

"Everybody thinks chemistry is this wonderful, sort of euphoric thing, and everybody gets along and puts their arms around each other and sings songs and goes out to dinner.... Team chemistry is not always what people think it is."

—Former major-league outfielder Randy Winn

In 1944, during World War II, the US Office of Strategic Services (OSS) issued a classified training manual to their agents stationed in enemy-occupied territories.* The OSS was the precursor to today's CIA. The "Simple Sabotage Field Manual" instructed factory workers and other "citizen saboteurs" on "effective weapons" to undermine the enemy.

One such weapon was a negative attitude.

Workers were directed to create "an unpleasant situation

---

* The manual was declassified in 2008.

among one's fellow workers." They should be "as irritable and quarrelsome as possible without getting in trouble." This would "induce others to follow suit" and result in a slowdown in productivity and thus a drag on the enemy's war effort.[1]

This is kind of stunning. US intelligence officers believed a single person's negativity could be contagious enough to affect the work product of an entire factory. It was the "bad apple" theory, which at least in apples is easy to understand. When an apple ripens, it emits a gaseous hormone called ethylene. The ethylene triggers ripening in surrounding apples, which then emit their own ethylene until the whole barrel has gone bad. The OSS's theory was that one malcontent could turn a barrel of good guys into a dysfunctional, low-productivity group.

There's plenty of research to support the theory. Humans are more sensitive and vulnerable to negative influences than positive ones.[2] Of the six basic emotions that nearly all societies have in common—sadness, anger, fear, disgust, happiness, and surprise—four are negative, one is neutral, and only one is positive.[3] We evolved this way for logical reasons. Our brains had to sound the loudest alarms—through immediate and strong emotions—to the threats in our environment, not the beauty. Negative experiences rock us in ways positive ones don't; they can burrow deep into us and stay there. There is no positive counterpart, for example, to the word *trauma*. There's also no positive equivalent of *contaminate*. We don't have a word for the act of transforming a disgusting thing into something pleasant simply through contact. A cockroach or a string of saliva needs only to appear *near* our food to render the entire dish, perhaps the entire meal, revolting. But a plump, juicy strawberry on a moldy scone does nothing to make the scone more appealing. Unsurprisingly, there is no "good apple" adage.

The Russians have their own version of the bad apple: "A

spoonful of tar can spoil a barrel of honey, but a spoonful of honey does nothing for a barrel of tar." For all the charisma and the high emotional IQ of Jonny Gomes, his power as a Super-Carrier requires at least a somewhat fertile environment. Yet one really bad influence in a clubhouse, like the citizen saboteur in a factory, seems able to disrupt a whole team.

When I canvassed a dozen baseball writers, Barry Bonds was at or near the top of everyone's list of Super-Disruptors. He topped mine, too. When I covered him as a sports columnist, I navigated the clubhouse with delicacy and vigilance, on alert for Bonds loudly embarrassing a reporter, a staffer, or occasionally a team-mate. Bonds's arrogance and rudeness earned him a tie for third on *Bleacher Report*'s 2010 list of "The 20 Worst Teammates in Sports History."*

For fifteen years, from 1993 to 2007, Bonds anchored the San Francisco Giants' lineup and dominated the sport. During that time, he was a twelve-time All-Star, a five-time Gold Glover (given to the best defensive player at a position), and a nine-time Silver Slugger (awarded to the best hitter at a position). In 2001, at the age of thirty-seven and under gathering clouds of suspicion for steroid use, he broke the single-season home-run record with seventy-three. In 2007, at forty-three years old and with federal prosecutors investigating him for possible perjury, Bonds passed Hank Aaron's 755 career home runs to become the all-time home-run king, finishing with 763.

Bonds's swing had the power to make forty-five thousand people in a ballpark and millions of TV viewers at home stop whatever they were doing and just watch. You couldn't take your eyes off Bonds when he stepped to the plate. When he had a bat in hand, his body

---

* Football player Terrell Owens shared the number-three spot with Bonds. Figure skater Tonya Harding was second, and basketball player Delonte West took the top spot.

became a seamless sequence of notes: quiet at first, then exploding, and then soaring. He was born to the game. His late father, Bobby Bonds, was an All-Star outfielder. His godfather is baseball legend Willie Mays. No one in baseball, and few athletes in any sport, had such a pedigree, and Bonds carried himself with a rough imperiousness that signaled, like royalty, he was not to be approached.

When the team moved to the new park in 2000, Bonds had access to four lockers. One was for his son, Nicolai, who often worked as a ball boy during the summer. Another was a locker used mostly by the clubhouse manager for storage; Bonds kept his extra bats there. Then a Brookstone massage chair showed up. A TV was hung on the opposite wall. Bonds had a personal massage therapist who did double-duty as his bouncer, keeping away media and staff when the star was resting or otherwise occupied. He had a physical trainer, too, hired by the Giants. Even if people knew he paid the massage therapist himself to treat back and leg problems, that he paid for the massage chair, that the clubhouse manager installed the TV because there wasn't one in Bonds's line of sight, he'd still be perceived as lordly and detached. The scope of Bonds's isolation was unusual even by superstar standards. He operated as an independent contractor, following an individual routine and schedule in preparing for games. He didn't stretch on the field with his teammates before batting practice, a custom so entrenched in baseball that his absence drew reporters' attention until the day he retired. Late in his career, when he had a day off, he refused to pinch-hit unless the game was on the line.

As he chased various home-run records, and as increasingly credible allegations of steroid use escalated, Bonds isolated himself even more. He refused most days to talk with the reporters who descended on the Giants' clubhouse from across the country. Teammates were left to answer for Bonds, trapped at their lockers by swarms of media day in and day out, their own performances brushed aside. "You don't think that pissed guys off?" broadcaster Mike Krukow said.

As if Bonds weren't enough disruption for one clubhouse, in 1997 the Giants doubled down. They signed another of *Bleacher Report*'s "20 Worst Teammates in Sports History," a hard-edged, hard-assed second baseman named Jeff Kent.

Kent was a different breed of cat. He grew up on the beaches of Southern California and was educated at UC Berkeley, but he was as ornery and hardheaded as the bulls he later raised on his ranch in South Texas. He doesn't much like people, which is why he left California for Texas. Lots of space. He has few friends. He once told a teammate he'd probably leave baseball without any. Social and emotional connections seem to baffle him. During premarital counseling, he told the counselor he'd rather his future wife show her love by doing something for him instead of by hugging and kissing. When he and a Giants teammate picked up their children at the same preschool, Kent didn't say hello or even make eye contact with the teammate—even if they were waiting right next to each other. With the Giants in 2000, he hit a grand slam to reach one hundred RBIs (runs batted in) in four straight seasons, and the San Francisco fans shook the ballpark with a thundering ovation, demanding a curtain call. Kent didn't budge from the bench. The cheering hung in the air like an unreciprocated handshake until the crowd sank back into their seats. It was bizarre. All he had to do was step out of the dugout and doff his cap.

Bonds and Kent were opposites in many ways. First-round draft pick versus twentieth-rounder. Son of a famous athlete versus son of a cop. Bonds flouted his wealth with sports cars and mansions; Kent tithed to the Mormon Church and sank his money into land for ranching and hunting. Bonds was divorced. Kent married his high-school sweetheart.

They were strikingly similar, too, of course. Neither had much interest in the company and opinions of other humans. Neither suffered fools gladly. Both were loners. Both sought to live up to their hard-driving, larger-than-life fathers. Both would gnaw through a cowhide catcher's mitt to gain a competitive edge. Their personalities often combusted into loud arguments and on at least one occasion a fistfight. It happened in full view of television cameras during a 2002 game in San Diego. At the end of the second inning, during which the Padres scored four runs, Kent exploded at third baseman David Bell, whose crime was fielding a slow grounder and throwing to second base to get the lead runner. Kent had been yelling at him to throw to first because they had no chance of getting the runner at second. Kent continued the tirade in the dugout.

Bonds snapped at Kent to chill out. Kent told him to fuck off. Bonds leapt from the bench and lunged at Kent's throat. Teammates, manager Dusty Baker, and trainer Stan Conte had to pull them apart.

Between battles, Kent and Bonds were like two generals in their bunkers. Bonds camped in his recliner behind his two aides-de-camp, and Kent hunkered across the room, his back to his teammates, reading hunting magazines. I envisioned their negativity rising off their bodies and curling through the clubhouse like cartoon aromas, sapping motivation and productivity from whomever it touched. Bonds on his own should have chipped away at the team's energy and performance. Together, Bonds and Kent should have been a chemistry disaster.

But that's not what I found.

The story that unfolded from their teammates and coaches wasn't the one we had seen from the outside. I realized that what we'd been watching all that time was the view from Plato's caves: We saw the shadows and pieced together a narrative. We couldn't see what else was going on—inside the clubhouse and inside their heads. I came to a conclusion I didn't expect:

Bonds wasn't a Super-Disruptor. Neither was Kent.

The analytics back this up, which I'll get to shortly. The more interesting and trickier question is *why* they weren't Super-Disruptors. Finding the answer meant flipping my understanding of chemistry on its head.

I was not confident Barry Bonds would show. We had made plans three days earlier to meet for coffee in a picturesque seaside town north of San Francisco. I had been trying to schedule the interview for almost two years. He ignored emailed requests to his assistant. He shot me down several times when I encountered him at the ballpark, once by dismissing chemistry as irrelevant to baseball, and another by asking how much I was paying him. Nothing, I said, same as the 160 other people I had interviewed. But one day he didn't walk away. We talked in the hallway to the clubhouse. No notebook, no recorder. Just small talk. After a while, his body relaxed, his face softened, and the pitch of his voice rose. He held eye contact. He giggled. He talked about everything from his social awkwardness as a child to his daughter's plans for graduate school to his affection for his old Pirates manager, Jim Leyland. He was no longer Barry Bonds. Just a guy named Barry.

Forty-five minutes passed. With the game about to start, he agreed to make a date for coffee and texted his assistant, Lisa, to confirm. But later the date was canceled. I exchanged emails with Lisa to reschedule. In the meantime, I'd occasionally run into Bonds in the office of Mike Murphy ("Murph"), the Giants' legendary clubhouse manager. Bonds has known Murph since he was a kid toddling around the clubhouse with his father. As we chatted in Murph's office, Willie Mays — Barry's godfather — would often appear in the doorway. Mays was in his mid-eighties, legally blind, and still built like a brick wall. Mays and his assistant Renee would relax in Murph's office for an hour or so before making their way to an upstairs suite to watch the game.

"Y'all workin' in here?" Mays would say. "You need the room? Stay! Stay!"

I'd leap up from one of the tiny office's two armchairs, and Bonds would get up just as quickly from the other. I'd always reintroduce myself to Mays. "I know who you are!" he would say, even if maybe he didn't: He was still a gentleman from Alabama. Bonds would pull a folded card table from its slot between Murph's desk and the back wall. He'd click open the legs and set it in front of Mays, who was now settled in the chair Bonds had vacated. With Renee in the other chair, Bonds perched against Murph's desk, half standing, half sitting, and asked his godfather how he was feeling, what he'd been up to. The two men would fall into the easy, jokey back-and-forth of old mates. If Mays was hungry, Bonds fetched soup or a plate of chicken from the players' dining room. One day, after Mays had arrived and I had said my goodbyes, I was a few steps down the hall when Bonds hollered at me to come back. I returned to find the two men standing in the middle of the room, Bonds's arm slung around Mays's shoulders.

"Willie!" Bonds said. "Do you believe in team chemistry?"

Mays scrunched his face as if he'd bitten a lemon. "Chemistry? *Chemistry?* There's no *chemistry!*"

Bonds howled, and Mays beamed, delighted to be in on Bonds's teasing.

These impromptu, casual conversations went on for the better part of a year. Finally, Bonds set a date for an interview.

In my memory, the Kent-Bonds teams weren't very good. I'm not sure why I remember them this way. Maybe because the Giants' subsequent championships give the Kent-Bonds era the whiff of failure in comparison. But the record shows that in the six years Kent and Bonds played together, the Giants flourished. When Kent arrived, the team had finished in last place two seasons in a row. In his first year, the Giants won the division. They over-achieved, which is almost always a sign of good chemistry. They won ten games more than their statistics predicted. Dating back to 1901, just one percent of major-league teams have turned in a sea-son at least ten wins above expectation.[4] No Kent-Bonds squad ever finished lower than second. When they reached the World Series in 2002, they became just the second Giants team in forty years to do so and came within six outs of winning it.*

Until the last three years of his career, Bonds's teams won a ton of games. The Giants finished first or second in their division in ten of his fifteen seasons, including eight in a row from 1997 to 2004. He changed the Giants' fortunes the moment he signed on in 1993. The club won 103 games that season—up from just 72 (and a last-place finish) the year before. It was only the second time since 1913 the team had surpassed one hundred wins.

Unfortunately, the Atlanta Braves won 104 games that year. (The Braves were in the same division as the Giants at the time.) And doubly unfortunate, only division winners advanced to the postseason. The wild-card format wasn't introduced until the fol-lowing year.

"That was the best team I ever played on," Matt Williams said of the '93 squad. "We all benefited from Barry showing up. He was

---

* It was the only time Bonds played in a World Series, and he shined. He had the highest on-base percentage (.700), the highest slugging percentage (1.294), and the most walks (13) in World Series history. Four of his eight hits were home runs.

the best left fielder I've ever seen. The best hitter I've ever seen. So what if he wasn't out there to stretch with us? I didn't care."

I began to wonder if high-performing stars, and particularly superstars, *could* be cancers. Their enormous contribution to winning—scoring runs or preventing opponents from scoring runs—perhaps outweighs the impact of their negative behavior.

Three sabermetrics geeks, who met as analysts at the Federal Reserve Bank of Chicago, crunched the numbers on Bonds in a paper they called "In Search of the Holy Grail: Team Chemistry and Where to Find It," which they presented at the MIT Sloan Sports Analytics Conference in 2017.*

"By our analysis Bonds would not have been a cancer. His individual performance is just so strong that it seeps through to teammates," one of the authors told me. "Bonds's fWAR [the acronym for FanGraphs.com's wins above replacement] numbers are so far out there, he's still going to have positive pcWAR [player-chemistry wins above replacement] almost no matter what. He's making those around him better."[†]

Bonds's presence in the batting lineup boosted the performance of virtually every player who hit in front of or behind him. From 1997 to 2002, the greatest beneficiary was Kent. Bonds was such a dangerous home-run hitter that pitchers walked him more than anyone else in baseball—sometimes intentionally, some-

---

* The paper's authors, Scott A. Brave, R. Andrew Butters, and Kevin A. Roberts, wrote in their abstract, "Using FanGraphs' wins-above-replacement metric, fWAR, over the 1998–2016 seasons and a spatial factor model embodying the strength of teammates' on-the-field interactions, we show that approximately 44 percent of the unexplained variation in team performance by fWAR can be explained by chemistry." The paper was originally called "In Search of David Ross."

[†] FanGraphs.com's wins-above-replacement metric compresses into one number all the ways a player can help his team win—at the plate, in the field, and on the mound.

times semi-intentionally, and once with the bases loaded.* Better to give Bonds a free pass to first base than a home run. This meant the pitcher had to throw strikes to the batters in front of and behind Bonds to avoid walking two players in a row. Thus Kent saw more pitches over the plate, boosting his chances of getting a hit. And with Bonds on base so often from walks, Kent saw his RBI totals rise. His highest total before joining the Giants was 80, in 1993. With the Giants, he hit 121, 128, 101, 125, 106, and 108 his first six years.† He posted the most consistently high numbers of his career while he was with the Giants. He had never been an All-Star or won a Silver Slugger Award before joining the Giants; with them he made three All-Star teams and won three Silver Sluggers. During his career, he had five seasons that could be considered Hall of Fame caliber, with a WAR over 4.0; all were with the Giants. His performance soared so dramatically in 2000, his fourth season in San Francisco, that he won the National League's Most Valuable Player Award. Bonds finished second.

Did Kent have any effect on Bonds's performance? Dusty Baker often compared the two to Sidney Poitier and Tony Curtis in *The Defiant Ones,* the 1958 film about two escaped convicts in the South, one black and one white, shackled to each other as they evade police. "They were good for each other," Baker said. But Bonds was Bonds, so extraordinary year in and year out that he

---

* It happened on May 28, 1998, against the Arizona Diamondbacks. The D-Backs led 8–6 with two outs in the bottom of the ninth. The Giants' next batter, Brent Mayne, lined out to right field, ending the game 8–7. Until then, a batter in the major leagues had not been intentionally walked with the bases loaded in fifty-four years. It has happened once since Bonds. In 2008, the Rays' Grant Balfour walked the Rangers' Josh Hamilton with the Rays ahead 7–3 in the bottom of the ninth.

† A good way to compare Kent before and after Bonds is to look at RBIs per at-bat. In '95 and '96, Kent drove in a run during 13 percent and 12 percent of his at-bats, respectively. In his first four years with the Giants, he drove a run in during 20, 24, 19, and 21 percent of his at-bats.

seemed a wholly contained entity, immune to external forces. "Ain't nobody going to protect Barry but Barry," Bonds told reporters in 2001 when asked about the protection he'd get in the lineup from newly signed slugger Andrés Galarraga. "There ain't no other Barry. He'll help Jeff."

But if you compare the six years he was with Kent (1997–2002) to the six preceding years (1991–1996), Bonds performed better with Kent. On average per 162 games, he put up better numbers in home runs (53/41), on-base percentage (.471/.441), slugging percentage (.689/.608), and on-base plus slugging percentage (1.161/1.049). Runs batted in (125/123) and batting average (.310/.309) were essentially the same.

Kent seemed to stoke Bonds's competitive fire in a way few teammates ever did. Bonds won three Most Valuable Player Awards early in his career and then went six years without placing higher than fourth in the voting. Then, after finishing second to Kent in 2000, he recaptured the award in 2001, 2002, 2003, and 2004.*

By the time their six years together ended, the two men had a combined 454 homers, 1,348 runs batted in, three Most Valuable Player Awards, and one World Series appearance, making them one of the most productive batting-lineup partners in baseball history.

At forty-eight, Jeff Kent still looked like a drill sergeant: broad-shouldered and square-jawed with short, choppy hair the color of

---

* Interestingly, after Atlanta Braves third baseman Terry Pendleton edged out Bonds for the MVP in 1991, a year when Bonds had better numbers but Pendleton had a greater impact on his team, Bonds responded by winning the award in 1992 and 1993. His seven MVP awards obliterated the previous record of three, held by eight other players: Stan Musial, Mickey Mantle, Albert Pujols, Joe DiMaggio, Alex Rodriguez, Mike Schmidt, Jimmie Foxx, and Yogi Berra.

ash wood. But his face no longer looked as if someone had just threatened his children. He was smiling. He was at ease. We were on a back field at the Giants' spring training complex in Scottsdale, Arizona, in February 2017. Kent was working as a visiting coach for two weeks. We sat in the empty dugout as his teenage son, Kaeden, gathered the hundred or so balls he had just smacked all over the field during batting practice with his dad. Kent had already made it clear that he thinks team chemistry is a crock. But he seemed happy to talk. Few creatures on earth are friendlier than retired star athletes. Like most of Bonds's teammates, he dismissed the notion that the star was a cancer. By way of explanation he told me about one of his cows.

"I'm moving 150 cows a few weeks ago, separating the babies from the mamas [for medical care], and this one cow won't come in the gate. That cow did not want to do what everybody else wanted to do," Kent said, a toothpick bobbing from the side of his mouth. "She was the strongest and fiercest and smartest of all the cows, and she knew it. But I have to get rid of her. You know why? Because she's the leader. I don't want her teaching my other cows to do the same thing."

Bonds was like that cow in behavior but not in influence, Kent said, because Bonds wasn't a leader. He didn't attract followers. He didn't seek recruits. So he didn't spread his negativity.

While the two men's isolation looked from the outside like a fracture in the team and thus a blow to chemistry, instead it was a blessing: It took them out of the equation and allowed chemistry to define itself among the rest of the players. What they created wasn't one big band of brothers. It was an interconnected web of small bands. Moving counterclockwise around the clubhouse, the Latin-American position players had lockers along the wall to the right of the entrance. Bonds's lockers and lounger were against the side wall, along with the lockers of a few more Latin-American position players. On the back wall were most of the African-American position players and, continuing along the wall and around the corner, were the white-American position players, including Kent. Completing that side wall and turning the corner to the front wall were the white pitchers and then the Latin-American pitchers.

Just as Bonds's and Kent's isolation could look like a rupture in team chemistry, so, too, could these physically segregated sections. But according to psychology professor Kate Bezrukova, these separate neighborhoods—created in part by management, in part by the players—can actually facilitate chemistry and higher performance.

Bezrukova studies workplace "fault lines," potential divisions based on race, gender, income, age, religion, and so on. If workers clump together with those most similar to themselves, fault lines can fracture into rifts. Employees start focusing on the concerns of their own subgroup and less on the company as a whole. Distrust and conflict spread. Sharing of information decreases. Productivity suffers. High-functioning workplaces, Bezrukova says, learn how to recognize and bridge fault lines.

At a professional conference some years back, Bezrukova met Chester Spell, a Rutgers University business professor and huge baseball fan. Spell wondered if fault lines on a baseball team might offer a way of measuring team chemistry and predicting performance. They decided to collaborate on a study.[5] The types of demographic data Bezrukova had to arduously collect for her workplace studies were publicly available for major-league baseball teams in newspapers and on websites such as Baseball-Reference.com and MLB.com. They looked at age, race, nationality, salary, tenure with the team, and tenure in professional baseball for every player on every major-league team over five seasons.

They devised an algorithm to assess the demographic overlap on each team. They rated each team's chemistry by how much the players had in common. Let's say a team has three young Venezuelan players, two young Japanese players, and the rest are older American players. There's a chance the team will fracture into three isolated factions. But if one of the Latin-American players is also an older player, he is a link between his group and the older American group. If one of the Americans had played ball in Japan and could speak some Japanese, he is a link to the Japanese guys, and so on. These webs of connections hold the groups together as a unified team.

Bezrukova and Spell found clubhouses functioned much like any workplace: the more overlap between groups, the better the team performed. But you never want to eliminate factions altogether, Bezrukova said. Subgroups are islands within a team where individual players can take refuge. Players from Venezuela know each other in a way their other teammates can't. They speak the same language, understand the same cultural references, laugh at the same jokes. They can provide the individual mentoring and emotional connection necessary to perform their best.

"[The subgroup] is how you get this extra-healthy support system for the players," Bezrukova said. "There's so much pressure in sports. Unbelievable stress. You really need to have that support."

The worst thing for a team, Spell and Bezrukova said, is a one-person subgroup. They call that person a token. "Tokens are kind of deadly," Spell said. They experience higher rates of anxiety and depression because they don't have the comfort of a tribe. Cirque du Soleil, which brings in performers from all over the world, has had a long practice of hiring at least two people from a country.[6]

Spell says leaders, whether in sports or business, must consistently reinforce the group's shared identity. "I know it sounds very

politically incorrect," Spell said, "but fights can be a good thing."
At least in sports. A bench-clearing brawl, as every fight between
baseball teams is called, can be amazingly effective in bridging
fault lines. Case in point: the Dodgers in 2013.

Motivated by the rising fortunes of the Giants, their division
rival, the Dodgers spent $600 million in one six-month span in
2012 to bring in stars such as Hanley Ramirez, Adrian Gonzales,
Carl Crawford, Josh Beckett, Yasiel Puig, Zack Greinke, Hyun-Jin
Ryu, and Shane Victorino. "We're talking about huge turnover,
perhaps unprecedented turnover for a contender," baseball journalist Ken Rosenthal wrote.

"People thought we'd be dysfunctional bringing in so much
talent," said Ned Colletti, the team's general manager at the time.
They *were* dysfunctional, and they failed to win the division in 2012.
The following season began with a rash of injuries. They'd been
sitting in last place for a month when they faced the Diamondbacks
on June 11. In the sixth inning, the Diamondbacks' pitcher nearly
nailed Puig in the head, though the pitch managed only to graze
his nose. Greinke, the Dodgers' pitcher, retaliated immediately in
the seventh, drilling the D-Backs' batter on the back. Benches
cleared, but no punches were thrown. In the bottom of the seventh, Greinke came to bat. The first pitch sailed toward Greinke's
head, hitting his shoulder then ricocheting against his helmet.

The Dodgers went wild, charging across the field, fists flying.
It was a real fight, with punches landing and bodies slammed to
the ground. When it was over, one manager, two coaches, and
three players were ejected. The Dodgers rallied from a 2–0 deficit
to win, 5–3.

The next morning "there was a rejuvenated aura in the
clubhouse," one Dodgers player told reporters. Colletti saw the
change, too.

"[The fight] wasn't pretty to see," he said, "don't get me wrong.

But you don't want to see people with the ball coming at their head, either. So we kind of took it to 'em. In the clubhouse afterward, guys who kind of had a passing friendship with each other suddenly had a real friendship. It brought us together. It really brought us together."

During July and August, the Dodgers lost just twelve games and went on to win the division. Despite differences in salary, nationality, age, and tenure within the organization, the players felt like a unit. The factions were no longer as pronounced.

In the Giants' clubhouse in the early 2000s, the tiny segregated neighborhoods had enough overlap to hold the team together while also serving as bulwarks against the potential distraction of Bonds and Kent. The subgroups helped to keep the players grounded.

"There was an article by a *Sports Illustrated* guy—not [Tom] Verducci but some other asshole," Kent said, continuing his argument that Bonds wasn't a cancer. (The writer was Rick Reilly in the August 27, 2001, issue.) "He asked me, 'Does it bother you that Barry's over there in his chair?' I told him, 'No. Big fucking deal. We got problems with Barry every day, but he ain't a problem.' But he didn't write that part. So that's the offense I had toward a lot of media. You don't write the whole picture. Yeah, I run my mouth too much sometimes, too. But what this guy wrote—it was so full of shit....It made out like it was kind of a war between Jeff Kent and Barry Bonds, and it wasn't."

There *was* a kind of war. But it didn't affect their performance. Kent openly acknowledges that Bonds helped him, and not just from hitting before or after him in the lineup. He learned from Bonds it was OK to embrace selfishness and arrogance, even if everyone thought you were an ass. "Listen," Kent said, "the best players are some of the biggest pricks to ever play the game. The biggest assholes. Selfish. Greedy. But you can also use these words: confident, self-motivated, competitive. They don't like to be second. Some guys don't even like their own teammate to have one more home run than they have, one more stolen base, one more win if you're a pitcher. There's an arrogance. It feeds players, and I really think it feeds championships."

The concept of conventional team chemistry is anathema to Kent's individualistic orientation to the world. "I'm not a friendly person. I don't really like people that much. Because I'm self-satisfied. I'm self-motivated. I don't dance. I wasn't a part of a fraternity. I don't cheer when I go to sporting events. I don't celebrate birthdays and anniversaries even though my wife kills me when I don't. Friends don't motivate me. Friends don't make me better, personally. Doesn't fuel me." He conceded that feeling comfortable in a clubhouse and having relationships with teammates probably affect the performance of "people who aren't self-motivated and [are] a little bit weak."

I shared a comment from a player who said teammates lifted his performance in ways he couldn't do for himself.

"Can he quantify it?" Kent asked.

"No," I said. "Does that mean the effect isn't real?"

He said maybe for highly emotional players, it's real. "And even if it's real," he said, "if you can't quantify it...."

I interrupted. "OK, you say you love your wife. But you can't measure it, right? So how do you know it's real?"

"Because I'll take a bullet for her."

"And there's the baseball equivalent of that, right?"

The toothpick bobbed. "Sure. I'd take a bullet for a guy on the mound whether I like him or hate him," he said.

He smiled. "Yeah, I get your point."

If his willingness to take a bullet for his wife means his love is real, then his willingness to do the same for a teammate means that something deep and even profound existed between him and his teammates. Maybe even between him and Bonds. I could almost see the wheels turning in Kent's head. He was thinking this through.

"That [connection] is built on the field; that's not built in the clubhouse," he said. "That's not built in team dinners. That's built when, if a pitcher is going to throw at the head of one of my team-mates, I got your back. And if you don't get a hit, I'm going to bust [the pitcher's] ass and take him deep. I picked you up. That builds that camaraderie. That builds that trust. That builds that chain of an unbreakable relationship that you can have for a time until it gets broken because nothing's perfect.

"You can listen to the same kind of music in the locker room. You can relate because 'Oh, you have two daughters, too? Yeah, let's go get drunk together.' But those are all so superficial. They don't last. What lasts is out here." He nodded toward the field and offered a story about pitcher Orel Hershiser.

The Giants were playing the Seattle Mariners. Alex Rodriguez ("A-Rod"), with the Mariners at the time, took out Kent on a slide into second base. The next day, A-Rod stepped to the plate in the first inning. Hershiser was pitching for the Giants. Despite run-ners on first and second and just one out, Hershiser plunked A-Rod, loading the bases. "He backed me up, and he didn't need to do that. That showed me a lot," Kent said. Hershiser gave up two runs that inning, and the Giants lost, 4–1. Kent was OK with that because, he said, sometimes you sacrifice one game so you can win two. Here was this militantly self-sufficient, friends-don't-motivate-me man saying that such a demonstration of loyalty has a powerful enough impact to lift a player's or a team's performance beyond that single game.

"It's something that I can't quantify for you," he conceded when I asked him to explain. "It's not a stat. But it's a pride. The old cliché is 'I'm in the foxhole with you.' It's just an emotional attachment. Does it lead to an extra hit? I don't know. But it can lead to this:

"If Orel's pitching, I might not ask the coach to give me the day off. I might not go stay out late at night. I might say you know what, my buddy Orel's pitching tomorrow so I need to go prepare. You may have a little more of an aggressive attitude that could lead to more success.

"Your question was why I could perform better just knowing Orel's pitching. I can't tell you why I performed better for Orel. There's no way. No way in the world that I ever [consciously] performed better for one player than another. But I can tell you that I had more *pride* in playing for one player over another. Did it translate [to a better performance]? I have no idea."

The conversation eventually turned again to Kent's relationship with Bonds. Kaeden had joined us in the dugout. He sat on the bench a polite distance away, far enough to be unobtrusive, close enough to hear. Kent was still rolling over in his mind this idea of players affecting one another. He had traveled to a different place on the topic from where he began when we sat down. I had, too. I was understanding that the human drive for connection can look like a knock-down pitch or an early exit from a bar. It can look like a cold rivalry.

"Even though I knew I wasn't a great player, I wanted to be great," Kent said. "I wanted to be the best player. I wanted to be better than Barry Bonds, even though I wasn't. And I wanted Bonds to know I wanted to be better than him so he could be better than me.

"OK, is that the team chemistry? Yeah, because I can kind of consider team chemistry along those lines of what I just described, which is internal competition—understanding it, managing it, not letting it get away."

A cold wind was kicking up off the water, but I took a table outside anyway. We'd have the patio to ourselves. It was mid-afternoon on a weekday, and few tourists were wandering the narrow street of quaint, upscale boutiques and restaurants. The ferry to San Francisco had already pulled away. It was quiet enough to hear the dull slap of waves against the dock. I saw Bonds strolling up the street, head high, a faint scowl across his face. He gave me a quick hug in greeting, but he was not Barry from Murph's office. He was Barry Bonds. The wall was up. After buying an oatmeal-raisin cookie inside, he positioned himself sideways in the wrought-iron chair, his back against the café's window, his legs stretched in front of him. I was not sure what the hard face was all about. I made some small talk. No dice. So I just dove into the interview. Yes, he believes chemistry exists. Yes, he thinks guys in the clubhouse have an effect on each other. His answers were clipped, and I asked the reporter's *pick-pick-pick* follow-up questions, trying to draw him out. A woman rode up on a bike, leaned it against the patio railing, and asked if we'd keep an eye on it while she got coffee.

"No one steals here," Bonds told her.

"Why do you look so familiar?"

"I don't know. No one steals here. You don't have to worry about your bike."

The woman laughed. "Can you tell I'm from New York?"

Bonds's face softened. He started talking about how much he loves this town, where he had moved a year earlier. He told me how everybody says hello to everybody, how his buddy in the deli will go into the back to get him a different kind of smoked turkey, how he directs baffled tourists on how to get back to the city. He's divorced and lives alone high on a hill with expansive views of the bay and city. He said he's been a loner all his life but that his older daughter, Shikari, is coaching him on how to boost his social life in retirement. "She says, 'Dad, you've got to get out. You can't sit in this house by yourself all the time,'" he said, laughing. "It's just who I am. It's peaceful."

Bonds had always seemed utterly incapable of, and uninterested in, cracking the code of social connection. Though extremely bright, he learned differently from other kids, something he realized only when one of his children struggled with similar challenges. School was difficult. Further isolating him was being an athletic prodigy and the son of a famous baseball player. His young brain became a baseball Library of Congress, filled with wisdom from his father and Willie Mays, his coaches at Serra High and Arizona State, his minor-league coaches, and then Jim Leyland, Dusty Baker, and various respected teammates. "I was lucky," he said. "Everybody I played with mentored me. I was able to take a lot of pieces from a lot of great players and create myself."

Bonds came with all the quirks and gaps that often accompany specific, exceptional gifts. He often felt on shaky ground when conversations turned to topics beyond sports. Social situations were stressful, boring, and often confusing. People made a big deal out of the stupidest things. He has little understanding and patience for certain niceties. "Let's say someone says they have a cut on their leg," Bonds said, brushing crumbs into his palm and then into the empty cookie bag. "Most people would say, 'Oh do this or that, blah, blah, blah.' I'd say, 'Get a Band-Aid.' Someone might say, 'That's kind of rude, Barry.' Rude? I'm like, what do you want me to do? Look at it all day? Whine about it all day? I don't have that bone in my body."

The social aspect of building team chemistry—going to dinner, hanging around drinking beers and talking—made no sense to Bonds. "Look," he said, "in left field I covered thirty yards in four directions. I got up to bat four or five times a day. Most of the time I walked two of them, hopefully get two hits, and get on base four times.... All of that is hard as hell to do. And now you want me to sit and play cards with you, too? I don't have time for that. I didn't do that. I went home and went to sleep so I could come back the next day and give my teammates the best I have."

His high-school coach told the *New York Times Magazine,* "He wanted to be liked, tried so damn hard to have people like him... But then he'd say things he didn't mean, wild statements. Still, he'd be hurt. People don't realize he can be hurt, and is, fairly often."[7] This might explain why his former Giants teammates were unusually protective when I asked about him. They seemed to have seen glimpses of that high-school kid. They spoke of him as you might a difficult, oddball brother.

"He was his own faction," said Dodgers manager Dave Roberts, a former Giants teammate. "It's almost sad that he was kind of on his own island."

Teammates disliked his self-absorption and arrogance. They disliked the invasion into the clubhouse of his two personal attendants. But for as tone-deaf and derisive as he could be with fellow players, he was generous and engaging with their kids. That went a long way. To them, he was more Sherlock Holmes than Moriarty: the pompous genius who had no clue how he came across to those around him and thus operated outside the embrace of the tribe.

I use *genius* purposefully. It is the key to understanding why Bonds was not a cancer. I know it seems hyperbole when that term is applied to anyone, much less a guy who hits a five-ounce ball for a living. Let me make my case.

Geniuses have always been recognized as anomalies, individuals whose minds work in ways so different from the rest of us that in ancient times they were thought to be touched by the divine. In the eighteenth century, Samuel Johnson wrote that genius was "like fire in a flint, only to be produced by collision with a proper subject." This definition makes clear that genius is innate, waiting for a specific catalyst. For Mozart, it was music. For Shakespeare, words. For Steve Jobs, design and technology. Thus the word *genius* requires a descriptor: musical genius, literary genius, technological genius. Genius is a vein of gold in the mine, distinct and specific. Thus it isn't intelligence in a conventional sense like IQ. It's an ability to see and think in ways that others don't. Walter Isaacson, Steve Jobs's biographer, described the late Apple founder's mind in the *New York Times*:

"[Jobs's] success dramatizes an interesting distinction between intelligence and genius. His imaginative leaps were instinctive, unexpected, and at times magical. They were sparked by intuition, not analytic rigor.... [He] came to value experiential wisdom over empirical analysis. He didn't study data or crunch numbers but like a pathfinder, he could sniff the winds and sense what lay ahead."

Isaacson could have been writing about Bonds.

Though he referred to himself in our conversation as "a baseball geek with no personality," Bonds was way beyond geek. He was a savant. At the plate, he could slow a pitch with intense focus, allowing him to see the baseball's spin and movement with such clarity he rarely swung at a pitch outside the strike zone. The faintest flaw in a teammate's swing leapt out at him like a singer's flat note. (Sometimes he'd point it out, sometimes not, and almost never to a teammate who didn't ask.) When stapled packets of batting analytics and spray charts landed in his locker, he dropped them in the trash. His mind could anticipate and read game situations with more precision than any computer. He detected the tiny, elemental details others missed. He often knew what the pitcher was going to throw before he threw it. ("Woulda been nice if he'd a told *us*," one teammate lamented.)

Once, in the middle of a chat outside Murph's office, he dashed into the clubhouse and emerged with his teammate Shawon Dunston, now a Giants coach. "Shawon, tell her what happened in the dugout," Bonds said, his face lit up with a smile.

Dunston looked from Bonds to me and back again. Game time was just thirty minutes away.

"The pitches," Bonds prompted.

"Oh, oh," Dunston said, then quickly recounted how during a spring-training game a month earlier, Bonds correctly predicted the next three pitches the opposing pitcher would throw. Dunston said it blew his mind. Bonds beamed.

"Talent hits a target no one else can hit," wrote the German philosopher Arthur Schopenhauer. "Genius hits a target no one else can see."

Still, when Bonds told me he was so gifted that he purposely hit all his milestone home runs at the Giants' home park, I laughed. Then I saw that he was not kidding.

"You either *have* to know what the hell you're doing," he said, "or you'd have to be the luckiest son of a bitch on the planet. I was the master. My IQ and skill on the baseball field was such that I could do it whenever I wanted to. Whenever I needed to. Didn't matter who was on the mound. And the only time I was going to do it [hit milestone home runs] was at home in front of my family, and San Francisco is my family."

I looked it up later. Sure enough he hit his 500th, his 600th, his 660th (tying Willie Mays's record), his 661st (breaking Mays's record), his 715th (breaking Babe Ruth's record to move into second place of all-time), and 756th (breaking Hank Aaron's record) in San Francisco. He also hit his single-season-record 73rd home run in 2001 at home.*

The team aspect of baseball meant something different to Bonds than it did to most people. He saw baseball not so much as a team sport but as twenty-five individuals preparing for a team event. The "team" part of baseball began with the first pitch and ended with the final out. The rest of the time was devoted to preparation, and that job was individual. You alone were responsible for getting yourself ready to play. This is why he didn't understand the ridicule he received for not stretching with the team before batting practice, for napping in his Barcalounger before games, for having special pregame meals prepared for him, for having the two personal trainers/aides for massages and physical conditioning. He was still baffled about it all these years later.

"I wanted to give myself the best opportunity to play the best I could," Bonds said. "Look at all those things I was criticized for— the Giants have all that now! Sleeping rooms. Massage chairs. Lots more trainers and massage therapists. A chef. It's a spa in there! So was I just ahead of my time in realizing what was needed to play 162 games at your best? Or was it for someone to make a joke out of it?"

By "someone," he meant the media.

"My baseball IQ was above theirs, and it was the only thing I

---

* OK, I hear the cries from every corner of the baseball world: What about allegations of performance-enhancing drugs (PEDs)? Were they Bonds's true genius? I asked myself the same question. The answer required that I examine my assumptions. Even if PEDs were the sole reason Bonds hit more home runs than anyone else (and charges were dropped), then any elite baseball player who used PEDs should have had a more or less equal chance to hit just as many. That wasn't the case; no other PED user came close to Bonds's numbers. Remember, the issue we're addressing here concerns Bonds's capabilities, not his ethics. To that one point, his capacity for predicting pitches, seeing the exact trajectory of the ball hurtling toward him, and timing his swing precisely far surpassed everyone else in the game and perhaps in history. PEDs inflated his records. They don't negate his genius in hitting a baseball.

knew better than them," he said. "I felt sometimes they were insulting the intelligence I had about the sport of baseball. The one thing I knew really well was baseball. The problem was I had people writing stories about things they didn't understand."

He let out a mirthless laugh. "We as athletes only want to pass on to generations our knowledge, our skills, something we have really mastered. I've mastered baseball, the art of hitting. The baseball field was my classroom. I don't like these hit charts and all of that. I didn't know what OPS [on-base plus slugging percentage] meant for half my life. Who cares about all that stuff? Who cares about what they do with this flight ball or whatever it's called? Hit the damn baseball.

"So when I had to talk to reporters and they're asking me a question like, 'Do you think you guys are going to win the World Series?' and it's spring training...A person of my intelligence of baseball, I'm thinking, 'Are you insane to ask me an idiotic question like that?' My baseball IQ is saying, 'I don't fucking know.' It doesn't compute. I'm having a hard enough time trying to figure out goddamn Greg Maddux tomorrow, who is going to be out there trying to kill me."

He sounded in this moment like Ted Williams, the Hall of Famer whose 1941 season batting average of .406 hasn't been matched since.* "You're gonna meet some guys that don't know *shit* about baseball that are writing about it," Williams once said. "And that bothers you a little bit, ya know? *Jesus*."[8]

Williams's contempt for the media during his nineteen seasons with the Boston Red Sox rivaled and perhaps surpassed Bonds's. Bonds never spit at the press box, for instance, which Williams did twice in one month, each time after hitting a home run.

---

* Williams's career batting average of .344 is the highest among players with five hundred or more home runs.

I include this aside on Williams not to promote the idea that reporters "don't know shit about baseball." Reporters know lots about baseball. I include it to underscore a particular mentality of certain gifted performers like Bonds, Williams, and, again, Steve Jobs.

The New Yorker writer Malcolm Gladwell described Jobs's boorish behavior:

> He screams at subordinates. He cries like a small child when he does not get his way. He gets stopped for driving a hundred miles an hour, honks angrily at the officer for taking too long to write up the ticket, and then resumes his journey at a hundred miles an hour. He sits in a restaurant and sends his food back three times. He arrives at his hotel suite in New York for press interviews and decides, at 10 P.M., that the piano needs to be repositioned, the strawberries are inadequate, and the flowers are all wrong: he wanted calla lilies. (When his public-relations assistant returns, at midnight, with the right flowers, he tells her that her suit is "disgusting.")

For all their unpleasantness, Bonds, Williams, and Jobs were still accepted by their teams. If your extraordinary contribution to the group's mission outweighs your brutish behavior, teammates will learn how to work with you. It's the "genius exemption." In identifying players as team cancers, only teammates get a vote. If they can accept the player *as he is*, then he can't undermine their chemistry. If he can't undermine chemistry, he can't affect performance. Thus he can't be a cancer.

But he *can* be what the military calls a LIMFAC, or a limiting factor. How much better could Bonds's teams have been had he regularly engaged teammates in discussions about strategy, technique, mind-set? So while he probably didn't diminish the team's collective skills and commitment (at least not until his last few years), he didn't lift them either, as a singular talent like his could have.

Acceptance of a misanthrope doesn't happen easily. Bonds was accepted in part because of Giants manager Dusty Baker's astute people skills. Baker had been a great player himself and, as a friend of Bobby Bonds, had watched Barry grow up. Baker learned early on about the privileges of superstardom. As a rookie with the Atlanta Braves, he played alongside such heavyweights as Hank Aaron, Clete Boyer, Joe Torre, and Felipe Alou. "You have to let guys bend the rules depending on how great they are," Baker said. He was ready not only for managing Bonds but for teaching the rest of the team what Aaron had taught him.

"Day one of spring training, I had to call five or six guys into the office that were already pissed off. Barry was joking around saying some things, and people took exception to it. So I had to call everyone in to smooth things out."

Even rules Baker figured were cut-and-dried were sometimes sacrificed. Baker had required all players to attend official team functions, a rule he adopted from a treasured mentor, the late San Francisco 49ers coach Bill Walsh. "That philosophy was tested with Barry and Jeff. Because if Barry didn't go, Jeff didn't go." Bonds went so far as to skip the team photo. The next year Kent skipped it, too. Both were photoshopped in.* The front-office

---

* The reason they didn't show? The photographer wanted the team at the ballpark at noon. The players didn't take batting practice until four. "I'm not sitting around the ballpark for two and a half hours, wasting my time, eating terrible food," Bonds told me. This was during the Candlestick Park days when the clubhouse was decrepit and the meals on par with a school cafeteria's. "Jeff agreed," Bonds said. "Me and Jeff stuck together." The team changed the time to three thirty after those two years. Bonds and Kent showed up.

executives had enough concerns about Bonds's impact that they surrounded him with seasoned veterans less likely to be affected. "You inject strength and leadership and healthy personalities all around to the point where you negate the potential destructiveness," one baseball-operations executive said.

As the sun dropped behind the hills and the air suddenly cooled, Bonds suggested we go inside. Customers glanced his way as he ordered a glass of fresh beet juice, but no one approached. We talked easily until suddenly he pumped the brakes, as if catching himself lowering his guard.

"Barry Bonds is a huge story," he said, locking his eyes on me as he leaned back into the banquette bench. "And I'm doing it for free. I don't work for free. I'm being a nice guy."

"I know and I appreciate it."

"You're getting free information you couldn't get from anyone else. So that's worth something."

"I would have been happy to buy your beet juice," I said, smiling.

"I'm helping you for your personal success."

"You are, and I totally appreciate it."

We were in our third hour of talking. I was thinking he was ready to leave. Instead he opened up again.

"I'm the villain because of something I'm trapped in," he said.

"I think you have more control than you're letting on."

He talked about racial bias—at school, in the media, in society. He isn't wrong. Arrogant, outspoken black players pay a steeper price in their public image than arrogant, outspoken white players. He mentioned jerky white players who weren't vilified and then ticked off a half dozen black players who were. He fell silent for a moment.

"If I would have talked more I would have been a helluva lot better off. Some people like the stage. It's natural. I wasn't one of them. I had great communication skills but only in baseball. I know how to teach it. I know how to make someone feel good about it. But just regular conversations…

"I know I created that monster," he said of his toxic relationship with the media. "I don't ever deny the monster that I created. I probably played better [because of it]. Once it happened, I used it to my advantage."

He told a story from the 2002 World Series. During the Game 2 loss to the Anaheim Angels, Bonds grounded out on the first pitch from an impressive twenty-year-old rookie named Francisco Rodríguez. Writer Peter Gammons said to Bonds after the game that he thought Rodríguez would become the best young reliever in the game.

"Peter, since you want to insult my ability and want to put this guy on such a high pedestal, when I face this kid again I'm going to hit the ball so hard you're not going to see it."

In Game 6, Bonds crushed a high change-up off Rodríguez that disappeared through the tunnel in the right-field bleachers. When he jogged to left field at the end of the inning, he looked up at Gammons in the press box and said to himself, "Now what are you going to say about it?"

Umbrage fueled him. Earlier in our conversation, he had said he believed that a single person on a team can get everyone on the same wavelength and create chemistry. He told me about a team-mate named Lloyd McClendon who would motivate guys by making them laugh or challenging them in some way. With Bonds, McClendon reported the shit opposing players were supposedly saying about him. *Dwight Gooden said in the paper today he owns you. You gonna let that guy walk on you?* "It would just fire you up so bad, and all of a sudden you get a hit," Bonds said.

"And then there are guys who are bad motivators. They think they're creating chemistry but really [they're] making it worse. When they try to challenge you as a person or your work ethic or 'this is the way the game's supposed to be played.' You look at him and think, 'Who in the hell made you God? You're not even the number one player on the team.'"

I asked if he was referring to Kent.

"Jeff Kent wasn't like that! Jeff Kent was never like that!" he said, his voice rising.

"Folks can say whatever the hell they want to say about that guy and me. We were both A-type-personality players. We didn't hang out. I didn't care what he was doing. You have players who care what another person's doing in the locker room. It's stupid. It's hard enough to prepare yourself to be good—why do you care what that dude is doing over there? Why do you care Jeff Kent is over there looking at properties for his hunting places? Who gives a crap?

"When it came to game time, what name would you want on the back of the uniform of the guy playing second base? I want Jeff Kent. Because he's a ballplayer. When it comes to guts, someone who goes out there to do his job—they can say whatever they want about Jeff Kent, they can say whatever they want about Barry Bonds—when it came to who they want to play in left field, who they want to play at second base, it would be Barry Bonds and Jeff Kent."

This is chemistry. Like more conventional emotional-social chemistry, it is built on trust. But it's trust earned through performance. You might not like your teammate, coworker, or boss, says Rod Kramer, the social psychologist who studies trust at the Stanford Graduate School of Business, but you trust his or her abilities and commitment. Again Steve Jobs: "A lot of people found him difficult, but they trusted him and his genius," Kramer said. "You can have coaches who are great intimidators and not very likable, but their teams trust they know what they're doing."

Hall of Fame manager Tony La Russa described it this way: "Trust is dedication to doing whatever you can, every game, to help the team win. You can be a selfish player, but if we can trust that you're going to use your talent to do your best every day, you're OK. But if we can't trust you're going to do that, we don't want you."

Skeptics often bring up the dysfunctional but hugely successful Oakland A's of the early 1970s to debunk team chemistry. Those A's were the original "twenty-five players, twenty-five cabs" team. Their clubhouse fairly seethed with animosity. One day before a game in Detroit in 1974, superstar slugger Reggie Jackson took offense to a comment from Billy North and lunged at him. Jackson and North pounded each other until teammates pulled them apart, only to watch the two go at it again. When the fight was over, Jackson was nursing a sore shoulder, and catcher Ray Fosse had hurt his neck from breaking the fight up. (Fosse soon found out he had herniated a disc and couldn't play for several months.) But North, Jackson, and Fosse all played that night. The A's won in a laugher, 9–1.

But Jackson plunged into a hitting slump after the fight. He hit .228 with just four home runs in the next forty-eight games. North still disliked Jackson, but he pulled his teammate aside. He told Jackson the team needed him. He was their star. They couldn't win without him. In his next twenty-seven games, Jackson batted .600 with nine home runs. The A's won their division, beat the Orioles for the American League pennant, and then beat the Dodgers to win their third consecutive World Series championship.

Whatever trust the A's players lacked in the clubhouse, they had it in spades on the field. Each man trusted his teammates to play all out every day because they were absolutely united in their goal. But North's pep talk to Jackson—showing his belief in and need for his teammate—also seemed to matter. Team chemistry is never the product of a single influence but the interplay of many.

Bonds and Kent deeply trusted each other, but only on the field. Each was wholly committed to his craft and to winning and recognized those qualities in one another. They even showed a task-oriented version of caring: They happily celebrated each other's on-field heroics. A case in point: Just minutes after their fist-fight in the dugout in 2002, Bonds hit a home run, and Kent was waiting in the dugout, all smiles, to greet him with high fives.

This "task chemistry" is about the work and only the work. Aristotle alluded to the concept when he categorized friendships under three labels: love, pleasure, and utility. Love friendships are the rarest because they require of each friend unconditional acceptance. Pleasure friendships are based on shared interests and activities. And utility friendships serve a particular, often short-term purpose. Task chemistry is a relationship of utility. Former Giants outfielder Randy Winn had described the concept to me a few years ago, though I didn't categorize it as such at the time. Winn played thirteen years in the major leagues before becoming president of the Baseball Assistance Team and special assistant to the Giants' general manager. He's a deliberative thinker and team-chemistry agnostic, so he was a useful devil's advocate for my theories-in-progress. Over cocktails and dinner one night in Arizona, when I still thought of Bonds as the poster boy for clubhouse cancers, I asked if the Giants would have been better off without him. Winn said that whatever chemistry might be, I was thinking about it too narrowly.

"Everybody thinks chemistry is this wonderful, sort of euphoric thing, and everybody gets along and puts their arms around each other and sings songs and goes out to dinner," Winn said. "Some places it's like that. But more often, what makes good chemistry is if you do your job, and especially if you do your job really well. That makes a good teammate. So I didn't have any problems with Barry. We don't talk. We don't go out to dinner. We don't hang out. But that's a good teammate. Team chemistry is not always what people think it is."

Jim Leyland made this point when we talked a few years earlier. When his players fought in the clubhouse, he left them to it. "What do I need to worry about it for? They played the game. They played their ass off. One was going to go out there and show *the other guy* he could play, and *the other guy* was going to show *him* he could play. They fed off one another."

That was task chemistry. Long before the contentious "Bronx Zoo" Yankees and the combative "Swingin'" A's, long before Bonds and Kent, Babe Ruth and Lou Gehrig showed you didn't need to like each other to play well together. Gehrig's mother reportedly criticized how Ruth's wife, Claire, dressed their daughter, and that was it. The two men were quiet enemies for life. In the famous double-play trio of Tinker to Evers to Chance, Joe Tinker and Johnny Evers didn't talk to each other for thirty-three years. Apparently Tinker claimed a taxi for himself, leaving Evers on the sidewalk.[9]

"Of course, how would you have known," *Sports Illustrated*'s Richard Hoffer wrote, "unless you wondered why Gehrig was always examining the dirt in the on-deck circle after the Babe had crushed another one. You certainly didn't read it in the papers.... We never doubted all that camaraderie was forced; that's actually why we admired it. Pretending to get along is one of the most useful lessons sports can give us. The day after Evers was left steaming on the curb, he grabbed Tinker and said, 'You play your position and I'll play mine, and let it go at that.'"

There was a famous study in the 1960s about task chemistry, though the phenomenon wasn't called that. A researcher named Hans Lenk, a former Olympic rower, was skeptical about the notion that a team had to get along to be successful. He spoke from experience. His successful 1960 West German rowing team—an amalgamation of two different rowing clubs—battled openly. Yet it went undefeated in winning the Olympic gold medal. Lenk posited that the performance of a high-achieving team wouldn't be negatively affected—and perhaps would even be improved—by "violent internal social conflicts."[10] Later he found the same dynamic in the bickering, cliquish West German team that won the World Rowing Championships in 1963.[11] Their hostility toward each other had no effect on their performance: They knew they could count on each other when they climbed into the boat.

So was the Office of Strategic Services's sabotage manual wrong about the contagion of negativity? Is the bad-apple theory—and the Super-Disruptor role—a myth?

No. Negativity can definitely spread and diminish performance. But the culprits are not arrogant superstars or antisocial workhorses like Kent. They can be grit in the gears, but they're not enough to ruin the engine.

The true Super-Disruptor, and perhaps the most potentially dangerous creature on any team, is the complainer looking for recruits. In baseball, he's known as a clubhouse lawyer.

"Clubhouse lawyers can do more friggin' damage than anybody on a ball club," Keith Hernandez told me. He played seventeen years in the major leagues, including on the 1986 World Series champion New York Mets. "Usually the clubhouse lawyer is someone who is dissatisfied himself. He's not happy about how he's being used, and he just can't internalize it. He's got to spread it like a weed, like a poison throughout the team. He needs to be traded as soon as possible."

The clubhouse lawyer is often a fading veteran riding the bench who pulls others into his bitch-fest. There's always someone ready to be convinced that—yes!—he's getting screwed, too. "That's why you want character guys who won't get sucked into the misery," one coach said.

At the winter baseball meetings a few years back, then-New York Mets general manager Sandy Alderson told me he had just shot down a deal with a free-agent reliever who was a notorious complainer. "We're not even going to consider him," Alderson said. "He's negative, complaining, pessimistic. If you have a guy like that in the bullpen, sitting there night after night with seven or eight guys, you worry he takes some guys with him, especially the young guys."

Every team and every company has complainers who infect others, like ethylene in an apple barrel. Because we mirror each other's body language and facial expressions, this negativity can spread quickly. "We can retain a mood that stays with us long after the direct encounter ends—an emotional afterglow (or after-glower, in my case)," Daniel Goleman wrote in his 2006 book *Social Intelligence: The New Science of Human Relationships.* "Like second-hand smoke, the leakage of emotions can make a bystander an innocent casualty of someone else's toxic state."

Attempts to rise above the negativity are emotionally exhausting for the team as a whole and peter out. Effort dwindles. Performance drops.

The antidote is a wise and at times ruthless leader who prevents the Super-Disruptor from gaining influence. He or she can concentrate the group's sense of unity onto the complainer, who either conforms or finds himself isolated. The legendary

Manchester United manager Sir Alex Ferguson felt so strongly about the toxic effect of complainers that he got rid of them regardless of their stature. In 2005, after longtime captain Roy Keane criticized teammates in the press, Ferguson terminated the star player's contract. Leading scorer Ruud van Nistelrooy was sold to Real Madrid in 2006 when he openly complained about being benched.[12]

"There are occasions when you have to ask yourself whether certain players are affecting the dressing-room atmosphere, the performance of the team, and your control of the players and staff," Ferguson said in a 2013 *Harvard Business Review* article. "If they are, you have to cut the cord. There is absolutely no other way. It doesn't matter if the person is the best player in the world. The long-term view of the club is more important than any individual."

The second most disruptive creature is the malingerer.

The malingerer always seems to need a day of rest when the opponent's ace is scheduled to pitch. While others play through aches and pains, the malingerer sits out to protect his stats. Teammates get cranky. Why should they play with iffy ankle sprains and swollen knees when this guy is on the shelf with *fatigue*? They start to ask for days off, too. "People will cooperate if they think everyone else is cooperating," said Paul Ferraro, a behavioral economist at Johns Hopkins University. If others are not, "you feel like a sucker." He conducted a field experiment in an Atlanta utility district that wanted customers to conserve water. Penalties weren't working. Ferraro tried different types of motivational messaging, including an argument for protecting the environment. Nothing was more effective, however, than letters to customers showing how their water usage compared to others'. When people saw that their neighbors were sacrificing, they sacrificed, too, particularly the highest consumers. Usage quickly dropped 5 percent.[13] When we believe others are doing little or nothing at all, we're reluctant to do our part.

Nearly every player I know has crossed paths with a malingerer.

"You're all wasting energy, physical and mental, thinking about what that guy's doing, why he's doing it, what's going on, how he's getting away with it," said former major-league reliever Javier Lopez. "You start building conspiracy theories, all kinds of things. And it takes away from your performance because you're not focusing on your own job."

The good news is that a true Super-Disruptor is a rare thing because humans yearn to belong. Paul Zak, the neuro-economist, found that "almost always if you set the right conditions, most people who are not pathological will be part of the group."

In the 2002 World Series, Bonds, Kent, and their Giants teammates were six outs away from winning the championship. Up three games to two against the Anaheim Angels, they held a 5–3 lead going into the eighth inning in Game 6. A victory would deliver San Francisco's first World Series championship since the team arrived from New York in 1958. But the Giants let it slip away, losing 6–5.

They still hadn't recovered from the crushing defeat when they arrived at the park the next day for Game 7. "I walked into the clubhouse in Anaheim, and they were not calm," recalled Mike Krukow, the Giants' broadcaster. "They were rattled from the night before in a game that they should have won. Little fissures of negativity that were starting to crack the egg. And in the end it wasn't even a close game." The Giants lost, 4–1.

Talking to Krukow made me wonder about the limits of task

chemistry, which seemed to be the foundation of the 2002 Giants. Was the all-important resilience a product only of band-of-brothers clubhouse chemistry? I was in Kansas City when the 2014 Giants were demolished in Game 6, 10–0, and, like the 2002 team, had to come back the next day and try to win. Their vibe before that final game stood in stark contrast to Bonds's and Kent's group.

"That [2014] bunch was extremely calm," Krukow said, "and that is a huge advantage when you're in an environment of adrenaline. That's the one thing that jumped off the page every game, including the seventh game. They were calm." The Giants won, 3–2, holding off the Royals one pitch after another for the final five innings.

After the 2002 World Series, Kent left the team, and Bonds stayed another five years. The Giants continued to do well in 2003 and 2004 and then plummeted his final three years. Bonds's chase of Aaron's all-time home-run record, and the hordes of media covering that *and* the ongoing steroid investigation, were distractions too massive for the rest of the players to absorb. "I don't know what the point is here anymore — to win?" one player asked in 2006.

Clearly in the decade-plus since his retirement, Bonds has become more introspective. He has regrets. Inside the café, Bonds glanced at his watch but made no move to leave.

"I could have done it a different way," he said. In the window behind Bonds, the sky was beginning to darken. "Just roll with it. Be fake and act like they [the media] are the nicest people in the world....If I was smarter, I would have just said, 'I think we have a great chance to win and da-da-da-da.' If they ask if I have four lockers, if I was smart I could have played along and explained, 'Oh, they assigned me these two, and the other two are storage.' When they asked about the massage chair, I should have just said, 'Yeah, isn't it great?'

"But at the time, I'm focusing on the game, and I really don't want to have that conversation. That's why I say now, in retrospect, I see how I could have diffused that."

His voice had taken on an edge, maybe a sense of urgency. He leaned forward, his arms on the table.

"I tell the guys now, don't be me...Don't allow them to hurt you. I catch guys all the time: Don't do that. If they could have cut my head off, they would have. Don't go down that road. Be kind. Be nice. Give the reporters what they want. Accept the way things are. They're never going to change. Play hard. Be blessed. You're making more money than most people will ever make. Go off in the sunset. Be with your family. That game's going to continue after you're gone, and the same stories are going to keep on coming, and the next person's going to come up, and he's going to go through it, and I hope you catch him the same way I caught you. Stop it before it gets bad."

"Was there anyone who tried to catch you?" I asked.

He said Tony Gwynn, the late San Diego Padres star, did. Gwynn was as easygoing and accessible as any star in the game. He couldn't understand why Bonds couldn't just relax with the media. "You're smiling and joking around," Gwynn would tell him, "and as soon as these people appear, you're like—"

Bonds grimaces and growls, imitating Gwynn imitating him. "Can't you just give them a little bit?" Gwynn would say.

I asked Bonds, "You couldn't take his advice?"

"I did take his advice. It lasted for about two to three days. Then my teammates would say, 'We want the old Barry.' They said I didn't come out with the same drive: 'You're striking out and just putting your bat in the locker.' One thing about your teammates, they need to believe you're giving your best. When it came to playing baseball, the old Barry is who they wanted."

CHAPTER FIVE

THE SEVEN ARCHETYPES

"Real team chemistry is about accepting everybody for who they are. It's what I keep telling these guys: In the end we love people *for who they are to us*."

— Carolina Panthers head coach Ron Rivera

Matt Duffy looked like the pizza delivery boy, a skeletal twenty-three-year-old with dapples of acne and just enough chin hair to make a case for a goatee. Nobody had ever heard of Matt Duffy. He was an eighteenth-round draft pick out of Long Beach State. After two years in the minors, he was still far enough down the food chain in the San Francisco Giants organization that he had never been invited to big-league training camp. Now here he was in the summer of 2014, carrying his duffel bag past pale wood lockers bearing the names of the Giants' biggest stars. *Posey. Bumgarner. Crawford.*

Eighteen hours earlier, Duffy had been pulled off the Flying Squirrels' bus in Richmond, Virginia, as it was about to leave on a four-and-a-half-hour drive to the next game in Altoona, Pennsylvania. Suddenly he was on a late-night flight to New York to join the Giants at Citi Field for their series against the Mets. What was he doing here? He hadn't played a game past the Double-A level. *Holy shit,* he thought. Small groupings of leather armchairs spanned the length of the enormous room like a hotel lobby.

From the corner of the clubhouse, a pair of eyes followed the newbie. Giants star Hunter Pence watched Duffy find his locker, unpack his bag, and pull on his number 50 jersey. Pence was the legend whose rousing speech one afternoon in Cincinnati two years earlier had become lore, a story retold in every cramped, musty clubhouse in the Giants farm system. Duffy, of course, knew it well.

The Giants were down two games to none against Cincinnati in the best-of-five National League Division Series in 2012. To stay alive, they'd have to win back-to-back-to-back games against a first-place team that hadn't lost three in a row since early August. Manager Bruce Bochy had wrapped up his impassioned pregame remarks when, to everyone's surprise, Pence stood. The All-Star right fielder had come over to the Giants just a few months earlier in a mid-season trade. He was a bit of an odd duck who rode a souped-up scooter to the ballpark, was obsessed with coffee and kale, swung the bat like the Tin Man chopping wood, and could still do backflips from his boyhood days as a competitive power tumbler. His googly eyes gave the impression of never blinking. Quiet and introspective by nature, he was as likely to be reading Miyamoto Musashi's *The Book of Five Rings* as playing *World of Warcraft* video games.

But on that October day, Pence rose and said, "I have something to say."

He waved for his teammates to gather round. His eyes shined. "Get in here! Everyone get in here!"

The players glanced at each other and moved toward him.

"I want one more day with you! This is the most fun, the best team I have ever been on, and no matter what happens *we must not give in!*"

His voice was now full-pulpit.

"Look into each other's eyes!" he said, his own eyes now bulging. "*Look into each other's eyes!* We *owe* it to each other to *play* for each other!"

"*Yes!*"

"*Yeah!*"

"I need one more day with you guys!" Pence said again. "I need to see what [Ryan] Theriot will wear tomorrow! I want to play defense behind [Ryan] Vogelsong because he's never been to the playoffs! Play for each *other* not yourself! Win each *moment*! Win each *inning*! It's all we have left!"

Second baseman Marco Scutaro erupted in a roar and then everyone roared—players, coaches, trainers, clubbies. They pressed in around Pence, their arms slung around each other's shoulders and, in a single tight ball, bounced and hollered like high schoolers about to take on their crosstown rivals.

The Giants won 2–1 in extra innings.

In the dugout before every game, through the last of the World Series, the team huddled around Pence, shouting, "*Play for each other!*" and showering themselves with handfuls of sunflower seeds like wedding rice. Pence became known as The Reverend.

Now, in Citi Field's visiting clubhouse with the fancy lockers and armchairs and baseball stars Duffy had seen only on television, who walks straight toward him but The Reverend himself. He looked unlike any ballplayer Duffy had ever seen. His blazing eyes were even more so in person, his bramble of hair even wilder.

Pence shook Duffy's hand and congratulated him on making the bigs. Then he said something the kid never expected.

"You're just the guy we need right now to help us win."

He said it so matter-of-factly that Duffy believed him. Maybe, Duffy thought, he didn't need to be bigger or more experienced than he was. Perhaps all he had to do was be Matt Duffy and play his ass off.

By season's end, he had hit .267 in thirty-nine games — good enough to make the postseason roster and earn a ring from the Giants' third World Series in five years.

"Hunter got rid of all my anxiety in those first few minutes in the clubhouse," Duffy said later. "He convinced me I was ready, so I went out there like I was."

Most successful teams have someone like Pence. He's the party guest who circulates the room reinvigorating conversations and shepherding social strays back to the herd. He "lights the candle," as some players say. He gets everyone playing with what he calls a "burning enthusiasm." That was Pence's function in the chemistry of the Giants — to ignite in his teammates a sense of purpose, selflessness, and collective invincibility. That translates into increased confidence and effort, which leads to elevated performance and — in this example — to wins. Pence's role was what I call the Sparkplug.*

From the beginning, I wondered if team chemistry requires a particular mix of personalities the way an actual chemical reaction requires a particular mix of elements. Were there certain archetype characters, such as the Sparkplug, that every good-chemistry team had? I began keeping a list of character types I'd noticed on good-chemistry teams. I periodically ran the list by players and coaches. They validated some, shot down others, and offered suggestions. I culled the list to seven. To be clear, these

---

* My original name was the Energizer until I talked with Canadian psychology professor Mark Eys, who had identified a similar archetype called the Sparkplug, which was much better than the Energizer. With his permission, I adopted Sparkplug.

archetypes are not scientific findings. They are patterns I've observed that seem to resonate not only with people in sports, but also with those in business. Perhaps all high-functioning groups have a version of this list.

My other six archetypes:

The Sage

This is Obi-Wan Kenobi, the wise, kind veteran. He has been through the grind. He has weathered the storms. He lifts anxiety and eases the sting of humiliation. He soothes and advises. Biology as well as experience might be at work here, at least in men. Testosterone declines not only as men age, but also when they get married and raise children. "You need grandpa," said former catcher and now scout Brian Johnson. "It's nice to have grandpa because he has seen it all. You can sit on grandpa's lap and tell him everything."

The Sage is David Ross on the 2016 Chicago Cubs, Tim Hudson on the 2014 San Francisco Giants, Teresa Edwards on the 1996 Olympic basketball team. The Sage accepts players for who they are. She doesn't judge or micromanage but instead nudges: "Hey, this is maybe something to think about." He or she provides a safe refuge where teammates can be vulnerable, even if the teammate is also a veteran.

Ellis Burks was a two-time All-Star who played eighteen years in the major leagues. Chatting with him one day in spring training, I asked if the Sage character rang true. He said he'd known several over the years and never stopped needing them. "Confidence, you know, creates success, all right? If you're confident—and I don't care if you've been a ten-time All-Star—you can go through a slump and suddenly your confidence is a little shy. Sometimes you need that person to remind you who you are."

The Kid

The Kid throws off energy like a puppy shaking off water. He's Matt Duffy, in awe of the espresso machine in the dining room. The Kid is the first in line to give high fives. The one draping an arm around a teammate for no reason. He's at the far end of the dugout after batting practice, signing autographs and chatting with fans long after his teammates have ducked back into the clubhouse. He isn't yet interested in the Dow, the real estate market, or the resale value of a Lamborghini Veneno. He thinks the team plane is awesome.

To the veterans, the Kid reminds them of the person they used to be. He reminds them of what they love about the game. They remember the heart-pounding amazement of looking up from the field for the first time and seeing the rows and rows of people rising as high as a ten-story building. Watching the Kid jump on a teammate's back during a lull in batting practice is a hit of oxygen.

"Baseball gets to be like a business," said retired pitcher Jeremy Affeldt. "It's Groundhog Day every day. For those young guys, it's all new, man. And you're like, 'All right, I need some of that.'"

The Kid carries the dream. She doesn't know what's impossible. She believes it's all there for the taking. "Time teaches many things," Warren Bennis and Patricia Ward Biederman wrote in their book *Organizing Genius: The Secrets of Creative Collaboration,* "including limitations. Time forces people, however brilliant, to taste their own mortality. In short, experience tends to make people more realistic, and that's not necessarily a good thing... Great Groups are not realistic places. They are exuberant, irrationally optimistic ones."

The Kid's irrational optimism challenges veterans to shrug off the limits they've put on themselves. Anthony Rizzo, the Chicago Cubs' young team leader in 2016, never stopped reminding his teammates that, in general manager Theo Epstein's words, "they were going to make history together; they were going to have a parade and be linked in eternity forever." In the dugout, Rizzo always looked like he was having the time of his life. He was authentic and genuine without being childish.

Twenty-three-year-old Buster Posey was a rookie in 2010 when the Giants beat the Phillies to win the National League Championship Series. When the impromptu party in the hotel ballroom afterward began to break up at four thirty in the morning, broadcaster Mike Krukow found himself in an elevator with a few players, including Posey.

"I hope," Krukow said, "you don't think this happens every year."

Posey, with his crew cut and pink cheeks, turned to Krukow and said, "Well, why not?"

The Enforcer

The Enforcer upholds the standards of the team, taking teammates to task for slacking off in practice, making mental errors, missing signs. It's not a role for the thin-skinned. The Enforcer risks being accused of sticking her nose where it doesn't belong and getting the "Who made you God?" treatment. The Enforcer believes winning is more important than popularity. Consciously or not, she understands that too much camaraderie can be as dangerous a threat to winning as too little. A team that cares too much about each other's feelings might shy from delivering pointed feedback for fear of damaging relationships. Taken to the extreme, a team with too much cohesion can turn cultish in its attachment to being in total agreement. The Enforcer never chooses feelings over winning. When she notices small slippages in behavior and effort, she sounds the alarm, even if the team's on a roll and everybody's perfectly happy with how things are going. The Enforcer recognizes the signs of a team dancing toward disaster.

The Enforcer comes in two personality packages. One is the caustic version like, say, Jeff Kent. He's what I call the Agitator-Enforcer. When he calls the team out for slacking off, his teammates bristle, maybe even roll their eyes. "God, he's a douche," they grumble, "but he's right." Message received. The Agitator-Enforcer has influence only as long as teammates trust he has the team's best interest at heart. It's a self-correcting dynamic: A leader who's on a power trip soon loses his power.

The second personality package is the Sage-Enforcer. He is as steely as the Agitator with none of the sharp edges. He is well-liked and trusted. He has social skills. Few outside the team would ever peg him as an Enforcer. Javier Lopez was a soft-spoken relief pitcher who had graduated from the University of Virginia with a degree in psychology. The son of an FBI agent, Lopez had a languid, self-possessed manner that brought to mind a quick-witted chairman of a college English department. He was a star among bullpen groupies, one of the most fearsome lefty specialists in the game. During his six seasons with the Giants, no one in the clubhouse was more respected.

That's how he was able, against the odds, to keep in check a young teammate whose mood swings and sometimes off-putting behavior threatened to disrupt the clubhouse. Lopez was old school and thus uneasy treating grown men with kid gloves. But getting in the face of the teammate would have backfired, only enlarging the chip on his shoulder and fueling his self-absorbed behavior. So Lopez adapted. He spent hours with the young player talking and listening, counseling and encouraging. He'd lead with two positives before calling the player out on his behavior. "That way I feel like that eases the blow. It shows that I care," Lopez said. "You never want to embarrass somebody or break them down."

Lopez knew this teammate needed a caring Enforcer with a

very soft hammer. "I could micromanage and call people out on every single thing," he said, "but it's not ultimately going to get us where we want to go."

The Buddy

The Buddy is everybody's friend. No one eats alone when there's a Buddy on the team. No one is without a tribe. She asks about your dad's heart surgery, rounds up people for a movie on the road, learns the best Japanese swear words just to make the new Japanese teammate laugh. Basketball star Jennifer Azzi was a Buddy. In the '96 Olympic team's training camp, when young Rebecca Lobo failed again and again to run two miles in the allotted time, Azzi ran alongside her every day until she passed. Lobo was the weakest but most well-known player on that Olympic team and felt like an outsider among the older, more experienced veterans. It was Azzi to whom she finally let her guard down, sharing her doubts, her loneliness, her discomfort with getting so much public attention. "We've all been where you are, one way or another," Azzi told Lobo. "We do understand." Soon after the heart-to-heart with Azzi, Lobo scored twenty-four points against South Korea in the China tournament, looking like her old University of Connecticut self again. She began joining teammates in their games of Spades and in their banter and jokes. She finally felt like she belonged.

Mark DeRosa, a utility player for most of his sixteen years in the major leagues, is another example. Always smiling and talking, he was naturally social but also believed personal connection helped his teammates play better. When you're embraced and accepted, you're more relaxed. When you're more relaxed, your mind and body are more in the flow, producing a better performance. DeRosa took more guys to lunch than anyone else on the team. The rookies, the Latin-American guys, the end-of-the-bench relievers. He bridged every cultural, racial, age, and position boundary in the clubhouse. He wanted to hear everybody's story.

"On any team, our upbringings are so different," DeRosa said, "so I'm always looking for the things that we have in common or the one thing that makes that guy tick. [Juan] Uribe, it's his sense of humor. [Travis] Ishikawa, his wife is pregnant and going through rough patches, and I went through similar experiences with my wife's two pregnancies."

Even when DeRosa was injured and couldn't play, he continued to have influence. He noticed players' moods. He cracked jokes and told stories. He talked ball all the time, keeping his teammates' focus on the game. He looked for opportunities to lift guys up. "I get my ass off the bench to tell someone they did a good job," DeRosa said. When Javier Lopez came back to the dugout after mopping up a game the Giants were losing badly, DeRosa was waiting for him at the dugout stairs. Lopez had slogged through one of the more thankless tasks on a baseball team. "Hey," DeRosa said, slapping Lopez's back, "I appreciate what you did out there."

The Buddy is *always* a good audience. He laughs at everyone's jokes and listens to their stories. He's perfectly happy playing the straight man, the good-natured butt of the joke. David Ross was a Buddy as well as a Sage for the Cubs in 2016. General manager Theo Epstein said of him, "Rossy was always reaching out to befriend the loneliest players, organizing team dinners, breaking down the barriers that sometimes arise between players of different backgrounds in the clubhouse."[1] Epstein hired Ross as the cubs' manager in 2019.

The Warrior

The Warrior is so exceptional and intimidating he gives the entire team swagger. Barry Bonds is a Warrior. LeBron James. Sue Bird.

Tom Brady. Megan Rapinoe. Mike Trout. The Warrior is the linch-pin of the team's belief in itself. *We have her, therefore we can win. We have him, therefore we are special.* The Warrior doesn't have to be a pleasant person. She doesn't even have to be a team player. She just has to be extraordinary and fearless. Former baseball player and manager Dusty Baker refers to these players as carriers. "Everybody can carry your team for a day or two," he said, "but the carrier, he can carry you for a couple weeks. Everyone else is a helper."

When a young Cuban slugger named Yoenis Céspedes arrived at the Oakland A's in 2012, he lit up a team that had won just seventy-four games the previous season. He hit moonshots into the second deck. He threw strikes to the plate from deep left field; he had muscles on top of muscles and blazed around the bases like an Olympic sprinter. Loving the spotlight, he played with joy and ease. In his first season, the A's rocketed from third place to first, winning twenty more games than the year before. They fin-ished first again in 2013. Céspedes was their Warrior, the larger-than-life presence who came to define the team.

By the All-Star break in 2014, the A's had the best record in all of baseball. To be sure, it wasn't all Céspedes. The A's were loaded, sending five players to the All-Star team along with Céspedes that year: Josh Donaldson, Derek Norris, Brandon Moss, Scott Kazmir, and Sean Doolittle. Céspedes, of course, won the Home Run Derby, making him the first player since Ken Griffey Jr. in 1999 to win two in a row.

Then a bombshell. On July 31, the A's traded Céspedes to the Boston Red Sox. They swapped their star slugger for Boston's star pitcher, Jon Lester. Oakland's bold move was applauded by much of the baseball world: Pitching won championships. The A's had been knocked out of the playoffs in the first round in both 2012 and 2013. In other words, what good was Céspedes helping us get to the playoffs if we can't win when we get there?

So, on paper, the trade made sense. In the clubhouse, not so much.

The A's won sixty-six games in the first four months of the season with Céspedes. They won just twenty-two in the last two months without him, losing thirty of their final forty-five games. They went from the best record in baseball to not even winning their division. All-Star Brandon Moss had hit .259 with twenty-three home runs and seventy-two RBIs (runs batted in) in the first four months and .162 with two home runs and nine RBIs in the final two. Josh Donaldson slipped from twenty-three home runs and seventy-six RBIs with Céspedes to six home runs and twenty-two RBIs without.

The collapse could be blamed on some injuries and players regressing to career averages. But in the clubhouse, the consensus was Céspedes.

"There's no doubt in my mind," said Dallas Braden, a former A's pitcher and now a baseball broadcaster. The A's had lost its Warrior, and other players tried to fill the gaping hole. "That's when you see guys come up and try to hit what I call the five-run home run. To make the play that just cannot be made. That's when you start to see performance wane."

The A's eked into the playoffs as a wild-card team and promptly lost to Kansas City.

"Céspedes had that star aura," said one A's insider, "and everyone felt it. Moss and Donaldson went in the tank after that. It's like, 'He's hitting behind me or in front of me, so I feel OK. We're going to be OK.' A lot of it was mental. He was the heart and soul of the team. [The team] honestly wasn't the same for years."

A Warrior must have a track record of winning. If he hasn't won in the pros, he better have won in high school or college. Every great team needs players who know how to win. That's why Pat Burrell was so instrumental to the 2010 Giants. He brought both his University of Miami and his Phillies championships into the clubhouse with him. He showed them how to deal with pressure, how to slow the game down.

A general manager told me about a mistake he made in trading for a solid outfielder at the trade deadline, hoping he'd launch the team into the playoffs. He didn't. "We did a lot of soul-searching after that deal," the general manager said. "I talked to another GM who had signed [the same guy] as a free agent and asked him, 'What do you think it is?' He said, 'He doesn't know how to win. He's the greatest kid in the world, but he's never won.' I said, 'You know what, you're right.'" The GM had passed up on Manny Ramirez because of his reputation as a disruptor in the clubhouse. The Los Angeles Dodgers signed Ramirez, and he rocketed them into the playoffs.

The Jester

The Jester is a shape-shifter. He can pump up his teammates like the Sparkplug. He can call out disruptive behavior like the Enforcer. He can foster connections like the Buddy. He can break tension with a well-timed prank, boost camaraderie with back-and-forth joking, ease anxiety with artful teasing. Because he can poke fun without ticking people off, he can say almost anything to anybody. He can shoot the sharpest dart without leaving a scar because no rebuke lands more softly than one wrapped in humor. A truly gifted Jester can wield more influence on a team than the strongest Warrior. "A fool's strength," writes Shanti Fader, writer and editor of philosophy and myth, "lies in the very qualities that separate him from the conventional image of the heroic: humility and the willingness to support others rather than seeking power or glory directly."[2]

Teams are never made up of equals. But for chemistry to

thrive, there needs to be a sense of equality. And, as we learned, joking cultures break down barriers. A Jester's savvy needling of a team leader—and the team leader's willingness to accept the needling—sends the message that we're all in this together. The leader gets to show he's a good sport, that he's one of the guys, which makes him more approachable and thus a stronger leader.

Every team develops its own inside jokes and gags, and the Jester sets the tone. These references are touchstones. They're repeated throughout the season and understood only by the team. They become integral to its identity, separating the outsiders from the insiders. When players refer to a running joke, they're reinforcing the trust they've established with each other. Ragging can serve as a test: Can you take it, or will you sulk and stew? Are you in or out? A team cannot function well without humor. It solidifies the players' sense of themselves as a single unit, as an island unto themselves. Only they could trust each other enough to accept the mockery and insults for what they are: signs of acceptance and even affection.

The Jester's gift for making people laugh brings them together in a way few things can. It is believed that laughter preceded language. It has its own vocal register, separate from speech. Its purpose is primarily social, bonding one person to another. A Vanderbilt psychology researcher named Jo-Anne Bachorowski wrote that "laughs of individuals play off one another like the sounds of different instruments in an orchestra."[3]

This is especially true with close friends. Their individual laughs start to overlap and shift so that the separate vocals begin to mimic each other. The laughter, Bachorowski believes, reinforces their affection for each other.

Robin Dunbar, the evolutionary psychologist at Oxford who studied grooming among macaque monkeys, characterized social laughter as "grooming at a distance," whether among humans or lower primates.[4] And it's contagious. Laughing is the ultimate example of mirroring. We see and hear someone laughing, and we feel the beginnings of a laugh, too. Try to stop yourself from laughing when you watch someone totally lose it.* Our brains make us feel that person's mirth.

A good laugh is like a cleanse to the system. The contractions of laughter force air out of our lungs, dropping our heart rate and blood pressure. Dopamine, the so-called pleasure hormone, floods our brain. We feel more connected and trusting, more relaxed and optimistic—a physical and emotional state more conducive to high performance.

I was still honing my archetype list the day I interviewed Mark Eys, the professor at Wilfred Laurier University in Canada who studies the psychological underpinnings of team performance. I was interested in his research on how cohesiveness affects performance. But the conversation turned when I mentioned archetypes. I heard him chuckle: He was studying this very thing. He had his own list of what he called players' "informal roles."

Eys arrived at his list by analyzing, with the help of other researchers, the content of every issue of *Sports Illustrated* published between January 2004 and December 2005.[5] They identified roles and then consulted a panel of coaches and athletes, coming up with a list of twelve: cancer, distractor, malingerer, sparkplug, enforcer, mentor, nonverbal leader, verbal leader, team player, star, and social convener. Eys emphasized that this was an initial finding that likely would be sharpened in further studies. Still, we laughed at how similar our lists were. "For a lot of different groups, not only in sports, people's eyes light up and go, 'Yeah, I know those people,'" Eys said.

---

* Check out this video of contagious laughter: https://www.youtube.com/watch?v=kHnRIAVXTMQ. I'm laughing now just thinking about it.

I received the same reaction from Dodgers manager Dave Roberts. "Utley and Ellis are the old men, the Sage," he said of his 2016 team. "The Kid is Corey Seager. Clayton's the Hero. The Enforcer—I want to say Justin Turner. Adrian Gonzalez was a little bit the Agitator-Enforcer because he would say things to stir things up. But in a kind of loving way. Our Jester is Puig, and Kike Hernández. Kenley Jansen is kind of like the Buddy. He's a big teddy bear and everyone loves him. Kenta Maeda, too."

Roberts rattled off the archetypes on his 2004 Boston Red Sox, too: Kevin Millar as the Jester, Doug Mirabelli and Jason Varitek as Enforcers, Tim Wakefield as the Sage, David Ortiz and Manny Ramirez as the Warriors, Bronson Arroyo as the Kid, and Pokey Reese as the Buddy.

Matt Williams did the same with his Arizona Diamondbacks team that won the World Series in 2001. He and Todd Stottlemyre were the Enforcers. (As an example, he told me about the time new teammate Reggie Sanders stood at home plate and admired the lovely arc of his home run as it sailed into the bleachers. Williams met him at the top step of the dugout. "Nice hit," Williams said. "And don't ever fucking do that again.") Luis Gonzalez was the Warrior, David Dellucci and Danny Bautista the Kids, Steve Finley the Sparkplug, Greg Colbrunn and Craig Counsell the Jesters.

This happened again and again. Players and coaches identified the archetypes on their teams. But could a smart general manager go looking for a Jester or a Sparkplug? Or do these archetypes simply emerge serendipitously?

I asked Ben Cherington. He was the GM who turned a contentious, complacent, last-place 2012 Boston Red Sox team into World Series champions. He had unloaded three of the team's highest-paid stars and added a bunch of so-called character guys. Cherington figured the team would be better—how could it be worse?—but he wasn't expecting to be wiping champagne from his eyes in October.

When I reached him by phone, in 2017, he was vice-president of baseball operations for the Toronto Blue Jays. He had left the Red Sox in 2015 and taught a class in the leadership program at Columbia University in New York. On his syllabus, one lecture had surprised me:

"High-Functioning vs. Dysfunctional Teams, and Team Chemistry."

Cherington had spent all but one year of his career with the Boston Red Sox, an organization so sabermetrics-focused it hired the father of sabermetrics himself, Bill James. James's impact was swift and profound. In two years, the Red Sox won their first World Series in eighty-six years—then another in 2007 and a third in 2013. Cherington fully embraced analytics, while not quite fitting the stereotype of the new breed of numbers-obsessed Ivy Leaguers. Growing up in a small town in New Hampshire in the company of writers and thinkers, he honed his intellect not on economics and finance, but on literature and the humanities. One grandfather won both a Pulitzer and a National Book Award for poetry. The other taught at Harvard and served in Richard Nixon's cabinet. At Amherst, Cherington was a baseball-playing English major focused on British literature. So while he trusted analytics to tell him a deeper and more accurate story about the game, he also understood the vagaries of being human. The prickliness and affection, the kindnesses and betrayals, the selfishness and generosity. They told a story, too. Cherington didn't know how to measure the impact of these forces, however, and thus his class at Columbia was more an exploration of chemistry than an explanation.

"When you're around groups that have that really strong connection, and you see how the total output of the group is more than it might be for any individual, it's clear that there's something to it and it's real," he said. "It's not hard to see chemistry happening when it's happening. The hard part is predicting it. I don't know how to do that."

Some thought he had cracked the code of chemistry by signing Jonny Gomes, David Ross, Stephen Drew, Mike Napoli, Shane Victorino, Koji Uehara, Ryan Dempster, Mike Carp, and Jake Peavy to the 2013 squad. But that wasn't how it happened. Cherington said he looked for the most talented players he could find who, first, filled positions he needed and, second, fit his budget both in salary and length of contract. Only then did he consider character. Archetypes? Never crossed his mind. The only archetypes he knew were in classic literature and Jungian psychology. Yet soon after the reconstituted Red Sox arrived at spring training in Fort Myers, Florida, Cherington saw a change from the year before. As he walked by the players' tables in the lunchroom, the conversation was about what had just happened on the field or what they needed to do better tomorrow. He'd hear Ross talking about a detail from a spring game that might help against the Yankees on opening day.

"It never sounded like a lecture, like he was talking down to anyone," Cherington remembered.

When the team hit a tough patch in May, Cherington noticed Ryan Dempster "had the comedic timing and skill to let the air out of the balloon at the right time, get everybody laughing to ease tension."

Ross and Dempster were emerging as the Sage and the Jester. Victorino and Clay Buchholz were also Jesters. Other players found their roles, too. Cherington predicted none of this. He takes no credit.

"The narrative around that team and how it was built—that it was built on high-character guys—was not a narrative written by us," he said. "That team wrote their own narrative."

I originally imagined team chemistry much as I did actual chemistry, with players as elements in the periodic table; each player, like each element, had unique behaviors and properties. But humans are nothing like elements in the periodic table. Our behaviors and properties change not only year to year due to age, health, experiences, but moment to moment in response to the people around us. Who we are in one group is not who we are in another. Hunter Pence became the Sparkplug for the Giants in 2012 even though he had not filled that role on previous teams.

I now believe that good-chemistry teams manifest what they need. Here's how I think it might work:

Every player on a good-chemistry team is highly motivated to contribute to winning. His role on the field is prescribed: pitcher, catcher, outfielder. His role in the clubhouse is not. He has to discover it. He gathers signals from teammates about what they value in him. Maybe he makes them laugh, and the reward center in his brain lights up. So he finds a way to make them laugh again. And then again. The player's teammates are showing him, quite unconsciously, how to be useful. The Jester emerges. This happens down the line, over and over, as players fill one archetype role or another. Some fill more than one.

They don't know they're filling a role. They just do it. Their physiological state—flush with oxytocin and dopamine—compels it.

CHAPTER SIX

JUST US

Tara VanDerveer was unpacking her bags at her Palo Alto home when she came across the box. She picked it up, headed for her backyard patio, and set it on the outdoor table. Inside was a set of drinking glasses. VanDerveer had just returned from coaching the US women's national basketball team in the 1994 FIBA World Championship in Australia. She had won the souvenirs in a raffle while she was there. On the patio, she lifted one of the pretty glasses from the box and hurled it to the concrete floor. She shattered each one in turn until they lay in shards at the foot of her potted azaleas.

Her team had fallen in the semifinals, and the loss was an embarrassment. They'd let Brazil score 108 points on them. The fourteen-hour flight back from Sydney did nothing to calm VanDerveer's fury. The team had practiced together before the tournament for two weeks at Stanford University, where VanDerveer had built one of the most successful basketball programs in the country. Some of the veteran players showed little enthusiasm for the coach's exhausting twice-a-day workouts and what they considered a stifling style of play. VanDerveer preached the "gospel of five," all five players maneuvering to create openings and set traps like pieces on a chessboard. But what the coach saw in Australia was her star players scrapping her plan in favor of winning games all by themselves. VanDerveer was apoplectic on the sidelines. Maybe raw athleticism once worked against international competition. It was 1994 now. Other countries had caught up to the Americans. VanDerveer saw a team that was undisciplined, sloppy, and weak.

Losing in the semifinals to Brazil was bad enough, but losing like *that?* After the tournament, the coach sent a pointed, four-page letter to the players. "Shakespeare said, 'The hungry lion hunts best.'...As a USA Team, we are in denial. We are arrogant and soft," she wrote. For months afterward, as she ran on her treadmill before heading to Stanford every morning, she watched the videotape of the Brazil loss. It played on her VCR repeatedly until every rushed shot, careless turnover, and missed rebound had been seared into her memory.

Teresa Edwards, the most seasoned and decorated player, returned from Australia with a bad taste in her mouth, too. She knew VanDerveer didn't like her, but she didn't know why. If anyone should be ticked off, it should be *her.* At the training camp at Stanford, VanDerveer had hollered at her constantly: about how she ran, how she shot, how she passed. What was it with this lady? Edwards had played in two Final Fours, three Olympics, and two FIBA World Championships. She had two Olympic gold medals. Her whole life had been basketball since her childhood in rural Cairo (pronounced *kay-row*), Georgia, playing with her four brothers at Holder Park. Now she was thirty years old with eight seasons in the European pro leagues under her belt. She wasn't one of VanDerveer's college girls. Sometimes she had snapped back at the coach. Why so many running drills? Why pass the ball when she had an open shot? She and her teammates knew what they were doing, and they played hard. If there were a more focused, competitive, and team-oriented athlete than she was, Edwards hadn't met her. But when the team lost to Brazil, VanDerveer seemed to blame *her*. Edwards didn't answer the coach's four-page letter.

Nearly a year passed before the two women saw each other again.

It was a spring day in 1995. The Olympic Training Center gym in Colorado Springs, Colorado, squeaked and thumped with the sound of sneakers on hardwood. The weeklong Olympic trials would whittle twenty-four candidates to the eleven who would comprise the US national team. (The twelfth player would be added later.) Edwards was easy to spot. She was the least flashy player on the court. Tight, plain cornrows began at her hairline and continued to the base of her neck, where they sprouted into short, stiff braids. Her easy, almost languid gait in the midst of the other players' jukes and spins and dazzling ball-handling might, in another person, suggest indifference. But her quietude had a fierceness to it, a commanding, intimidating quality. She, too, could juke and dazzle but preferred efficiency and calm. Her even gaze gave away nothing except the impression that she'd already figured out how to beat you.

By all accounts she was a shoo-in to make her fourth Olympic team, which no American basketball player, male or female, had ever done.

This team, Edwards and all the other players knew, would be unlike any previous Olympic team. It would require putting their lives on hold for a year. They would have to leave their families and give up salaries from their pro teams. VanDerveer would have to leave her job, too, at the university where she had won two national championships. Their singular purpose: to win the women's basketball gold medal in the '96 Olympics in Atlanta. No other American basketball team had spent more than a few weeks preparing for the games. USA Basketball wanted to make sure these women would have enough time to mesh as a real team. It was a yearlong experiment in team chemistry.

On the court in Colorado Springs, Edwards was nervous. Between warm-up shots, she found herself glancing at the sideline. There, with a big silver whistle around her neck, stood VanDerveer, the Olympic coach. VanDerveer's furrowed brow and watchful eyes gave Edwards no reason to believe the coach had forgotten Australia. She feared VanDerveer would keep her off the team.

The coach glanced Edwards's way, too, but only briefly. Her eyes moved on to the rest of the two dozen hopefuls: players whose jerseys had been retired by their colleges, who had won NCAA championships, who had starred on pro teams overseas, who had lucrative shoe contracts, who owned medals from the FIBA World Championship and the Olympics. VanDerveer was looking for players who were talented *and* would buy into her program. That was essential if they were going to train and travel together for a year—and win the gold. USA Basketball had too much riding on this for VanDerveer to carry a player who would be grit in the wheels, no matter how well she could play. The coach understood that extraordinary talent was no guarantee of victory.

The once-dominant US women's team had been slipping for almost a decade. It had lost not just the '94 FIBA World Championship in Australia but also the '91 Pan American Games and, most distressing, the previous Olympics in '92. There was more at stake than the gold medal. A dominating Olympic team—coupled with a yearlong marketing campaign of television interviews, autograph sessions, magazine covers, commercials, billboards—would help launch a professional league, a long overdue and critical step in growing the sport in the United States. So USA Basketball needed this team to capture the country's imagination, to show

America that women's basketball had evolved way beyond the college game.

The marketing side of things mattered little to VanDerveer. She cared only about winning. *Dominating.* To that end, she had made it a priority to produce the best-conditioned team in the history of women's basketball. If they didn't win, it would not be because they were outhustled, outworked, or outlasted.

This was another reason she was so cool on Edwards. Veteran players like her weren't accustomed to rigorous weight lifting and conditioning. They hadn't done much of it in college back in the day, and they certainly weren't doing it in the undisciplined pro leagues abroad.

Edwards was right to worry about VanDerveer trying to keep her off the team. The coach did try. But the choice wasn't hers. USA Basketball made the decision. Edwards was in.

An icy wind hit the women's faces like needles. It was just past dawn in early October, four months after the tryout. On the cinder track behind Eagleview Middle School, ten miles from the Olympic Training Center in Colorado Springs, the eleven players zipped their jackets up to their chins. VanDerveer briefly considered relocating to an indoor track or rescheduling altogether but quickly thought better of it. The weather was a gift. She wanted their year together to be difficult.

The players had already gotten a clue of what that might mean when, just days after the tryouts, they gathered at Dulles International Airport in Washington, DC, to fly to Lithuania and then Italy to scrimmage against several European teams. Before the team had even boarded, VanDerveer told one of the players, Rebecca Lobo, to take her bags and go home. Among the team rules—which included wearing specific socks, shirts, athletic bras, wristbands, and headbands so no player stood out from any other— was a requirement to wear closed-toe shoes on flights. VanDerveer was a nervous flier and had visions of fire and shattered glass destroying her players' feet. Lobo, the University of Connecticut superstar and the youngest member of the US team, had shown up in sandals. Lobo hurriedly found a teammate with an extra pair of size-12 sneakers in her carry-on. VanDerveer allowed her to board.

If any player had expected star treatment, she was quickly set straight. The team flew coach, stayed two to a room, hauled the team's eighty-seven pieces of luggage and equipment themselves, and received all of thirty-five dollars each, per diem, for meals. Many of the players' feet dangled off the ends of the beds in the two-star Lithuanian hotel.

From a neuroscience point of view, VanDerveer and USA Basketball could not have designed a better plan to begin melding eleven star players into a single unit. When I asked Paul Zak, the neuro-economist who studies oxytocin and trust, how he would go about building trust on a sports team, he described almost exactly what VanDerveer had done.

"There's got to be a stressor," he said. "It should be a little hard. Maybe twice-a-day workouts. But isolating. You can't see your family. This is boot camp. They're suffering together. They help each other. We get away from the cattiness. Let's get down to what's really important, which is being super fit, working as a team, and connecting to each other on a level that's just about us."

He continued. "I need to build trust with you, and the question is how do I do this efficiently? The only way I know is high stress and isolation. The military model. There may be other ways I don't know about, but that seems to be the most effective way."

After the trip to Lithuania and Italy, the players had returned home for the summer. VanDerveer wasted no time in jump-starting her conditioning program. Each player had an individualized daily training schedule to follow. She was to record each day's workout on a form that accompanied the schedule. The written log was as important to VanDerveer as the training. She believed that attention to detail was both a discipline and a test. It signaled a player's commitment to the team.

Upon the players' return to Colorado Springs at summer's end, only four players had completed the training and had filled out every form. Edwards was one of them.

Now in the biting wind behind the middle school, the players shook their arms and legs, jumped, and stretched. VanDerveer and her two assistant coaches held stopwatches. Eight laps. Two miles. Each player had a target time to meet. The run began. The women gasped for breath in the thin mountain air. Even the best-conditioned athletes ran slower than usual. Three players failed, requiring them to return to the track again and again, between practices and workouts, to make their times. Those three had also failed to do their summer training. So in addition to the extra running, they were rising every morning at dawn, along with the four other players with incomplete workouts, to make up every minute.

VanDerveer was secretly pleased by all this. It set the tone early on: There would be no shortcuts. During sprinting drills from one end of the court to the other, the players literally had to touch their fingers to the baseline. No waving at it. VanDerveer's voice rang in their ears all day like a car alarm. "Move it! Move it!" she hollered, clapping her hands, blaring her whistle, barking corrections and instructions. "Palms up! Palms up!" Even a water break wasn't a break: *"Jog!"*

After drills, legs burning and drenched in sweat, they scrimmaged, knocking into each other for the ball, setting picks, firing passes, grabbing rebounds. "Stay low! Stay *low*! Run! *Ru-un!*"

VanDerveer yelled. Even Ruthie Bolton, whose muscles had muscles, was a wet rag at the end of the day. "If you don't feel like quitting at least three times," she said, recalling those days, "you're not working hard enough."

They practiced twice a day every day. On Monday, Wednesday, and Friday they added an hour of weight training. Each evening, they retreated to their separate apartments in Colorado Springs. Edwards and Katrina McClain were best buddies, but most of the rest were colleagues rather than friends. Unlike NBA players, they rarely had opportunities to play together; the overseas teams usually employed just one American. So after practice in Colorado Springs, they didn't hang out. At night they talked by phone to their actual friends and family, watched TV, or read until they fell asleep and then started all over the next morning.

After being so upset that Edwards had made the team, VanDerveer regrouped. She wiped the slate clean. Every player would be allowed to define herself anew. VanDerveer had called Edwards in Atlanta on her birthday during the summer, and they had a pleasant chat. "A year from today we'll be walking into Olympic Stadium," the coach had said. The truth was she never had a problem with Edwards personally. She admired her intelligence and drive. Edwards once told her about the long summer during college when she took a job at the factory where her mother had worked for as long as Edwards could remember. The days were backbreaking. Edwards became more focused than ever on earning her degree. She graduated from the University of Georgia, went on to command big contracts in the European leagues, and, as soon as she could, bought her mother a house.

Still, VanDerveer worried that Edwards might be too set in her ways to work with a coach so set in hers. And now at training camp in October those concerns became manifest. During a scrimmage against Ukraine, VanDerveer watched Edwards take shots without passing and go one-on-one instead of setting up plays—in other words, Australia all over again. VanDerveer yanked her off the court and exploded. Edwards listened, keeping whatever she was thinking to herself. If Edwards was as hardheaded a player as VanDerveer had ever coached, Edwards could say the same of VanDerveer. They were so much alike. Serious, intense, unglamorous. The celebrity that came with being on the national team was lost on them. They were in it for the basketball and the gold.

If the two women didn't yet fully trust each other—and they didn't—each recognized in the other the thing that burned brightest in herself: the fire to win.

On the first day of November, VanDerveer ushered her team into a bus waiting outside the Westin Hotel in Atlanta. They were in town to play the University of Georgia, the first stop on their twenty-game college tour. "What's that crazy lady got for us today?" one player groaned. The bus headed down Peachtree Street. A few minutes later it pulled into a loading dock at the massive Georgia Dome. Inside, the field was set up for an Atlanta Falcons football game. VanDerveer led the women to the fifty-yard line. "I want you to see where you're going to win the gold medal." She had them visualize the court and the scoreboard and the crowd. She wanted to transform the concept of winning the medal into a concrete experience.

The venue's facilities director explained that the dome would be divided in half for the Olympics: gymnastics on one side, basketball on the other. He directed the players to a spot several yards to their right. "This," he said, "is where the stand will be set up for the gold-medal ceremony."

A huge video screen in the end zone suddenly blazed to life. There was President Clinton against a backdrop of the American flag speaking about the honor of hosting the Olympic Games in 1996. Then came a montage of past Olympic highlights—Jackie Joyner-Kersee leaping into the long-jump pit, Mary Lou Retton landing her vault, Carl Lewis lunging past the finish line. By the time "God Bless America" rose from the speakers, the players and coaches were wiping tears from their eyes. VanDerveer talked about the higher purpose of lifting women's basketball for every woman who came after them.

Then Carol Callan, the team's program director, pulled a flat wooden box from her briefcase. Inside were two gold medals she had borrowed from Edwards without telling her why. VanDerveer wanted the players to see and touch the gold medals in the same arena they'd have the chance to earn their own. They took turns draping the medals around each other's necks. Some raised their arms in victory as if standing on the actual podium. They hugged one another.

"Every time I tell this story it still makes me want to cry," Ruthie Bolton said. "Tara told us, 'This could change women's basketball. It's not going to be easy. When you feel like giving up, remember this moment.' It was profound. We made a commitment to ourselves without realizing it."

We take for granted that purpose matters to performance. This is why coaches don't deliver locker room speeches about analytics, physical conditioning, or talent, though all three are essential to winning. Giants manager Bruce Bochy was particularly skilled at stirring in his players a sense of playing for something larger than themselves. He was neither a frequent orator nor a gifted one, though his voice could be mesmerizing—as low and slow as an ambling cowboy's. He wasn't one to scour Winston Churchill's collected speeches for inspiration. But what Bochy might have lacked in eloquence he more than made up in conviction.

Each of San Francisco's three World Championships—2010, 2012, and 2014—was preceded by an epic Bochy speech.

In 2010, the Giants had been chasing the resurgent San Diego Padres all season and caught them in September. Or kind of did. They'd take over first place one day, and the Padres would reclaim it the next. With two weeks left in the season, the Giants fell one and a half games behind the Padres. Before batting practice at Dodger Stadium, at the start of a three-game series, Bochy called a team meeting. He gave some background on William Wallace, the thirteenth-century Scottish hero who took on the mighty British with his ragtag army.

"Boys," he said, "there's a team ahead of you that has faltered. It is now your time."

Bochy wheeled a television into the clubhouse on a cart and hit "play." Up came Mel Gibson as Wallace in *Braveheart* rallying his troops to seize this moment in history. "Will you fight?" Gibson challenges them, leading to the iconic final words:

"They may take our lives," Gibson shouts to the rising cheers of his soldiers, "but they will never take our *freedom!*"

It was a bit over the top for a baseball game, and some players found it hokey. Yet for the rest of the season through their final unlikely, historic victory in the World Series, cries of "Freedom!" rose from the dugout whenever something good happened.

In 2012, Bochy cast his players as Gideon's army. The team was down two games to none in the best-of-five division series against the Cincinnati Reds. Before the must-win Game 3, Bochy gathered his guys. First he cited examples of similar comebacks in baseball— his own 1984 San Diego Padres winning three straight games against the Cubs to reach the World Series, the Red Sox winning four straight games against the Yankees to win the American League Championship Series in 2004, the A's sweeping the Rangers to win their division in 2012. The manager acknowledged that, yes, they were short on firepower—the team had scored just two runs in their eighteen innings against the Reds—so they would win with guile and skill. Then he told them a story from the Old Testament.

Gideon was a farmer chosen by God to lead the Israelites against the mighty Midianites. He had thirty-two thousand volunteers, but God told him to winnow the group to just the bravest, smartest, and most selfless men. When he had done so, he had three hundred men left. Those three hundred defeated the Midianites' hundred thousand men. When Bochy finished, Hunter Pence was so fired up he leapt from his chair to deliver his now-famous "Play for each other!" speech, which became the team's rallying cry for the rest of the postseason.

This is what sweeps us off our feet, the exhilaration of being part of something extraordinary. Together we feel invincible. We feel within us a sense of completeness—of being the perfect you in this moment, with these people, for this purpose.

The Giants beat the Reds that night in extra innings despite producing just one hit in the first nine. They won the next two games as well and moved on to the National League Championship Series against the St. Louis Cardinals. Again, they fell behind and had to win three straight games to stay alive. In all, they won six do-or-die games during those two series. In the World Series, they beat the Detroit Tigers in four straight games.

In 2014, the Giants faced Game 7 in the World Series in Kansas City. The Royals had murdered them, 10–0, the day before. No team had won a Game 7 on the road since 1979. Bochy had no story to tell his players this time. He just reminded them who they were.

"We wouldn't be here if it wasn't for Mike's home run against St. Louis," he said, gesturing toward his pinch hitter, Mike Morse. "Brandon, remember that home run you hit in Pittsburgh? On the road. You weren't supposed to do that." He went down the line, one player after another, recalling what each had done to get them to this day. He singled out Huddy, the beloved veteran Tim Hudson, their Sage, who was in his final season without ever having played in, much less won, a World Series. When Bochy had finished, he told them to look into the eyes of the guys around the room. They knew who they were as men and as players, he said, and they knew what they were about to accomplish on behalf of history, an entire community, and each other.

"It was getting us to *see* it," said Jake Peavy, who pitched for the Giants that year. "He believed it so much that we believed it, too. In that moment we came together in a way that nobody thought we could. Everyone was jacked up. It was time to go on the field. I truly believe that was a huge deciding factor in us winning that game."

There's no way to prove that Bochy's speech had anything to do with the Giants winning that game, 3–2, or any other games during their World Series runs. The belief, of course, is that "playing for a larger cause cranks up the 'want to' factor," as Bochy put it. But why did the players need that? Wasn't a World Series ring incentive enough? Wasn't money?

Material rewards, particularly money, aren't the great motivators we think they are. When the first Macintosh design had been finalized, Steve Jobs gathered his team and had all forty-five sign their names onto a sheet of paper. The signatures were then etched into the inside-rear-panel case mold, like artists claiming ownership of their work. No one who bought the computer could see the signatures, but Jobs had understood that creating something exceptional and revolutionary had driven his team through the long days, and now their names would be preserved for history.

Adam Grant, an organizational psychology professor at Wharton, has done heaps of research on motivation in the workplace. In one of his well-known studies, he invited thousands of executives to solve a particular workplace problem.[1] Students who had part-time jobs calling alumni for donations, most of which funded scholarships, were becoming demoralized by the repetitive and often thankless work. Because alumni often hung up or brushed them off, the students' morale withered along with their efforts. Donations were not pouring in. The executives had lots of ideas to boost productivity: pay increases, promotions, recognition, food, and breaks. The fundraising managers had already tried each of those ideas to no avail.

Grant, however, had another idea. He invited one of the scholarship recipients to visit the call center and briefly tell the workers how the scholarship had affected his life and how much he appreciated what they were doing. A month later, the workers had spent 142 percent more time on the phone and brought in 171 percent more money. Grant repeated the experiment with other groups and saw similar or greater results each time. "There was no added compensation for the harder work," psychology professor Barry Schwartz observed, "just a deeper sense of purpose."[2]

The eleven women on the '96 national team left the Georgia Dome that November day energized and inspired to win the gold. But the Olympic championship game was still nine months away. What is the shelf life of inspiration? How does a team hold onto it day after day after day? The answer, I discovered, is they can't.

Noble purpose, essential as it is, carries a team only so far. Enduring motivation comes from something much closer at hand: each other.

The military has always understood this.

Who you are fighting alongside is, ultimately, more important than what you're fighting for. This is why in the SEALs' Basic Underwater Demolition course, trainees are assigned swim buddies. They must go everywhere together, even the dining hall. When someone is caught without his swim buddy, another trainee is punished at random for allowing it to happen. "This is about more than the feel-good effects of 'bonding,' " retired general Stanley McChrystal wrote in his 2015 bestselling book *Team of Teams*. "It is done because teams whose members know one another deeply perform *better*. Any coach knows that these sorts of relationships are vital for success."[3]

How was he, and the military, so certain that bonding elevated performance? I flew across the country to Alexandria, Virginia, to find out.

At sixty-four years old, General McChrystal was as lean as a new recruit. He was a decade removed from commanding the joint NATO-US mission in Afghanistan in 2009. Before that, he spent five years running the Department of Defense's super-secret black operations and, unlike any other senior commander, personally accompanied his men on dozens of nighttime raids. His squads captured Saddam Hussein in 2003 and killed Al-Qaeda leader Abu Musab al-Zarqawi in 2006.

Now he's a civilian, or at least approximates one. His consulting company, McChrystal Group, occupies the ground floor of a redbrick building in the leafy Old Town neighborhood in Alexandria. He greeted me in casual office attire of a button-down shirt and khaki pants. But the shirt was army green, the sleeves were neatly folded to about two inches above his elbows, and the slacks had a military crease. His close-cropped hair looked freshly trimmed.

He is an army man, and he can trace his family military history back to the Civil War. His father and grandfather, plus all four of his brothers, also spent their careers in the army. His sister's husband is an army man, his wife is the daughter of an army man, and all *her* brothers are army men. The army has been McChrystal's pack, and, when he retired in 2010, the sense of being part of a pack was the one thing he could not leave behind.

"Quite honestly, that's why we have a company, so that part of our lives, the camaraderie, is filled," he said. About a third of the ninety-person staff are his friends from the military, including his old sergeant major.

McChrystal has created packs, it seems, in every aspect of his life. There's one in New Haven, Connecticut, where he teaches a leadership course at Yale. He initiates his class of twenty under-graduate and grad students—culled from 250 applications—into his circle with a party at his house in Alexandria with his wife of forty-three years and alums from previous classes. "We tell them they're all going to be buddies," McChrystal said. Regular classes last four hours, the last two dedicated to beer and conversation at a local watering hole.

McChrystal even writes his books in a pack—three coauthors for *Team of Teams* and two for *Leaders: Myth and Reality*.

The general led me with brisk efficiency through the company's newly renovated headquarters. It has minimal interior walls, creating an open workspace of tables and desks arranged more like a web than a grid. No cubicles and few enclosed offices. The gate-way to the workspace is an enormous kitchen where, when we passed through, several staffers were chatting and eating lunch at a long counter. It reminded me of the description, in *Team of Teams*, of the antiterrorism task force headquarters during the Iraq War. Every partition in the main bunker at Balad Air Base had been torn out to create a nerve center that allowed all factions of the quick-response task force—intelligence analysts, operations offi-cers, military liaisons, surveillance and reconnaissance operators, Department of Defense lawyers, medical staff—to be in constant connection and communication with one another. The carefully designed physical space elicited what McChrystal calls "the emer-gent intelligence we believed resided in the force as a whole."

Not far from the kitchen is McChrystal's tiny office. There is room for a desk and chair, two guest chairs, and a shallow closet for books and binders. The walls have none of the usual posed photos with presidents and other luminaries. The one decoration is a large print of a painting depicting a rugged, sweaty crew of World War I fighter pilots, laughing and slapping each other's backs as they walk away from a biplane. It was a gift from the first drone squadron assigned to McChrystal's special operations.

Though a glass wall and glass door allow the retired general to look out at the workspace, he usually works from a cushioned rocker positioned next to his assistant's desk and in the direct path of everyone coming from or going to the kitchen. No one passes without stopping to ask a question or share a thought. McChrystal thrives on the connection.

In person, he had the eyes of a kind interrogator, folding his hands on his desk and leaning attentively toward me, all the while taking my measure. There was a restive quality, too, as if behind those eyes he was ticking off the minutes until he could tackle his next task or rejoin his pack beyond the glass wall.

McChrystal said the first time he consciously noticed the power of bonding, at least in retrospect, was in Little League. Like Jonny Gomes, he loved wearing the same uniforms, following the same rules, and needing to rely on teammates, and to be reliable himself, to win a game. As one of six kids in a military family, McChrystal unknowingly had been absorbing the team mind-set. His family lived on army bases, surrounded by men (and some women) in matching fatigues, each individual a part of a company, a battalion, a division. His father had gone to West Point. Though "we weren't one of those Kennedy-like families playing touch football on the lawn," he said, "there were times you could feel the family come together."

One such instance is lodged in his memory. The year was 1965, and he was ten years old. His father had to go to Fort Benning, Georgia, for a weeklong course in preparation for deployment to Vietnam. As a family, they piled into the station wagon, something they had never done together, and took to the road for what was billed as a two-and-a-half-week vacation. Mom and the kids would be dropped off with her kin in Lookout Mountain, Tennessee, and Dad would go on to Georgia. At the end of the first day of driving, however, Mom—who had just had her sixth baby—began to feel sick. When they arrived in Tennessee on the second day, she was rushed to the hospital with appendicitis.

With Mom in the hospital and Dad in Georgia, the kids were farmed out to various family members. McChrystal and one brother ended up in LaFayette, Alabama. Two weeks later, Mom was out of the hospital and recuperating, and Dad had finished his course. The family headed home. "We had this vacation that wasn't," McChrystal said. But it was the closest they'd ever get.

Three days later, they drove Dad to the airport. "It was devastating to me, to all of us, that my father was going away for a year, and going to war, and might not come back," McChrystal said. "He told us we had to sort of be a team to look out for my mother. We're thinking, 'How are we going to make this work for the next year?' But we did." They learned to take care of their mother by taking care of each other, the older kids helping the younger ones with homework, everyone chipping in on the chores.

The family held together through Dad's second tour in Vietnam a few years later. But when he returned, everything fell apart. He wasn't himself and struggled with alcohol, which had not been an issue before. McChrystal, by then, was sixteen, playing sports, going to school, and preparing to apply to West Point. Then one day, his mother fell ill and died eighteen hours later of kidney failure at the age of forty-five. His father sent the youngest two children to live with their older sister, who was about to be married.

"My father was unable to provide that gravitational pull," McChrystal said. "So a number of other things pulled on us, and we just never really got back. It was never the same. Even to this day."

The cataclysmic disruption to his family changed forever how he would think about the bonds that hold people together. "I became very sensitive to the fact that this sense of team is more fragile than we think," he said. His mother was the hub of the wheel, and when she was gone, so was the wheel. McChrystal came to understand that a team has to be a network, a latticework, with ownership of the team's quest spread to the outermost edges. The bonds have to hold together even when the leader falls, even when comrades fall.

McChrystal was a commander in the 82nd Airborne Division at Fort Bragg in 1994 when two planes collided and burst into flames during landing, a tragedy that came to be known as Green Ramp for the area where paratroopers on the ground were hit by an enormous debris-filled fireball. McChrystal's 2nd Battalion, 504th Parachute Infantry Regiment, was hardest hit: nineteen killed and more than forty severely injured. Nineteen dead meant up to nineteen widows. Forty severely injured meant as many as forty young wives or girlfriends suddenly caring for men with severe brain damage or horrific disfigurement. Neighbors and friends on the army base helped plan funerals and took care of children suddenly without fathers. No member of the 2nd Battalion was untouched.

In three weeks it would be their turn to be what the 82nd Airborne calls Division Ready Force-1. It meant the 2nd Battalion would be on highest alert, the first one deployed to war should the situation arise. To prepare, they'd have to make sure their vehicles, communications systems, weapons, night-vision goggles, and all other equipment were serviceable and ready for combat.

"The question was, 'Could we do it?'" McChrystal said. "There are a lot of things to do to get ready. We had to look everyone in the eye and say, 'Can we fight as a team?' Everybody came to the conclusion we could. There was a sense of, 'If we can't do our job, what are we? We're just sort of this injured thing.' So instead it became, 'Yeah, we're knocked down, but we're better than that.'"

Their bonds held, and, in their pain and grief, they performed.

I was reminded of a conversation I had with Jake Peavy on the balcony of his high-rise apartment in San Francisco several years earlier. Peavy won the Cy Young Award as the league's best pitcher in 2007 and had two World Series rings, one from the Red Sox in 2013 and another from the Giants in 2014. On the mound, he was a stomper and a snorter, barking at himself, vibrating with ferocity. He was a big believer that team chemistry raised performance, but I wondered how that was possible in his case. He was already giving 100 percent on every pitch.

"Your teammates bring out a fight in you that you can't willingly summon for yourself," he said.

No other athlete had framed team chemistry in that way. It was an echo of the open-loop system that Thomas Lewis had talked about: "[No human] is a functioning whole on his own; each has open loops that only somebody else can complete." Only Peavy's teammates—or more precisely, his emotional relationship with his teammates—could bring out his true, full potential.

In the 2008 Summer Olympics, a swimmer named Jason Lezak was pegged to swim the final 100 meters for the US 400-meter freestyle relay team. The anchor for the French, in the next lane over, was Alain Bernard, the world-record holder in the 100-meter freestyle. The United States was behind when Lezak dove into the pool; Bernard was ahead by a full second, a substantial margin. At the turn, Bernard was still up a body-length, an impossible distance to make up in 50 meters. Michael Phelps and Lezak's two other American teammates screamed wildly at the edge of the pool as, stroke by stroke, Lezak gained on Bernard. In one of the greatest moments in swimming history, Lezak lunged at the wall and beat the world champion by eight-hundredths of a second to clinch the team gold. His time was a ridiculous 46.06 seconds, faster than he had ever covered the distance, even accounting for rolling starts on relays.

Two days later, Lezak was back in the pool for the individual 100-meter freestyle. He tied for third in 47.67 seconds. (Bernard finished first.) Lezak raced significantly slower for himself than for his team. Maybe it was just an off day for Lezak. But two German psychologists proposed a different theory.

Joachim Hüffmeier and Guido Hertel decided to analyze the results of sixty-four Olympic freestyle swimmers from thirty-one countries in the 2008 Olympics. Like Lezak, all had competed in both individual and relay events. Those who swam the first leg of relays showed no difference between their relay and individual times. But those in the second, third, and last legs swam faster in the relay than in their individual events.

These Olympic athletes were the best in the world, which meant they already were pushing themselves to the limits of their abilities. Yet when competing as part of a team, they kicked into a higher gear. The data suggests that the drive to come through for their teammates produced a boost in performance they couldn't generate for themselves.[4]

Competing as a team seems to boost endorphins, the feel-good brain chemicals that, among other things, lift mood, foster bonding, and diminish pain. Researchers at the University of Oxford used levels of pain tolerance to compare endorphin production in rowers when they trained with a team and when they trained alone. The endorphin levels during team training were significantly higher.[5]

"There's just something about sports in that regard that can create a bond that's a little bit deeper," Peavy said. "Especially when you play at the highest level in front of so many fans, you can't do it alone. It doesn't matter how crucial a guy is to a team, he cannot be the team."

The power of bonding has been recognized throughout history, from Aesop's fable of the Bundle of Sticks ("union gives strength") to Ben Franklin's "We must all hang together, or, most assuredly, we shall all hang separately." But nowhere more so than in the military.

"We few, we happy few, we band of brothers," Henry V says, in Shakespeare's telling, to his vastly outnumbered soldiers before the Battle of Agincourt. The king makes the case that the experience of fighting together, with these exact men, is a privilege to be envied.

> For he to-day that sheds his blood with me
> Shall be my brother; be he ne'er so vile,
> This day shall gentle his condition:
> And gentlemen in England now a-bed
> Shall think themselves accursed they were not here,
> And hold their manhoods cheap whiles any speaks
> That fought with us upon Saint Crispin's day.

Letters from the battlefield are filled with soldiers' devotion to one another. "It always seems to me," a company commander in the English army wrote to his mother in 1917, "that I'm not fighting for King and Country but just for the company, which seems to be everything to me these days. I hate to be away from them, and I don't worry the least about leave."[6]

Ninety years later, the writer Sebastian Junger embedded him-self with a platoon in Afghanistan to find out what war actually feels like for soldiers. He calls the bond among soldiers "the core experience of combat and the only thing you can absolutely count on.... [T]he shared commitment to safeguard one another's lives is unnegotiable and only deepens with time. The willingness to die for another person is a form of love that even religions fail to inspire."[7]

I asked McChrystal if *love* is the right word to describe these bonds.

"People call this comradeship," he said. "Love is sort of the heart of it. It's the love of a lot of things. You love the people you work with because you admire them and you're close with them and you just start loving them. The next thing you love is being a part of something. You love the idea that if you throw something in the air, somebody is going to catch it.

"You love—in the Rangers we have the Ranger Creed. Six stanzas. It says you never leave a comrade behind. What that is, is a promise. Everybody's promising every other Ranger that they'll die for him. You think, 'Wow, that's stronger than your wedding vows.' Two thousand people every morning are promising they'll die for me without a second thought.... It makes you more confi-dent because you know someone has your back or, as we say, your six o'clock," he said, tapping his back.

This love seems to me as intense and selfless as romantic love and surely as transformative. Romantic love makes us feel more than we are, as if our flawed little solitary self has absorbed some powerful piece of this other person. I imagine it might be like that for soldiers. In this way, each soldier is the unit, and the unit is each soldier.

"You like the way it makes you feel about yourself," McChrystal said. "You like to be in an organization that is committed to each other, that is brave—because it makes you feel that you are that, too. It can make you *be* that."

When the US Olympic basketball team began their college barnstorming tour, Edwards was on the bench. She could barely remember the last time she wasn't in a team's starting lineup. It stung. But she managed to joke about it. She was back where she was as a twenty-year-old on the 1984 Olympic team. "Twelve years of playing," she cracked to a teammate, "and I ain't gone anywhere."[8]

Riding the bench alongside her was Lobo, a hardworking center fresh from college who wasn't prepared for the bruising world of international competition. Her teammates knew she was a marketing choice for USA Basketball, not a sports one. She was enormously popular, having just led the University of Connecticut to an undefeated season and an NCAA championship in front of a national television audience of 5.4 million people. She attracted the most media and the longest autograph lines while also occupying the lowest rung on the roster. Her teammates liked her well enough—she was unfailingly nice and persevered through VanDerveer's brutal critiques—but they made little effort to connect.

One game was particularly demoralizing for Lobo. She couldn't seem to do anything right, and VanDerveer went off on her. Afterward, the usually sunny twenty-two-year-old slumped at her locker. She felt embarrassed and defeated. From across the room, Edwards motioned her over and told her to sit.

"Let me tell you somethin'," Edwards said. "She's going to make you feel bad about yourself when you shouldn't. You gotta keep your head up. You know you're good. Don't let anybody shake what you know about yourself. Stay with it. Be strong. That's how you survive."[9]

The team finished the college tour undefeated, 29–0. They had touched down in twenty-six airports and traversed 25,584 miles. Now it was time to play potential Olympic opponents. First stop: Siberia in January.

Temperatures dropped at night to twenty below zero. They played in a freezing gym on a court laid over an ice rink. The officiating was atrocious. Still, VanDerveer fully expected her team to beat this team of second-tier (though enormous) Russian players sponsored by a local machinery company. But the American team fell behind. When Nikki McCray, one of the younger players, committed two consecutive turnovers, VanDerveer leapt from the bench and called a time-out.

"Don't pass to Nikki," the coach told her team. "She obviously doesn't know what to do with it." McCray's eyes welled up, and, as if choreographed, Edwards, Jennifer Azzi, and Lisa Leslie quietly repositioned themselves so VanDerveer couldn't see.

Protecting each other like this was becoming commonplace. The schedule was grueling, the physical demands exhausting, and the coach's expectations seemed to ratchet higher every day. Even Azzi—who had played for VanDerveer at Stanford—finally cracked one day, though later in the season. A Cuban player had inadvertently elbowed Azzi in the face, crushing her nose. When she returned to the court after surgery and a painful recuperation, she wasn't herself.

"Jennifer, do I need to replace you?" the coach barked. "Do I need another point guard on this team?" Exasperated, VanDerveer stopped practice and told everybody to just go shoot free throws.

Azzi could feel the tears beneath her protective face mask. Suddenly Sheryl Swoopes was at her side. Swoopes owned nearly every college scoring record and was the first woman ever to have a signature shoe, the Nike Air Swoopes. She and Azzi had never been close. Now the superstar put an arm around her crying teammate and led her toward the far basket.

"Let's go over there," Swoopes said. "Keep your back to her and don't let her see you cry." She shot baskets as Azzi gathered herself.

A note about crying.

In all my interviews with male players, very few mentioned crying. I knew these women were hard as nails. They'd been through much worse in their lives than a coach yelling at them. Yet there it was. Lots of crying. Women just cry more than men. We cry thirty to sixty-four times a year on average compared to men's six to seventeen times. One reason is we produce more prolactin, a hormone associated with emotion, so we are moved to tears more often, though in childhood boys and girls cry with the same frequency.[10]

Another reason is our smaller and shallower tear ducts: Our ducts fill and spill more quickly.[11] The late Tennessee basketball coach Pat Summitt, who was every bit VanDerveer's equal as a yeller and taskmaster, dismissed the notion that crying was somehow a reflection on a player's grit. It is just what women do. "Crying is fine with me," Summitt once said. "I do a fair amount of it myself."[12]

Back in the cold Siberian gym, the Americans pulled together and began to play as if the game mattered. Which it didn't. None of the games mattered until they arrived in Atlanta. They scored twenty-eight points in six minutes, roaring back from an eleven-point deficit to win by twelve. They flew from Siberia to Kiev for five days to play the Ukrainians. There was no letting up between games and practices. VanDerveer drilled her players on strategy, at one point concocting a version of *Family Feud* that required them to diagram plays or answer questions about particular game situations. The hardships of training and travel created common ground, drawing the players toward each other. No one was surprised when, as their plane was stuck at the gate for four hours on the way home from Russia, Carla McGhee came strolling down the aisle with her arms full of McDonald's burgers for her teammates. Every day, it seemed, brought new gestures of kindness.

Hardship, though, comes in many forms, and two weeks after returning from Ukraine, VanDerveer unwittingly introduced a new one. Since the moment the US roster was announced, VanDerveer had obsessed about the lack of a big, Enforcer-type post player. Her worries deepened in Siberia when her team fell behind the Russians. VanDerveer knew, and so did the players, that USA Basketball could make changes to the roster up until eight weeks before the Olympics. So in an interview with a *USA Today* reporter, she mentioned Lobo by name as someone who could be dropped in favor of a more intimidating, more athletic post player.

The story hit the players like a slap. "Rebecca's not going any-where," Edwards said to her teammates. Everyone felt the same way. They had not been happy when the Olympic committee had chosen Lobo, but now they were a team. The players decided if Lobo was cut, they would all leave.

On paper, replacing Lobo with a more experienced player would improve their chances of winning the gold medal and elevating women's basketball in the United States. This was the lofty purpose that had moved the players to tears just months earlier on the fifty-yard line of the Georgia Dome. Yet now their loyalty to Lobo, their least valuable player, was stronger than their hunger for the gold medal. Their commitment to an external purpose had shifted to a commitment to each other. They had evolved from a group with shared goals into sisters willing to sacrifice and fight for one another. That's chemistry. It is *the* crucial turning point for any team.

As the physical training continued to pull the players closer, so did the isolation of travel.

The month of March found them in China, where cigarette smoke befouled their nostrils and lungs, even in the basketball arenas. People often gawked and pointed when they ventured outside their hotel, so they retreated to their rooms, eating the crackers and granola they'd brought from home. They had no cell phones. There was nothing to watch on television. Yet off the court, the women still kept mostly to themselves or split into small groups.

One night, Azzi posted a sign on her hotel-room door: "Jen Chu's Coffee and Espresso Bar." She had made herself a cup of the vanilla-macadamia-nut coffee she had bought during their stop in Hawaii and figured she'd offer it around. She wasn't sure who might stop in. "This wasn't like a high-school or college team," she told me later. "We didn't all hang out after practices. It literally was everyone went to their rooms." Lobo, who shared the room with Azzi, wandered back in from dinner. Then came Edwards and McClain, who were ready to spruce up the cornrows they'd braided into Lobo's hair weeks earlier. Next came McCray, Bolton, Dawn Staley, and Katy Steding. Leslie arrived with a CD player and turned on the music. Soon Bolton was taking McCray's braids *out,* and Leslie was dancing. Azzi looked around and said, "Oh my god, we're all in the same room!"

Steding said, "It was kind of like that moment we realized we kind of came together from lots of different areas, age groups, and everything to bring that team together. I don't know if it was a watershed moment or anything like that but—'Hey, we're a team!'"[13]

Steding had it right. The coffee and hair-braiding weren't fostering team chemistry, as I had once thought—and what I had assumed about every team that got together for barbecues and golf outings. This squad already had chemistry at that point. The coffee and hair-braiding were the evidence of it. When chemistry skeptics dismiss social outings as meaningless to performance, they might be right. These gatherings, though surely deepening existing bonds, are more likely the *result* of chemistry, not the cause. A commitment to one another strong enough to affect performance rises from deep emotional bonds that can't be produced by social interaction alone.

Still, the women's tight bonding off-court lifted VanDerveer's spirits. She understood as well as anyone how it could intensify their play. "There was an 'us against them' mentality a little bit," she told me later. "They stuck together. I don't remember people ever getting on each other. It was incredible, it really was. Now, they might have been sitting in a room complaining about me, but that's bonding, too."

The travel didn't let up. In the three months leading up to the Olympics, the women played in South Carolina, Atlanta, and Philadelphia and then swung through Australia—Melbourne, Sydney, Townsville, and Adelaide—and on to Rhode Island, Canada, down to Oakland, then Colorado Springs, Chicago, back to Colorado Springs, then Orlando, Indianapolis, Orlando again, and finally, mercifully, the Olympic Games in Atlanta. They had now won fifty-two straight games.

Uncles, neighbors, old classmates, distant cousins, and everyone else the players had ever met descended on Atlanta looking for extra tickets, a few moments of their time, just one photo— *What's a single photo?* Stepping outside the relatively quiet Omni Hotel was like plunging into a party in full swing. Getting back inside meant a gauntlet of security checks. The players and coaches first had to show an official Omni Hotel ID, then go through a metal detector, then scan their hands to verify their identity, and then punch in their personal four-digit code. Only then could they return to their rooms. VanDerveer, of course, was so focused on staying focused she rarely left the hotel except for early-morning runs, practices, and games. When Nike, with whom she had a shoe contract, asked her to appear at a news conference, she said no.

But she was surprised to find she wasn't nervous. "I felt," she said, "as if I were about to take a test for which I had studied harder than I ever had before in my life. I knew the material cold." If the players were nervous, they also didn't show it. They, too, knew the material cold. Their bodies had been transformed by their year of work. They beat Cuba in their first game by seventeen points, Ukraine by thirty-three, Zaire by sixty (despite VanDerveer keeping most of her starters on the bench), and Australia by seventeen. Four games down, four to go.

Instead of practicing the next day, the halfway point of the games, VanDerveer gathered the team in her suite. Just the players and coaches. She told them to bring whatever memorabilia, pictures, programs, and balls they wanted their teammates to sign. Before they started, she popped a tape into the VCR. She had asked NBA Entertainment for an advance copy of the video they had just finished about the year the team had spent together. There on the screen was their first practice together; their trips to Siberia, Ukraine, Australia, and China; the late-night bus rides between college towns; and their visits to classrooms and shopping malls. The players laughed and needled each other, reliving the journey.

It was brilliant. In all the hubbub of the Olympics, VanDerveer brought them back to each other. For the next two hours, they sat and talked and signed each other's souvenirs.

They beat Korea by thirty-nine points and then Japan by fifteen.

The players and coaches knew they probably could have gotten this far in the tournament with just a month or so of practice. Their year of work and sacrifice was all about the next two games.

In the semifinal, they played Australia yet again and dominated, winning 93–71. They had now won fifty-nine straight.

Brazil waited for them in the championship game. Of course, Brazil. The United States hadn't faced Brazil since the debacle in Australia two years earlier. The US-Brazil gold-medal game was the final event of the 1996 Olympics. Another sellout crowd of thirty-three thousand people packed the Georgia Dome.

In the first half, VanDerveer's players made *72 percent* of their shots and kept Brazil's famous "Magic Paula" to just a single basket. They were up eleven at halftime and scored the first eight points of the second half to take a nineteen-point lead. The twelve women played out of their minds. They had been dominating in their previous fifty-nine games, but none compared to this one. There were no-look passes, steals, dives for loose balls, three-pointers. VanDerveer called a play she hadn't all year. It was an inbounds play from under the US basket. Edwards floated an alley-oop pass. McClain leapt, caught it, and dropped it in for two points. Perfection.

It's no coincidence they played their finest game when the pressure was highest. That's when chemistry matters most. The adrenaline is flowing, providing focus and energy. We trust our teammates and know they trust us back, so we're awash in oxytocin. We feel a sense of calm and well-being, knowing we are completely prepared. With these exact people around us, we feel invincible. The stressful task ahead is a challenge instead of a threat. We're pumped but relaxed, on alert but unafraid.

The Americans' lead against Brazil stretched from nineteen to twenty-five to thirty. "The players looked bulletproof," VanDerveer said, "the way athletes do when their minds and bodies are working in perfect concert with their teammates' minds and bodies."

Every player got in the game if only for a few minutes. They won, 111–87, the most points ever scored in a women's Olympic game.

The players collapsed into a heap. They ran laps around the

court, waving American flags. Azzi did a cartwheel. They changed into their official USA Olympic team sweats and stepped as a single unit to the top tier of the medal stand. They stood exactly where they had nine months earlier. One by one, beginning with Edwards, they bowed their heads to receive their gold medals.

Now, twenty-three years later, all the women have retired from playing basketball. Several went on to coach, including Jennifer Azzi. During her coaching stint at the University of San Francisco, she came to a realization she had not grasped before, even during that extraordinary Olympic odyssey.

"I now know that winning comes from players," she said. "It's not the coach. It's good that the coach can articulate the vision, but ultimately it's the role of the players, the role of the team. A coach can have the best pregame speech ever, but you can't play for them. So that was an eye-opening moment for me in coaching. It's them."

Azzi invited me one night in 2018 to an event at the University of San Francisco where she interviewed Golden State Warriors coach Steve Kerr onstage. In a reception afterward, I met Warriors president Rick Welts. Two weeks earlier, the team and staff had received their 2017–2018 NBA championship rings. I mistook the gargantuan hunk of shine on Welts's finger for the championship ring. It was actually from his induction into the NBA Hall of Fame. But he anticipated someone (like me) might want to see the championship ring, so he had been carrying it in his pocket. I ogled the seventy-four diamonds and seventy-four sapphires representing the Warriors' seventy-four wins. Tucked on the side of the ring, in such small letters I almost missed them, were the words JUST US.

I had followed the Warriors that season like every good Bay Area sports fan, but I didn't know the significance of "Just Us." I learned it's what the players shout when they break a huddle: "One, two, three—*Just Us!*" There's a poster in their locker room that reads, mUSt be jUSt about US. The words hold such meaning for the players that Kevin Durant has it tattooed on his legs: just on the right, us on the left.

That was it. A team's true purpose, the deep meaning of its efforts, is always each other. The team itself is the "something bigger than themselves."

I remember reading how Pat Summitt rallied her Tennessee team in 1997 as they chased a third straight NCAA championship. She did not focus on historic achievement. "Tennessee has enough championships for the record books....But you have a chance to win your *own* championship. This is *your* team... *your* opportunity... *your* season."

What is the function, then, of the lofty purpose? Why bother bringing the Olympic team into the Georgia Dome to show them what they were playing for? Why does the military bother with pledges to God and country?

Because purpose is the stepping-stone to Just Us. Winning the gold medal, or protecting the country, inspires people to buy into the same dream. They willingly endure hardship in pursuit of that dream. And as they do, connections deepen. If the leaders have created a trusting, high-functioning culture, the individuals fuse into a team. They come to believe that these exact people, and only these people, can achieve this extraordinary, maybe impossible thing. *Just Us.* Commitment to the quest becomes commitment to each other.

Creating Just Us in the workplace is more challenging than in sports or the military, as McChrystal has learned since starting his company nearly a decade ago.

"It's hard because you can't wrap yourself in this sense of mission," he said. Soldiers can embrace the noble quest of defending the nation or making the world a better place. Doesn't work at, say, a Popsicle factory. Employees know they're not changing the world through Popsicles. The mission has been and always will be to make money. Therefore, businesses require a different kind of culture but with the same end game: a bonded, committed workforce.

In his own company, McChrystal set up the physical space to foster frequent interaction. He chose not to base pay strictly on merit. He believes paying huge salaries to stars creates a transactional culture instead of a team culture; you've made money the prime motivation for good work. He offers prospective employees fair compensation and fair benefits, with the promise they will be part of a workforce that is dedicated to each other.

The camaraderie, of course, must be balanced against productivity.

"You have to make tough decisions to protect the company," McChrystal said. "But at the same time, there's another factor: We committed to Joan, and she committed to us. The commitment goes further than just her batting average this week. The commitment goes a little deeper. So now you enter this unwritten contract between the individual and the organization that isn't as clean. It's much more emotional.

"What if Joan is trying really hard, which is what she said she'd do? Now every other member of the organization watches because they want to know how you're going to treat them when their batting average drops. So it's this balance."

His company comes down on the side of sticking with people who are holding up their end of the bargain by working hard and staying committed to the team. "We choose to be an organization that does that," he said. "We believe it pays off over time."

McChrystal's leadership model is the gardener: The gardener plants and harvests, but mostly he tends. McChrystal tends more than anything to the company's "team-ness." One way is by sitting in the rocker in the path of his employees so he can see and hear for himself how connected people feel. Another is the leadership retreat. Four times a year, he takes twenty-four staffers at a time to Virginia's Shenandoah Valley for the weekend. The outdoor equipment from the most recent outing was still in the alcove near the entryway on the day I visited. Past retreats have included whitewater rafting and ropes courses. This time they broke into small groups to learn land navigation and then, as always, spent time discussing leadership.

"It reinforces why they would want to be a part of this," McChrystal said. "It's a powerful connector to the organization and to each other."

After nearly a decade in the business world and thirty-four years in the army, McChrystal is more certain than ever that personal connection is at the core of every high-performance team. He said if he were put back in command in Afghanistan, he knows what he'd do first: Grab two cases of beer and get the president, the vice-president, the secretary of defense, and the director of the CIA to go white-water rafting with him.

"We don't talk about the war," he said. "Just bond."

As I rode the train that afternoon from DC to New York, transcribing my interview with McChrystal, I found myself thinking about the 1989 Giants. Nearly ten years had passed since I wandered through the party tent at AT&T Park in San Francisco, watching those players and coaches revel in each other's company twenty years after winning the National League pennant together. They were a Just Us team. They accepted each other. They played for each other. Their manager, Roger Craig, was a textbook example of leader-as-gardener, as was their clubhouse leader, Mike Krukow. Their reunion in 2009 was the start of what has become my near obsession with figuring out what team chemistry is. I knew their love for each other had to have played a part in making them a championship team, but how? I had no idea back then.

Now I did. When I got back to the Bay Area, I pulled out my notes and stepped back three decades, into the story of the best chemistry team I've ever known.

CHAPTER SEVEN

HUMM-BABY, KRUKE, AND THE PYGMALION EFFECT

"A gardener can't grow tulips or roses. He can only create the environment in which the flowers can do so."

—Anonymous

Never have a stadium and a baseball team reflected one another as much as Candlestick Park and the San Francisco Giants in the early to mid-1980s.

Fans called it "The Stick," but players preferred "The Dick" or the "John C. Holmes Memorial," after the 1970s porn star. St. Louis Cardinals manager Whitey Herzog called it "a toilet bowl with the lid up." It had been built south of the city on a windswept promontory on the shore of San Francisco Bay. Temperatures plummeted so sharply and gusts kicked up so violently that, during construction, radiant heaters had been installed under half the seats. They didn't work on opening day or any day thereafter. Summer nights were the worst. Fog settled in the stadium like a cold, wet blanket. Fans stayed away in droves. Sometimes so few dotted the vast expanse of seats that the place gave off the lonely feel of a half-lit motel sign.

Deep in the bowels of all that concrete existed a separate and self-contained world. You reached it one of three ways: through the dugout, through a door on the right-field wall, or through the players' parking lot. The Giants' clubhouse operated inside a windowless room with a spit-stained carpet and metal lockers. The low ceiling trapped nearly thirty years of stink: coffee, sweat, eucalyptus, cigarettes, laundry hampers, maple syrup, and beer. It smelled as if a high-school gym had landed on a diner. When I would arrive in late afternoon to cover a night game, I'd hear the clang of a dropped barbell in the workout room, the hum of washers and dryers down the hall, the scrape of brushes against mud-caked cleats, the soft slap of shower shoes, the crisscross of conversation. If the door leading to the dugout was open, the drone of a riding mower drifted in. The closer it got to game time, the louder the clubhouse got. The room thrummed with shouts and jokes in Spanish and English, twangs, and slang. The cassette player on the shelf near the laundry carts blasted Lynyrd Skynyrd or Johnny Cash, unless it was Sinatra Sunday, when clubhouse manager Mike Murphy controlled the music.

A pitcher named Mike Krukow arrived at the Giants in 1983, though not of his own volition. He'd been traded by the Phillies. At the press conference at Candlestick to welcome him, the Giants presented him with a game jersey—and a parka. Krukow had played at Candlestick enough to know the miserable conditions. What he had not counted on was the negativity and divisiveness in the clubhouse. One day he came home from the park and told his wife, "We're not staying." But when the Giants offered a three-year extension to his two-year contract, he took it. His wife was pregnant with their second child. The extension meant five years of guaranteed income, almost unheard of at the time, especially for a pitcher who had never made an All-Star team much less won a Cy Young.

The team finished in second-to-last place in Krukow's first year and was so hapless going into '84 that the Giants' marketing department, stumped for a slogan, went with "C'mon, Giants, Hang in There!" They finished dead last with ninety-six losses, barely escaping the ignominy of a hundred.

That came the following year.

As the losses mounted in 1985, Krukow watched new manager Jimmy Davenport chew handfuls of Rolaids and bite his nails so feverishly he once left streaks of blood on Krukow's fingers after shaking his hand. With a couple of weeks left in that murderous season, the Giants fired Davenport and brought in their third manager in less than two years.

Fifty-six-year-old Roger Craig ambled through the clubhouse door on September 18, 1985, with his cowboy hat, pointy boots, and folksy smile, to take over the worst team in baseball. Few men knew more about awful teams than Craig. He pitched for the 1962 Mets, which lost a modern major-league record 120 games; Craig lost twenty-four of them that season and twenty-two the next. (He also pitched twenty-seven complete games over those two seasons.) He knew about extraordinary teams, too. He pitched for three World Series champions (Brooklyn Dodgers, Los Angeles Dodgers, and St. Louis Cardinals) and was the pitching coach for a fourth (1984 Detroit Tigers).

As he pumped the hands of Giants players and clubhouse attendants, beaming with such optimism and speaking with such surety, Krukow couldn't decide if the guy was incredibly cocky or incredibly naïve. This was an organization that used Little League baseballs for batting practice because they were cheaper than major-league ones. The trainers ran so low on athletic tape by season's end they scavenged rolls left behind by the San Francisco 49ers, who also played at Candlestick. Position players raided the pitchers' lockers for bats because they were allowed just two dozen for the entire season. This was a team that lost ten of their first fourteen games of the season, ten straight in June and ten of fourteen again to kick off September.

None of it seemed to faze Craig. "I'll teach them how to win," he told reporters.

Days earlier, a new general manager named Al Rosen had walked through those same clubhouse doors. A no-nonsense navy man, Rosen had almost immediately fired Davenport and hired Craig. At sixty-two, Rosen had the blunt face and hard eyes of a man accustomed to battle. He fought in the boxing ring throughout high school and college. He fought in the Pacific during World War II. And he fought any opposing player in the major leagues ignorant enough to hurl an anti-Semitic slur his way. His nose had been broken eleven times. He was the American League's Most Valuable Player and a four-time All-Star third baseman for the Cleveland Indians from the late 1940s to the mid-1950s. At thirty-two he retired and worked the next seventeen years as a stockbroker and then a casino executive. In 1978, he returned to baseball as team president and CEO of the New York Yankees. The Yankees won the World Series that season, but Rosen found owner George Steinbrenner and manager Billy Martin so incorrigible he resigned after a season and a half. He ran the Houston Astros for five years before joining the Giants.

Now in the dank Candlestick clubhouse on September 18, Rosen and Craig addressed the troops. They introduced new team rules, emphasizing one in particular: No more complaints about Candlestick. The negativity was over. This park would become the greatest home-field advantage in the history of the game, they said. Visiting players so detested the cold, wind, and sparse crowds that they just wanted to get the hell out of town. Embracing the conditions would give the Giants a leg up.

Krukow suppressed an eye roll. He had been in the game ten years. He could sniff bullshit.

The Giants lost their hundredth game on the last day of the season, securing the team's place as the worst in franchise history.

For Al Rosen, a baseball season was a military campaign. The war was won through intelligence, grit, and pragmatism. His first priority was eliminating excuses for failure. He brought in a new head trainer and restocked his treatment room, which included all the athletic tape anyone could need. He ordered higher-quality uniforms. He brought in a new traveling secretary. He secured more comfortable planes and buses. He let players order as many bats as they wanted. During the off-season he created a family room at Candlestick for wives and children—complete with toys, games, and childcare—to lift at least one worry from the players' minds. The message: We are here to win and will do anything to help you do that.

Roger Craig ran training camp that first spring as if rebuilding a crumbling house inch by inch. Fielding practices began with fundamentals and repetitive drills. The team relearned baserunning and tightened its defense. Craig loved bunts, squeezes, hit-and-runs. He was a huge fan of the surprise play. We can't outmuscle too many opponents, Craig told his players, but we'll outmaneuver and outhustle them. During spring games, the manager often thought out loud about game situations and strategy. Krukow listened and found himself learning something new almost every day. "That's what impresses a veteran," he said. "The more I got to know him, the more I wanted to stand next to him."

When Craig looked you in the eye and started talking in that gentle, North Carolina drawl, you could find yourself believing almost anything. Krukow noticed how he called out guys not for doing something wrong but for doing something right. He'd make the player at the farthest end of the bench feel as if he were the linchpin of the whole operation. A guy might pinch run and break up a double play, and Craig would make a big fuss about how crucial that was in the game. That guy could look at the team's stars and feel he was an equal. They were all "Humm-babies," Craig's label for players who, as he once explained, didn't necessarily "have a lot of talent," but "gave you 180 percent."[1] Craig showed up every day in a positive mood and stayed that way.

"It spread from one locker to another," Krukow said. "We bought into it. By the time we headed north, the whole mood had started to change. It was like playing games in a big overcoat and then suddenly you get to take it off."

Robert Rosenthal's study began, as so many do, with rats.

In the 1960s, he was a Harvard psychology professor who was interested in how expectations affect performance. Telling a group of student researchers that he had lab rats that had been specially bred for high intelligence, he wanted the students to test these rats' ability to navigate a maze against other rats. The rats were in cages labeled "maze-bright" and "maze-dull." The maze-bright group consistently beat the maze-dull rats. In truth, all the rats were the same and had been assigned to the cages randomly. But researchers who thought they had maze-bright rats rated their experience with the rats more favorably and described their own behavior as more "relaxed, casual, and pleasant-voiced" than did the researchers with maze-dull rats. The maze-bright researchers also reported handling the rats more, and more gently, than did the other researchers. The rats that were expected to perform well did, in fact, perform better than the "normal" rats. Rosenthal theorized that expectation bias probably influences performance in humans, too.[2] This led to what became a classic experiment.

Rosenthal then conducted IQ tests on children in eighteen elementary-school classes.[3] He told the teachers which students showed extraordinary academic potential. As with the rats, these children were chosen completely at random. Rosenthal monitored the classrooms for months. Teachers touched, nodded at, and smiled more often at the "superior" children. They gave these students more approval and extra time to answer questions.

After eight months, Rosenthal gave each child a follow-up IQ test. The "superior" students gained three times as many IQ points as the control group. Rosenthal called this the "Pygmalion effect."

Now the question was, do teachers need to be duped into believing their students are bright in order to treat them as such? Or could they learn how to treat every student this way? Studies by New Zealand education professor Christine Rubie-Davies showed that they can.[4] She identified a variety of behaviors and strategies that convey high expectations, things like attitude, beliefs, touch, tone of voice, and other nonverbal cues. After holding workshops to instruct teachers on these "expectancy" behaviors, she ran multiple experiments to test their effectiveness. In one, she split eighty-four teachers into two groups at random. One group attended her workshops; the other attended regular professional-development classes. By the end of the school year, students taught by teachers who had attended the workshop were three months ahead of the control group.

The Pygmalion effect is seen not just in classrooms but in hundreds of workplaces from hospitals to factories to psychotherapy clinics. In the 1980s, Rosenthal tested it on the playing field. He led physical-education teachers to believe that some students—whom the teachers did not previously know—had the potential to be unusually good athletes and others did not. In reality, of course, they had been labeled randomly. The teachers tested the students by number of sit-ups (for girls) and push-ups (for boys), jumping distance, and speed in moving blocks from one point to another. The high-expectation kids performed better than past performance had predicted, and the low-expectation kids performed worse.[5]

The Giants had no rookies in '85. Now, a year later, they had seven, nearly a third of the team. The best of them was a loud, gregarious kid named Will Clark. Born in New Orleans, son of a pool shark, he had been an Olympian in '84, a first-round draft pick in '85, and now an invitee to big-league camp in '86, having spent all of forty-five days in the minor leagues. No matter. As he waited to take his turn at his very first batting practice at spring training, the twenty-one-year-old struck a pose that would become familiar to a generation of Giants fans: leaning on his bat, jaws working over a wad of bubble gum, one ankle crossed nonchalantly over the other, a crooked grin across his face. He looked like a land baron admiring his domain. His first cuts in the cage explained his confidence. His swing was a swashbuckler's flourish, a silky, sweeping stroke that sent one pitch after another into the outfield bleachers.

Clark had been so itchy to get the baseball season started that he had arrived at camp a week early, showing up with the pitchers and catchers. He promptly went around the clubhouse saying, loudly, how great spring training was, how wonderful the sport of baseball was, and how absolutely *thrilled* he was to be there.

"Will the Thrill!" Krukow had said, laughing with his buddy, veteran catcher Bob Brenly. The nickname stuck. Instantaneously, Clark filled the archetypal role of the Kid, and soon would add Warrior and Sparkplug.

A twenty-three-year-old second baseman named Robby Thompson was another Kid, but a more mature version. Thompson had none of Clark's star power. His arms were a little short. His range a little narrow. He wasn't a terrific hitter. He barely spoke. But he was hungry and focused, both born of a decision he and his fiancée, Brenda, had made four years earlier when they were still in college. They decided to adopt the newborn baby of Brenda's sister, who had died suddenly from complications during childbirth. Thompson and Brenda were nineteen years old. They brought baby Kristeena into their one-bedroom, off-campus apartment. Thompson was drafted by the Giants a year later, and he and Brenda married six months after that. As Thompson's minor-league teammates went out for beer and pizza, he happily spent evenings with Brenda and Kristeena, eating peanut-butter-and-jelly sandwiches to stretch his $650-a-month salary. In the off-season, they lived with his mother-in-law in Florida, and Thompson worked construction and valet-parking jobs to make ends meet.*

Thompson had never played above Double A in the minors. But when camp broke, he had earned the job as the Giants' starting second baseman and leadoff batter. He played so well that first season he finished second in the National League's Rookie of the Year voting, beating out future superstars Barry Bonds, Barry Larkin, *and* Will Clark. Thompson hit .271, higher than he ever had in the minor leagues. He led the team in sacrifice hits with eighteen. He turned ninety-seven double plays.

He wasn't the only player performing beyond expectations under the new leadership of Craig and Rosen. Krukow made the

---

* The minor leagues and winter leagues pay little more than minimum wage. Even high-round picks back then didn't earn the big signing bonuses they do today. In 1986, Thompson's first year in the majors, he earned $60,000. He still worked construction and valet jobs during that off-season. He stopped in '87 when his salary jumped to $140,000.

All-Star team for the first time in his life. He was 11–5 at mid-season and went on to win twenty games, the most of his career. He finished third in Cy Young voting and even garnered votes for the National League's Most Valuable Player.

The Giants won eighty-three games in '86, a twenty-one-win gain from the previous year. Attendance grew. The winning continued through the first two months of 1987. Then the team began to slide. There was a Super-Disruptor in their midst.

Chris Brown was a young third baseman who, as his team was losing one hundred games in '85, managed to make the All-Star team. A gifted and at times even hardworking player, he seemed to bench himself every other day with some malady or another. Teammates called him the Tin Man. Once he sat out because of a "strained eyelid" from sleeping wrong. Another time it was a "bruised tooth root." His hand hurt. His ankle hurt. His knee hurt. He had all that talent and parked it on the bench. He was a classic malingerer. Players complained about him during batting practice, on the team plane, in the hotel bar. Krukow once called him out in the clubhouse in front of everybody, hoping to light a fire under Brown and put an end to the griping. Instead, Brown sat at his locker without a word. "Nobody I played with ever came remotely close to dragging down a team like he did," Krukow said.

Rosen recognized the danger of a malingerer like Brown, especially to a team still knitting together a new identity as winners. He worried that the team might not be strong enough yet to keep Brown from infecting the clubhouse. But he had no viable replacement at third; Matt Williams wasn't yet ready. He kept a close watch.

High-performance teams are often compared to well-oiled machines. But the analogy isn't accurate. If it was, we could produce how-to

manuals and YouTube videos for their construction and mainte-
nance. We can't. This is because teams are complex systems and
machines are complicated ones.[6] Understanding the difference is
essential to understanding team chemistry.

A complicated system—a car engine, say—has standard parts
that interact with each other in a precise, prescribed manner.
When your spark plugs go bad, the engine's power weakens. When
you put in new spark plugs, the engine's power is restored. Cause-
and-effect is predictable and replicable.

A team, on the other hand, is like an ecosystem or a national
economy. There are so many interdependent parts that a change
in one can cause a cascade of changes throughout the whole system. This is the famous butterfly effect, proposed in the early
1970s by Edward Lorenz, an MIT theoretical meteorologist. He
was running numbers about a weather pattern on his laboratory's
1960s-era computer. Back then, calculations could take days. On
the second day, Lorenz found the results had taken off on a dramatically different tangent from the previous day.

What was going on? The only difference was an alteration so
miniscule he couldn't imagine it could be the culprit. He had
rounded off the fourth decimal place of the starting number of
the second day's run. But he found that was indeed the reason the
results had veered so wildly. That tiny alteration.

The discovery ran counter to our understanding of cause-and-
effect: that is, a tiny change in the cause produces a tiny change in
the result. In complex systems, a tiny alteration might, in fact,
cause a tiny change. Or it might cause an enormous one.[7] There is
so much less predictability. In other words, the fluttering of a butterfly's wings in Rio de Janeiro, amplified by atmospheric currents, could cause a tornado in Texas two weeks later. Or it could
have no effect at all.

The same is true on a team. Let's say there's a disturbance in a clubhouse environment—losing streak, injury, divorce, trade, individual slump. The impact will depend on the thoughts, emotions, expectations, personality quirks, and insecurities that each player attaches to the disturbance—more variables than any of us can count. Indeed, each of these individual reactions is its own mini-disturbance, which creates a new string of mini-disturbances and so on. Now multiply that by, say, 162 games. Every team ought to be haywire at all times. But they aren't.

That's because a team differs in one big way from the weather, the environment, and most other complex systems. Teams are made up of humans, and, unlike climate patterns and zooplankton, we have the capacity not only to notice the potentially destructive course we're on, but to alter the course. And we have the capacity to create the environment in which this noticing and altering happens.

Such an environment absorbs the disturbances. We know this as resilience.

When the Giants arrived in Chicago on July 3 for a series against the Cubs, they were five games out of first place. Rosen sat in the stands at Wrigley taking stock of his men as they took batting practice. A run-of-the-mill ground ball took a wonky hop and hit Chris Brown on the forehead. Brown collapsed to the ground as if he'd been shot. Batting practice came to a halt as two trainers helped Brown off the field, his feet inexplicably dragging behind him. Players stood in knots on the field and behind the batting cage, shaking their heads.

Rosen felt his anger build as Brown disappeared into the clubhouse. A staffer soon reported that Brown had taken himself out of the lineup. When the team needed to battle back from their slide in the standings? That was it. Time to alter course. He stormed down the stands and into the clubhouse. He found Brown on the training table.

"Son, take that uniform off because you're never wearing it again."

Within hours, Rosen had hammered out a trade with Padres general manager Chub Feeney, giving him Brown and three pitchers in exchange for All-Star pitcher Dave Dravecky, reliever Craig Lefferts, and utility man Kevin Mitchell.*

Rosen knew he got the better of the deal, mostly because he landed a frontline starter in Dravecky and a solid reliever in Lefferts. He wasn't so enthused about Mitchell. But he took him, trading his own problem child for San Diego's. In Mitchell, Rosen saw a street thug with a big gold tooth and fat gold chains and a reputation for fighting and flouting rules.

Craig and Krukow saw someone else.

Kevin Mitchell ("Mitch") was not your average American ballplayer. He grew up in an area called Southeast, a district of housing projects in San Diego with warring black and Mexican gangs. You were either predator or prey, so you quickly sorted out where to pledge your allegiance. By the time he was a teenager, Mitch and his best friends were running with a local gang called the Pierules, skipping school and battling boys from rival gangs. Mitch

---

* Chris Brown washed out of the major leagues within two years. The Detroit Tigers cut him in May 1989. He knocked around the minor leagues briefly before taking a job in construction, mostly as a crane operator. After the 9/11 attacks in 2001, he spent parts of three years driving fuel trucks between Iraq and Kuwait for Halliburton. He died in 2006 at the age of forty-five from burns he suffered in a mysterious fire at his soon-to-be-foreclosed home in Sugar Land, Texas. He left behind an estranged wife and a nine-year-old daughter. In retrospect, Krukow believes Brown's problems in baseball were born of a debilitating fear of failure.

enjoyed the fighting. Fighting was an act of brotherhood. Even an act of love. His boys took his side no matter what, and he theirs. Mitch's body was a testament to that bond: a white line on his right thigh from a .38-caliber bullet, a swoosh on his back from a shotgun blast of rock salt.

The welt on his right wrist was his oldest scar, a permanent reminder to be careful who he trusted. He'd gotten it from a pan of hot grease he flung at his father to stop him from hitting his mother. He was nine years old. For Mitch the house often felt more dangerous than the streets. He found refuge with his grandparents, who lived ten blocks away. He'd whack Wiffle balls in their driveway and go to church with Granny, who he adored, and clear the dishes from Sunday supper. Soon after the hot-grease episode, Mitch brought over a bag of clothes and never left.

Football was Mitch's sport and the athletic expression of his life in the neighborhood: rival packs of men committing intermittent acts of violence on each other. He only played baseball for two reasons: His granny loved the game, and he was a savant with a baseball bat. His forearms were as thick as hams, and he could crush anything that crossed the plate. Fathers at his Little League games would pay him twenty dollars to hit home runs on demand. While he never graduated, he attended four different high schools in four years and barely played an inning for any of them. He'd suit up for football in the fall semester, flunk out or get suspended before the end of the season, and be ineligible for baseball in the spring.

But one day a scout from the Mets saw him play in the Thursday-night winter-ball league on the campus of San Diego State. The guy offered a contract for $25,000, and Mitchell signed on the hood of the scout's car. He spent five uneven, sometimes tumultuous years in the minors before landing in the big leagues during the Mets' run to the 1986 World Series. Mets star Gary Carter nicknamed him "World" because he could play six different positions. Mitch had never felt anything like the joy and love in the clubhouse the night the Mets beat the Red Sox in Game 7. He and his teammates wrapped their arms around each other like brothers. He thought he'd be with them forever.

A couple of months later, however, he was traded to the Padres. And then to the Giants. Two trades in seven months. He felt like a bag of trash on a curb and wanted to quit baseball. Dravecky had to coax him onto the plane to Chicago to meet up with the Giants. He was one of the few people who could.

Dravecky and Mitchell were improbable friends. Dravecky was a kind, soft-spoken, evangelical Christian who belonged to the right-wing John Birch Society. He had taken Mitch under his wing in the Padres clubhouse, drawn to his warmth and vulnerability. Mitch opened up, sharing with Dravecky how much he missed his teammates at the Mets (so much so that he wore a Mets T-shirt under his Padres jersey), how belittled he felt by Padres manager Larry Bowa's constant judgment, how much he loved his baseball-crazy granny, who cooked for Mitch and Dravecky at her house in the old neighborhood. Dravecky called Mitch "Boogie Bear." Mitch called him "Snacks" for the sweets and chips that filled his locker.

Mitch's head still churned with plans to quit baseball when he arrived at the visitors' clubhouse at Wrigley Field. He watched his Padres teammates throw their arms around Giants players they knew from previous teams. Mitch knew no one. He didn't want to be there in any case. As Mitch hunted for his locker, Craig summoned the new player into his office. Of course, Mitch thought. The manager had just lost his All-Star third baseman for a twice-traded reject with a bad rep. Not wasting any time to grill me.

Craig rose from his desk and grasped Mitch's hand with his big paw.

"Glad you're here," the manager said. "I know you can play the game. That's why we got you. Just go out there and play and have fun. Enjoy what we got going on here. We got us a great bunch of guys."

Mitch emerged to find Krukow waiting for him. "Glad I don't have to see your mug at the plate anymore," Kruke said, smiling. Mitch undressed and pulled his new Giants jersey off the hanger. No name on the back. He looked over at Dravecky and Lefferts. Their jerseys had *their* names. See? he thought. I don't matter.

One day, after the team returned to San Francisco, Mitchell noticed Krukow and other veterans shooing reporters out of the clubhouse. "Kangaroo court!" someone yelled.

Players pulled their stools together to face a panel of judges that included Krukow. Bob Brenly served as the keeper of the infractions book, in which any player could register charges against any other player—or coach, clubbie, or trainer. Back then, most teams had kangaroo courts. In some clubhouses, judges wore mops as wigs like clownish barristers. The best courts were both hilarious and merciless. It was open season on complainers, who drew the most outrageous charges and biggest fines. The message was clear: either stop whining or continue to be mocked and fined.

Brenly opened the notebook and began reading the charges. No court could operate without Jesters, and Brenly and Krukow were among the funniest in baseball. Chris Speier was fined fifteen dollars for each use of *frick* when he meant *fuck*. Others were fined for peeing in the shower, fraternizing with an opposing player before a game, undertipping, getting a flat tire on the way to the ballpark, missing a steal sign. At least one guy in every court was fined for "dick in the spread," the legal term for partaking of the postgame food spread while naked.*

A player might get fined simply for not getting fined in the previous court. Rookie infielder (and future Washington Nationals manager) Matt Williams had a *Rain Man*-like recall of movie quotes, and, as the judges declared someone guilty, he'd loom over the offender's shoulder and do a whole scene from, say, *Scarface*: *"Yeah, you piece of shit..."*

Mitch watched from the back of the clubhouse and found himself giggling despite understanding almost none of the inside jokes. Then he heard his name. He'd been with the team barely a week. How could he have landed in the book already?

Brenly read off the infractions:

No name on his jersey.
Showing off by hitting two home runs in his first game as a
    Giant.
Having a bulletproof tooth.
Putting fourteen animals on the endangered-species list with
    one outfit.

* My favorite kangaroo-court story is about Frank Robinson and the Baltimore Orioles in the late 1960s. They had a bat boy named Jay Mazzone whose hands had been severely burned in an accident when he was two years old and had to be amputated. He used metal hooks to do his job. According to an Associated Press story, the kid and Robinson became good friends, but some players were awkward around him. "Frank Robinson broke the ice," Mazzone told the AP writer. "He was running his kangaroo court and calling a vote among the players about whether to fine somebody or not. It was either thumbs up or thumbs down. After the vote he said, 'Jay, you're fined for not voting.' Everybody laughed. After that, I was treated just like everybody else. Somebody even made a big cardboard hand with a thumb so I could take part in future votes."

Mitch laughed harder with each charge until he was stomping his feet. "We buried him," Krukow recalled later, "and he loved it."

As the season progressed Mitch was happier, but he knew better than to get too close. A baseball team, he had learned, was a business not a brotherhood.

Two months later, Krukow showed him otherwise.

In mid-September, the Padres came to town. Mitch would face his old team for the first time. Around the batting cage before Game 1, Padres starting pitcher Ed Whitson joked with Mitch that he better watch out—he might plant a fastball in his rib cage. Mitch laughed. He considered Whitson a friend.

But Krukow, the Giants' starter that day, heard the remark and wasn't pleased. Whitson had a reputation for beaning guys.

In the bottom of the first inning, the Giants' first batter hit a home run off Whitson. Then Mitch stepped to the plate. Whitson wasted no time. He hit Mitch on the back with the first pitch. Mitch took it without response. He dropped his bat, pulled off his batting gloves, and trotted to first base.

When Krukow took the mound for the second inning, his old, cranky back had started to spasm. Craig could see from the dugout that Krukow was in pain, and he signaled for a reliever. But Krukow wasn't leaving. As the Padres' batter made his way to the plate, Krukow summoned his third baseman.

"This one's for you, Mitch," he said.

Krukow reared back. The throw hit the batter as if he were a target in a carnival game.*

---

* The batter who happened to step to the plate for that one well-aimed pitch was Chris Brown. Instead of turning his body to let it hit his back, as Mitch had, Brown stepped right into it. The ball ricocheted off his hand so hard that it bounced on the dirt and soared into foul territory. Brown crouched in pain, cradling his hand. The Padres' trainer rushed out to take a look as Brown stalked away, hurling his helmet down the first-base line. The hand, it turned out, was fractured.

Krukow turned toward Mitch, who gave the slightest nod.

Then the pitcher hobbled to the dugout.

Mitch couldn't openly acknowledge what Krukow had just done. Throwing intentionally could draw stiff fines. But Krukow had his back. Mitch would never forget it. He still has a photo on his wall of Krukow's pained face as he left the mound that afternoon.

One day Mitch was checking the daily lineup card Craig had just posted in the clubhouse. "How come Skip [Craig] puts my name up there without knowing how I feel?" he asked Krukow.

The question was a bizarre one. It was not the practice of managers to check with players on their availability to play. If a player was hurt or sick, the trainer would let the manager know. Otherwise it was assumed he was good to go. Krukow could have explained this to Mitch. Instead, he took it to Craig. Good managers have partners in the clubhouse. Over a long season, players know other players in ways a manager never can. ("We'd joke that you can sit down in the shitter and look at the feet next to you in the stall and know who it is," Krukow said.) He knew Mitch wasn't looking for an answer from him. He needed something only Craig could give.

Before the lineup was posted the next day, Krukow watched Craig stop at Mitch's locker and ask how he felt. He did this every game from then on. "I was up late last night," Mitch would answer. Or, "My legs are really aching, Skip."

To which Craig unfailingly replied, "Mitch, we need you."

And Mitch would play, as Craig knew he would. This was a guy who once dislocated his finger taking grounders in batting practice, yanked it back in place, and took more grounders. Craig knew Mitch just needed to know he cared. The gesture took a minute of the manager's day.

Some players grumbled that Craig coddled Mitch. But if the so-called coddling made him a better player, it wasn't coddling. It was smart managing. "I did some special things for Mitch," Craig told me a few years ago when I visited him at his home in Borrego Springs, east of San Diego. "He was so important to us. And such a sweet kid. I just loved him. If you don't handle him right, he's going to crawl into his shell." Craig was tending his garden. The proof was in the numbers. In sixty-two games with the Padres and manager Larry Bowa in the first half of the season, Mitch hit .245 with seven home runs and twenty-six RBIs. In sixty-nine games with the Giants and Craig in the second half, he hit .306 with fifteen home runs and forty-four RBIs. And the best was yet to come.

One day I sketched a pyramid as a way to organize my thoughts on leadership. On the base I wrote *Trust*. On the next level, I wrote *Adaptability*. Leaders need to adapt to players, not the other way around. But that wasn't exactly right. You don't adapt for the sake of adapting. You do it with purpose. Craig accommodated Mitch's unusual request about the lineup because he understood the underlying emotional need. This is different from accommodating a player's request for, say, a bigger television over his locker.

So I scratched *Adaptability* and changed the second level of my leadership pyramid to a less snappy heading:

"Understanding and Utilizing Two Fundamental Concepts: The Constancy of Human Nature and the Wild Variability of Actual Humans."

In other words, humans share common needs and tendencies,* but we express these needs and tendencies in infinitely varied

---

* Abraham Maslow's pyramid model, "Hierarchy of Needs," endures as a schematic distillation of the complexity of human nature and motivation. His theory was first presented in his 1943 paper "A Theory of Human Motivation" in *Psychological Review* and refined over the years.

ways. A leader who recognizes and adapts to the unique needs of each person can unleash skills and talent that boost performance. The late basketball coach Pat Summitt was flummoxed one season by an extraordinarily gifted freshman named Semeka Randall. "Semeka's attitude was the one remaining loose thread that could unravel the team in the post season," Summitt wrote in her memoir about the '97–'98 championship season, *Raise the Roof.* "Our emotions as a team tended to mirror Semeka's.... [W]hen she was low and hung her head, she could drag us all down." Summitt called Semeka's high-school coach for advice. "Pat," he told her, "you've got to hug that kid." Summitt sat down with Semeka. "You need to trust me," she said. Semeka didn't answer. So Summitt said, "How about this? I won't ask you to trust me. Instead I'm going to trust you. Is there anything else you need?"

Semeka looked up at her. "A hug." Summitt became a hugger.

The University of North Carolina's Anson Dorrance, the winningest college soccer coach in history, told me about a note a player left on his desk one day. The player and the coach didn't get along. In Dorrance's view, she resisted his coaching and had a bad attitude. Her note read, "People don't care how much you know until they know how much you care." Dorrance, by his own admission, can be arrogant and abrasive; the emotional side of coaching doesn't come naturally. "What she was telling me was, 'You know, I'm not listening to you because you don't care about me.' And that was a great message, because it's the truth and I needed to be reminded of that."

The word *love* kept coming up with athletes and coaches, as it did with military people. Hall of Fame basketball coach Phil Jackson called it the essential ingredient of a championship team. So did VanDerveer, a Hall of Famer not known for her Zen-ness.

"Probably in everything we do for high performance, it isn't just about the X's and O's," she said. "It's a lot about how you feel emotionally, how you process things. Think about the greatest motivators: One is love. If you really love someone, you're going to do more for them." She said her best lesson about coaching came from her first gig with her little sister's youth team. "I never forgot that everyone on the team is someone's sister, someone's daughter, and you have to coach them like they're yours."

When Dave Roberts was hired in November 2015 as the Los Angeles Dodgers' manager, he sought leadership advice from coaches he admired, such as the Seattle Seahawks' Pete Carroll, the Golden State Warriors' Steve Kerr, and former Los Angeles Lakers and New York Knicks coach Pat Riley. Roberts came away with pages and pages of notes and distilled them to this: "Players want to know three things about a coach: Does he care about me? Can I trust him? And can he make me better?"

Roberts said, "If you can check those three boxes, then you can get a lot from a player. I think for me that foundation started with the phone calls in the winter." He talked to twenty-five or so players on the phone and met with half a dozen more before the team gathered for spring training. He flew to Texas to spend time with his biggest star, pitcher Clayton Kershaw, and his wife and baby daughter. He talked with his twenty-one-year-old rookie shortstop, the first-round draft pick Corey Seager. He called Seager's parents. As a father himself, Roberts figured they'd want to know someone would be looking out for their son. Throughout the season, he'd walk the field during batting practice, casually checking in with each guy: "How's the baby?" or "Your dad's surgery go all right?" If there was an issue to address, he could do it then, quietly and inconspicuously, instead of dragging the player into his office. Getting to know his players and building trust were huge time sinks. But as McChrystal wrote in *Team of Teams,* "Trust and purpose are inefficient... [but] these inefficiencies are precisely what imbues teams with high-level adaptability and efficacy."

When Kershaw landed on the disabled list with a back injury in July 2016, some players were waiting for Roberts to call a team meeting to address the enormous loss. Kershaw was their Warrior. Instead, Roberts kept to his routine of touching base with the guys, trusting them to step up their own play to make up for Kershaw's absence. "I think they felt empowered, like 'Yeah, we lost our best player, but so what?' From that point on we just played great baseball," Roberts said. They won eight of their next eleven games. (They reached the National League Championship Series but lost to the eventual World Series champions, the Chicago Cubs.)

Now in his fourth season with the Dodgers, his goal is still to check in with every player every day. "People talk about the millennials and that it's hard to get to know them, that they're not coachable," Roberts said. "I couldn't disagree more. They just want to be loved on."

Clubhouses, locker rooms, and workplaces are not such distant cousins from early cooperative tribes, European orphanages, the partnership between Tversky and Kahneman: All are expressions of our fundamental need for, and effect on, each other. When the manager of a Bank of America call center needed help figuring out how to boost productivity among his calling teams, he turned to professor Sandy Pentland, who directs the Connection Science and Human Dynamics labs at MIT.[8] Pentland is a bit like the Bill James of social analytics. *Forbes* named him one of the seven most powerful data scientists in the world. He's a geek for human interaction.

He and his researchers equipped employees at the call center with sensor "badges" that collected reams of digital data on their movements, conversations, body language, and tone of voice. They analyzed the data, teasing out patterns that connected specific behaviors with high or low performance. They found that the most significant predictor of a calling team's success was time spent talking with coworkers *away from their workstations*. Their data showed that informal interaction had as much impact on productivity as all other factors—individual intelligence, personality, skill, and the substance of discussions—combined. Like laughter, idle conversation is a bit like the human version of chimpanzees grooming each other. Non-human primates pick bugs off one another for many more hours than hygiene requires. What they're actually doing, without knowing it, is building trust and lowering stress. Coworkers at B of A were getting both those benefits, plus information and advice.

Pentland proposed an unusual solution to the call center's manager's problem.

Instead of staggered coffee breaks, Pentland said, let everyone on a calling team take their breaks together. An entire team away from their phones sounded inefficient, even crazy, to the manager. But it worked. Productivity went up. Workers handled calls more quickly and thus fielded more calls per day. The manager changed coffee-break schedules at all ten of the bank's call centers and saw productivity gains of $15 million a year. Pentland has since applied his research to start-ups, hospitals, and other workplaces with similar results.

Two years removed from losing a hundred games, the '87 Giants won ninety and clinched their first division title in sixteen years. Krukow, however, was breaking down. His arm was slowly giving out. Still, Craig believed in him enough to have him start Game 4 of the National League Championship Series against the St. Louis Cardinals. Krukow had never pitched in a postseason game, and this one was huge: The Giants were down two games to one. He pitched a complete game, 4–2 victory. The Giants pushed the Cardinals to seven games before falling. Rosen was named National League Executive of the Year.

Dravecky emerged as the team's ace and threw a shutout on opening day to start the '88 season. But after just seven starts he underwent surgery for a frayed tendon in his shoulder and was out the rest of the season. The team was also without Krukow, who had shoulder problems, for nearly half the season. Injuries ate away at the lineup, and the team finished fourth.

When Dravecky went home to Ohio for the winter, he visited the Cleveland Clinic to check out a lump in his pitching arm. It had been there for about a year, but he'd been told not to worry about it. Probably scar tissue. But it was a malignant tumor that had invaded the deltoid muscle, the primary muscle involved in throwing a pitch. In removing the tumor, surgeons had to slice away half the deltoid. They also had to freeze the humerus bone, which runs from shoulder to elbow, to kill invasive cancer cells.

With the muscle ravaged and the bone beneath it weakened, Dravecky was told his career was over. "My greatest hope," his surgeon said, "is you'll be able to play catch with your son in the backyard."

News of the cancer devastated everyone on the team. Dravecky had been one of their stars and was as beloved as anyone in the clubhouse. When he arrived at the Giants with Mitch and Lefferts, Krukow had watched him go about his business, and the man had impressed him more every day. Krukow saw how Mitch was with him — how when Rosen announced a (brief) ban on junk food in the clubhouse, Mitch showed up the next morning with a box of donuts so "Snacks" wouldn't go without. Dravecky's growing contingent of evangelical players had come to compose about a third of the team. This one-third eschewed drinking, swearing, and carousing, the favorite pastimes of the other two-thirds. But

Dravecky didn't judge. He was the Buddy, everybody's friend, and he played his ass off on the field. In Krukow's book, that made him a great teammate.

Most of us in the press referred to the Giants' evangelicals as the God Squad, reviving the nickname of an earlier group that had played for the Giants in the late 1970s and early '80s. When a San Francisco columnist back then wrote, tongue in cheek, that praying to God didn't seem to be helping the team and maybe they should try Satan, one of the Squadders remarked that the column didn't surprise him. "The Bay Area is the center of devil worship, radical groups, and homosexuality in this country," he said. "It's a satanic region."

Dravecky's crew had a lighter bent. God Squadder Atlee Hammaker delighted at stopping at the locker of ornery Mike LaCoss on Sunday mornings. LaCoss was the Giants' Enforcer, never hesitating to take a guy to task for slacking off or arriving late for stretching. He didn't mind if anyone thought he was a jerk.

"Buffy," Hammaker would say, "chapel in twenty minutes."

"In two years I haven't come," LaCoss snapped every time, "and you're still fucking asking?" Hammaker laughed.

When Dravecky and his flock held chapel, Krukow and *his* crew gathered next door in the clubhouse kitchen for Caveman Quiz. "Caveman" was Don Robinson, another Jester. He was this big, hilarious, gritty pitcher from small-town West Virginia whose battered twenty-nine-year-old body had more stitches than a bucket of baseballs. "He could break his humerus in three places," Krukow once said, "and still give you three solid innings."[9]

The *San Francisco Chronicle* published a trivia quiz on Sundays. Caveman read the questions out loud. He butchered the words so badly he had everyone in hysterics. The Christians at chapel could hear the roars of laughter through the wall. One Sunday, a player who usually attended chapel opted instead for Caveman Quiz. The next week, two more defected, "making the transition from heaven to hell," as Krukow put it. Soon, only a handful of players were showing up at chapel. Dravecky pulled Krukow aside.

"Kruke, this has got to stop. I'm losing all my guys!"

"No way," Krukow said. "This is the funnest thing we've ever done."

"I know!" Dravecky said. "I want to be there!"

Krukow agreed to hold Caveman Quiz after chapel.

When the team reported to spring training in February for the '89 season, Dravecky's number-43 jersey hung in his locker as a reminder that, even if he wasn't there, he was still a Giant. One morning, Dravecky walked through the door.

Teammates swarmed him, saying how good he looked, how great it was to see him. Handshakes and careful hugs all around. Dravecky pulled off his shirt to show his arm. The room fell silent. His upper arm was half gone, as if its meat had been scooped out with a broken bottle. The skin was puckered and discolored from skin grafts and stitches.

"Man," Mitch finally said, "you look like Jaws took a bite outta you!"

Dravecky laughed. Krukow then noticed the duffel bag. Dravecky unpacked his glove and other equipment into his locker and began pulling on his practice uniform.

"What the hell are you doing?" Krukow asked.

"I'm getting in shape," Dravecky said. "I'm going to pitch again. I'm a little behind."

Krukow and everyone else went along with it. If Dravecky needed to believe he could make a comeback, well, they were happy to believe it, too. Every day in the training room and gym, they watched the pain and beads of sweat spread across Dravecky's face as he strengthened what was left of his deltoid. He had to build up strength, too, in lesser-used muscles that now needed to take over. He learned how to engage these new muscles in a reinvented throwing motion.

Around this time, Rosen brought in a former Giant named Bob Knepper to shore up his pitching staff. Knepper was, by most accounts, a good guy, but his rigid and outspoken interpretation of the Bible clashed with many of his teammates' mainstream values. He espoused, for example, that God deemed women submissive to men and that they should therefore not hold leadership roles, a view that had earned him a nomination as Neanderthal of the Year by the Houston chapter of the National Organization for Women. His arrival portended Lorenz's butterfly effect, a small disturbance that could turn disastrous.

Sure enough, word soon spread that some of the Christians were criticizing teammates for what they considered immoral behavior. This didn't go over well with the carouser group, who grumbled about the Christians shrugging off losses as "God's will," though it was unclear whether any of the Christians ever actually said this. Matters were not helped when Craig and Rosen asked the Christians to stop holding Sunday chapel so close to game time because they believed it made the players less driven and aggressive when they took the field. Dravecky and his group changed the time of chapel, but the accusation stung.

The lines between the two factions were beginning to fracture the locker room. "You can't have two sides in the clubhouse over any one issue," Krukow said. "Everybody has got to be together or it doesn't work."

The brewing rift among the players was not going to be fixed by a coach or manager. The job belonged to one or, in this case, two of their own. Dravecky, still rehabbing his arm, and Krukow didn't call a team meeting to solve the problem. Instead, they did it with a conversation here, a joke there. They were Sages and Enforcers, with bits of the Jester and Buddy thrown in.

"If we're going to be Christians," Dravecky told his guys in a dozen different ways, "we can't challenge them in what we say. Only in the way we live."

Krukow, meanwhile, defended the Squadders at every turn. "Listen, these guys will fight for you. They're your teammates. That's all you or I need to know."

The two veteran leaders patched the rift so seamlessly they appeared to have done nothing at all. The regular postgame conclave, usually a dozen or so half-dressed players talking about what had happened on the field, would slowly draw the entire team and come to be known as the Circle. Krukow and a few other veterans led the discussion. They discussed mistakes and missed opportunities, strategy and effort. Who was dogging or killing it? They sought and offered advice and feedback. Why are guys running on me? Am I tipping my pitches? They analyzed the next day's opposing hitters and starting pitcher. Who's seen this guy? What do you know? Eventually, almost the whole team showed up. Rookies learned what to do and what not to do. How to tip, how to dress, how to pick yourself up after getting your ass kicked, how to take the needling and hazing in stride. In exchange for this education, they fetched beers from the fridge.

On the road, teammates would go to dinner and even to hotel bars together, Christians and carousers alike, to laugh and talk ball. "They drank tea and I drank nineteen beers," LaCoss said.

Krukow had known since the previous season that his days as a pitcher were numbered. He wore a hat off the field because he couldn't comb his hair. Over the course of spring training, he was able to pitch a total of three innings. He broke camp on the disabled list. Without him and Dravecky, the team headed north with just nine pitchers instead of the usual eleven. Preseason predictions had the Dodgers winning the National League West again, with the Padres and the Reds giving them a run for their money. The Giants were figured to finish fourth.

Krukow returned to the lineup in May with little more than a leaky cutter and floppy curve. "I didn't dare throw a fastball because I'd look like I was playing catch with the umpire," he said. Between starts, he didn't touch a baseball. His arm had only so many pitches left in it, and he wasn't going to waste them in the bullpen. With painkillers and wile, he compiled a 4–2 record going into June.

In the fifth inning against Atlanta on June 4, on a fastball to Darrell Evans, Krukow heard the rip. He fell to the mound, his eyes wet with pain and grief. He cradled his dead arm as he walked off the field and into the clubhouse. Rosen was already waiting. The usually stone-faced general manager had tears in his eyes, too.

"I'm sorry, Al," Krukow said. "That's all I have."

At the airport that night, the team bus stopped at the main terminal to let Krukow out. He was flying back to San Francisco for treatment. The team was taking a charter to Cincinnati. Krukow walked twenty steps from the bus and turned around. "Everybody's pressed up against the windows. I cried my ass off going into the terminal," he said.

After surgery, with his arm in a sling, Krukow refused to return to the clubhouse. He knew players were often superstitious about being around an injured teammate, as if they might catch his bad luck. Guys were calling every day, asking when he was coming back, saying that the clubhouse wasn't the same without him, but Krukow still wouldn't go. The team had gone on a wild winning streak in June, winning ten of twelve games, including seven in a row, leaping from third place to first. "I didn't want to drag them down. I thought I'd kill the chemistry," he said. "Then Dravecky comes in and saves my ass."

Dravecky began throwing in batting practice in June and then in simulated games. When he pitched in front of a sold-out crowd at a minor-league park in Stockton, California, he made national news. He pitched in another minor-league game and another, looking more and more like his old self. His story was gathering momentum, and Krukow was swept up like everyone else. He rejoined the team. He wasn't going to miss the greatest comeback in the history of baseball.

Just ten months after his surgery, Dravecky took the mound on August 10 in front of thirty-four thousand cheering, teary-eyed fans at Candlestick. Media from around the world jammed the press box and photo wells. Dravecky pitched shutout baseball into the eighth inning against Cincinnati, leaving with a 3–1 lead to thunderous ovation. The Giants won, 4–3.

Dravecky pitched again five days later in Montreal. He sailed through five innings, giving up no runs and just three hits, taking a 3–0 lead. He began the bottom of the sixth by giving up a home run to the first batter and hitting the second.

Now, facing Tim Raines, he reared back to throw a fastball. Before the ball had left his hand, Dravecky's arm snapped. The sickening sound—like a breaking branch—would haunt every-one who was on the field that day. Dravecky collapsed to the ground, thinking for a moment that his arm had sailed to the backstop with the ball. He clutched at it to feel that it was still there. Teammates rushed to the mound. Craig bolted out of the dugout alongside the Giants' trainer.

"It's broke," Dravecky said, his face twisted in pain. The humerus bone had split in two.

As he left the field on a stretcher, he told Craig, "Win this game. I want this win." The Giants won, 3–2.

The horrific ending to Dravecky's miraculous comeback risked throwing the Giants into a tailspin but instead seemed to strengthen them. They played as if victory was always within reach and that it hung on the contributions of every single one of them. Craig so completely believed this that everyone else did, too— even the bench players, which is not always the case. If a team has complainers, they usually emerge from the bench, and understandably so. Sometimes all a bench player has to show for his nine innings in uniform is a mound of sunflower-seed shells. But the Giants' backups so embraced their roles they called themselves the Killer B's, a reference to their designation as the "B" squad in spring training. Every day during infield practice, they competed against each other in a little game they made up called "Service." The Killer B's—Greg Litton, Donell Nixon, Ernie Riles, Bill Bathe, Chris Speier, Mike Laga, and Ken Oberkfell—lined up behind each other at third base to take grounders. Coach Wendell Kim hit balls at them as hard as he could. The player with the most errors had to serve the others the drinks of their choice after the game. "I served a lot of drinks that season," Litton said.

On September 4 in Cincinnati, the Killer B's played their way into Giants lore. The Giants were behind 8–0 in the seventh inning when Craig yanked almost all his starters and deployed the B's, who unleashed a month's worth of hits. "Roger was calling it, going up and down in the dugout, saying, 'Here's how it's going to happen. He's going to hit a double . . .' and so on," said Krukow, who stood at the dugout rail with the rest of the team, cheering and hollering as the B's kept circling the bases. Final score: 9–8, Giants. "It was unbelievable," Krukow said. "We felt bulletproof after that."

In the meantime, Kevin Mitchell and Will Clark were having the season of their lives. Clark batted .333 (losing the batting title

to the Padres' Tony Gwynn on the final day of the season) with a
.953 OPS (on-base plus slugging percentage), 23 home runs, and
111 RBIs. In the National League, only Mitch was better. He led the
league in six batting categories with 47 home runs, 125 RBIs, .635
SLG (slugging percentage, or total bases per at-bat), 1.023 OPS,
345 total bases, and 32 intentional walks. Both were Warriors that
season. Both were leading contenders for the National League's
Most Valuable Player Award (MVP). Each supported the other.

"Kevin Mitchell ought to win the MVP," Clark told reporters.
"Mitch is the one who carried us for three months. Without him,
there's no way I'm having the season I'm having."

Mitch shrugged. "I never won nothin' anyway, so it doesn't
matter," he said. "It would be nice. But Will deserves it as much as
I do." In the end, Mitch won it.

The Giants easily won the division and then beat the Chicago
Cubs in five games to win the pennant. But during the celebration
on the field, as Dravecky rushed toward the mound, his arm still
in a sling, someone ran into him from behind. Dravecky knew
immediately his arm had broken again.* As soon as doctors set
the break and released him from the hospital, Dravecky returned
to the team. His teammates were on the verge of history, and nothing was going to keep him away.

The Giants were back in the World Series for the first time in
twenty-seven years. They faced the mighty Oakland A's, who easily
won the first two games with a cumulative score of 10–1. Shortly

---

* A month after the season ended, the cancer returned and Dravecky offi-
cially retired. He was thirty-five. On June 18, 1991, after two years of chronic
pain and infections, his arm and shoulder were amputated. He is now a
Christian motivational speaker and author, and a community ambassador
for the Giants.

before Game 3 on an unusually warm and still evening in Candlestick Park, a 6.9 earthquake rattled the light towers and shook the entire stadium. I was up on the third deck in an overflowing press area. We swayed in our seats for fifteen seconds—in earthquake time, an eternity. When it stopped, the ugly old park, the "John C. Holmes Memorial," had held up, touching off peals of happy cheers and chants of "Let's play ball!"

But plumes of smoke rose in the distance from fires in San Francisco's Marina District. A portion of the Bay Bridge, the very symbol of this World Series, had collapsed. The top deck of an Oakland freeway crashed onto the lower deck, crushing motorists. The quake killed sixty-five people, injured three thousand, and caused $10 billion in damage. The World Series was postponed. Giants players and coaches visited shelters and listened to people's stories. "All this misery," Krukow said, "and, in the middle of that, baseball."

The Series resumed at Candlestick ten days later. The A's won 13–7 in Game 3 and 9–6 in Game 4 to win the championship in a sweep. The Giants' exhilarating, heart-wrenching season was over. The tragedy around them made the loss almost meaningless. But the many months that preceded it—come-from-behind wins, kangaroo court, Caveman Quiz, Dravecky's comeback, all the dinners, The Circle, the Killer B's, the million conversations and laughs and stories—ensured the season would always be remembered as the greatest season of their lives.

I met Krukow for lunch one day across the street from the Giants' ballpark. He was now sixty-four years old. But beneath the second skin of middle age, there was a boyishness that made the lines around his eyes and his white hair and beard look rakish. Still sporting the rangy build of a kid going through a growth spurt, he leaned his walking stick against our table, folded his six-foot, five-inch body into a chair, and with both hands positioned his braced legs. Since his diagnosis in 2006 of inclusion body myositis, a degenerative muscle disease, his legs had slowly atrophied. Now his hands were weakening, too. His precarious negotiation of stairs and crowds had curtailed his travel, so he wasn't broadcasting as many road games.

"I do believe the real significance of that team, what made us different, is we openly loved each other," he said. "And that entire emotion was picked up by people who watched us play baseball. That team made it cool to wear orange and black again. I think back on those days and always get this wonderful, warm feeling about it. All those guys brought their contributions. They brought their championship seasons with other teams into that clubhouse. We had Terry Kennedy's Padres in there. Ken Oberkfell's Cardinals. Mitchell's Mets. Everybody brought those components and shared."

Krukow was in the broadcast booth when the Giants finally won their first World Series championship in 2010, and he was there in 2012 and 2014 for two more. All those teams were said to have great chemistry. I asked Krukow if he saw a common component to team chemistry.

"There is one," he said, "and it has to be said in your book. There are a lot of different things you can play for: You can play for money, you can play for the crowd, you can play to get a date, you can play to make your mom and dad happy. The only way you'll ever find true chemistry is if you play 100 percent for each other. There was a mutual respect we had for one another, an expectation for one another. There was true joy—not fake bullshit joy, or jealous joy, or lip-service joy—there was true joy when somebody did something good. There was accountability when you did something bad, and there was a sincere, honest effort to figure out why you were going bad and get you out of your doldrums. It was like a clean start every day. When that season was over and I went home to my family, I had such a longing for those guys in the clubhouse."

He talked about Craig and Rosen and everything they did to change the culture and wring every ounce of talent and commitment from all those men. I asked if the Giants could have gotten to the World Series without Craig and Rosen.

Krukow smiled. "We wouldn't have wanted to."

CHAPTER EIGHT

SYNTHESIS

"Scenarios of the mind are all but infinite in detail,
their content evolving in accordance with the unique
history and physiology of the individual. How are we to
feed that into a computer?"

—Biologist E. O. Wilson in *Consilience:*
The Unity of Knowledge

The old practice facility and headquarters for the Golden State
Warriors sat atop a convention-center parking garage in the middle of downtown Oakland, California, nine minutes up interstate
880 from Oracle Arena, the team's home court.* The garage elevator opened to a well-appointed lobby decorated with outsized
photos of a franchise in full: the ticker-tape parades, the fans
going bananas, the gobsmacked teammates leaping into each other's arms. A sunny attendant at the reception desk checked my
driver's license against his list and directed me down the hall and
to the right.

---

* In the fall of 2019, the Warriors moved to the Chase Center, a new arena
and headquarters in San Francisco.

An army of reporters and photographers was clustered along the wall. From behind a set of closed double doors came the squeaks of sneakers, the *thwat-thwat-thwat* of basketballs on hardwood, the dull clangs of errant shots. The beat reporters—the regulars—exchanged the usual unequivocal opinions and hinted at nuggets of inside information, which, in the eternal ebb and flow of sportswriter hierarchy, momentarily elevates the nuggetholder. The rest of us, the outsiders, kept our mouths shut and cast glances at the double doors.

It was a Wednesday morning in early February 2019. I hadn't written about the Warriors since my sports-writing days in the late 1990s, when the team was in the midst of twelve consecutive losing seasons. Now the Warriors had won three NBA championships in the last four years. The run of success coincided with the arrival of new owners, a new management team, and a new forty-nine-year-old head coach named Steve Kerr.

The Warriors plucked Kerr from the TNT broadcast booth, where he had spent two four-year stints as an NBA game analyst. It was the rest of his résumé that landed him the job: five NBA championships in fifteen years as a player, and later a three-year stint as an NBA general manager. Until the Warriors hired him in 2014, Kerr had never coached. But he had been filling notepads and Word documents with thoughts and theories about coaching, drawn from his own observations, his long reading list, and his sit-downs with successful coaches who had fostered selfless, committed, high-performing teams, specifically Phil Jackson and Gregg Popovich from the NBA and Pete Carroll from the NFL.

Kerr inherited a talented Warriors team that had finished sixth in the Western Conference the previous season and lost in the first round of the playoffs. During the months before the season began, he partnered with the team's metrics guru, Sammy Gelfand, to figure out ways to boost this underperforming team.

The two men, along with other staff, spent hours together digging into metrics that might reveal unseen opportunities to improve. Kerr knew he wanted a style of play like the San Antonio Spurs, with lots of ball movement, though he had little hard evidence that more passes translated to more wins. Gelfand looked into it and returned with eye-opening numbers.

The team had averaged just 247 passes per game the previous season, by far the worst in the NBA. Gelfand also found that when the players passed the ball more than three times in a possession, they were "almost unstoppable." They led the league in points per possession on such plays. Kerr asked Gelfand to figure out the ideal number of passes per game for this team. The "magic number," he calculated, was three hundred.

Kerr immediately recognized that Gelfand had just handed him a cornerstone principle on which to build the Warriors' new culture, which was a synthesis of analytics and team chemistry. The benchmark of three hundred passes per game captured this dual nature of a high-performing organization: intellectual, information-age strategy coupled with tribal reliance on one another. First, as Gelfand had already figured out, the benchmark would mean more points. And second, an increase in passing not only would unite players around a specific goal, but it would also solidify a team-first mind-set by constantly sharing the ball.

So Kerr issued the three-hundred-pass challenge to his players, explaining the metrics. After a couple of weeks of sloppy turnovers, they fell into a new rhythm, moving the ball from one to another in quick, exquisite patterns, as if rising from one mind, as if it were choreography instead of improvisation. By season's end, they had averaged 315.9 passes per game, nearly 70 more than the previous year. They ranked second among all NBA teams in offensive efficiency and first in defensive efficiency and were on their way to winning the NBA championship, the franchise's first in forty years.

The media and fans raved about the team's chemistry, and the MIT Sloan Sports Analytics Conference named it the "Best Analytics Organization" in sports. Kerr emerged as the model of the cutting-edge leader who viewed analytics and chemistry as partners in an audacious quest: to be epic. His team set an NBA single-season record in 2015–2016 with seventy-three wins (against just nine losses), reaching the finals again, but falling to the Cleveland Cavaliers. The Warriors then added center Kevin Durant, one of the greatest players of his generation, to their already killer lineup. They won the next two championships, in 2016–2017 and 2017–2018. They had leapt from exceptional to dynastic, winning more games over Kerr's first four years than any franchise in league history.

In the fall of 2018, the start of Kerr's fifth season, his team was riding the momentum of back-to-back championships with their eyes on a three-peat.

Then the smartest, closest, most talented team in the NBA cracked, their dominance undone by the rupture of a single relationship.

At last the double doors swung open, spilling the gym's white light into the hallway, and we poured in. Players in loose T-shirts and shorts shot baskets in groups of two or three at the eight backboards positioned around the court. The head coach sat on a green, inflatable exercise ball behind a basket at the far end. Kerr was lean and athletic, with a look that could be described as boyish if not for the lightest shadow of pain that fell across his face. Two back surgeries in 2015 and 2016—the second to try to fix the botched results of the first—caused such agony he missed forty-three regular-season games and eleven playoff games over the course of two years. Migraines still plagued him, but he didn't talk about them. He seemed to have emerged from the egoistic world of professional sports as grounded and pleasant as a midwestern schoolteacher. His Twitter bio was all of five words: "Proud dad, husband and coach." His half-million followers on the social-media site were more likely to find political commentary than Warriors news. A vehement critic of President Trump, he openly supported liberal causes such as LGBTQ rights, Black Lives Matter, the #MeToo movement, and gun control. His father, Malcolm Kerr, president of the American University of Beirut, was assassinated by terrorists when Steve was in college.

As players were leaving the court, I was escorted over to Kerr for a prearranged interview. From a bench a few yards from us, Warriors superstar Steph Curry was watching a smattering of second-string players who continued to shoot. In a few hours he would have to report to Oracle Arena for the fifty-third game of the season, yet instead of bolting home for a few hours' rest, he lingered, just watching his teammates.

I asked Kerr if team chemistry actually matters.

"Of course it does," he said. "Having played for fifteen years and coached for five, you can feel it. Every team has a sort of a heartbeat. It's a living thing. And, as you go through the course of the season, things happen good and bad, and if you have the right group of players you can sort of nudge them back toward the positive direction when something goes wrong.

"You can try to foster an environment that creates a comfort level and a happiness factor where players want to come in and work together. When that happens, they're more likely to sacrifice for one another, play hard for one another. And in basketball, when players are playing for each other, you reach a level that wasn't possible when you started training camp and people didn't know each other well.

"I've always looked at a basketball season—it sounds corny—

but it's almost like a life form, like an organism. Look at our team. Earlier this season, we had a moment between Draymond and Kevin. There's a reason we lost the next four games. Our soul was damaged, our spirit was damaged."

It was an early November game against division rival Los Angeles Clippers. With just seconds left in the final quarter and the score tied, Warriors power forward Draymond Green grabbed a rebound. Kevin Durant signaled for the ball, ready to take the possible game-winning shot. But instead of passing, Green dribbled up court and lost control of the ball as time ran out.

Durant was furious. In the ensuing team huddle, he yelled at Green for being selfish and trying to win the game by himself. Green exploded, letting loose his resentment about Durant signing a contract over the summer that allowed him to walk away from the team at the end of the season. For Green, commitment and loyalty were everything. How could Durant be fully committed if his bags were already packed and at the door? Who was Durant to accuse *him* of being selfish? He repeatedly called Durant a bitch. Teammates and coaches stepped between the two players. It was a shocking display for a Warriors team so famous for its chemistry. Television cameras caught it all.

The Warriors lost in overtime, and the argument escalated in the locker room, with Green's accusations growing sharper, meaner, and more personal. The team had won a title without him, Green reminded Durant, and they'd win another when he was gone. Durant fired back with pent-up aggravation with Green's disruptive and coarse behavior. For all his brilliance—his smart playmaking and relentless drive, his ability to fire up exhausted teammates—Green could be spectacularly reckless and insensitive. On the court, Green threw tantrums and was notorious for kicking and kneeing opponents in the groin. In Game 4 of the 2016 NBA Finals against the Cleveland Cavaliers, Green's blatant punch between LeBron James's legs earned him a suspension for Game 5. The Warriors lost that game and the next two, losing the championship after a seemingly insurmountable three-to-one series lead.

Durant was Green's opposite. Soft-spoken and introspective, the ten-time All-Star played with artful efficiency, his six-foot-ten body gliding across the court, his jump shots floating off his long fingers with the delicacy of a butterfly. His competitive fire burned as hot as Green's, but he rarely showed it. Now, in the locker room after the loss to the Clippers, Durant had grown weary of pushing himself quarter after quarter, game after game, only to watch Green scream yet again at the refs and scuffle with opponents, wasting energy and disrupting the Warriors' flow. Durant couldn't fathom how Green could have kept dribbling as time ran out. Or how he could let himself get so out of control, so vile. Green had gone too far this time.

Kerr felt "the entire chemistry of the team was at stake."[1] Green's attack violated the sanctity of what it means to be part of a team. Kerr took the unprecedented step of suspending Green for a game without pay, costing the player more than $120,000.

"The energy got sucked right out of us," Kerr said, "because our family had been harmed." It showed in the players' performance, unfolding in small vignettes like scenes in a play.

"You see guys not as willing to dive on the floor for a loose ball, or put everything on the line," the coach said, "because they don't feel the same sense of responsibility to each other. When a team is together, the execution is better. They're more likely to set a good screen. And if you set a good screen your teammate is much more likely to get an open shot, right? It might seem little, but all these little things add up. And I've seen it my whole basketball career. When a team has good chemistry, there's a different level of play."

Four days after the blowup, Durant and Green met over a bottle of Spanish red wine at the Hotel Crescent Court in Dallas. Green reiterated that he felt Durant wasn't committed enough to the team. The players' loyalty to one another was what made the Warriors the Warriors, Green felt, and everyone needed to buy in or it wouldn't work. Durant assured his teammate he was fully on board and conceded he could have been more vocal about it.

Then it was Durant's turn to unload. Green's explosions on and off the court were self-indulgent. He needed to stop excusing his bad behavior as "passion for the game." Durant said he expected more from Green.[2]

Reporters dissected every small interaction between Durant and Green, declaring progress when they were seen chatting on their way into the arena, laughing during a huddle, reviving their special backhanded, double-tap high five. But a team that once had lost nine games in an entire season now lost seven in November alone. Then another five in December. But the culture of resilience Kerr and his staff had fostered over the years held the team together, however imperfectly. They won eleven straight games in January. Ensconced once again atop the Western Conference standings, the Warriors were looking like their old selves.

But in the first round of the playoffs, they blew a thirty-one-point lead to the Clippers in the *third quarter*, the greatest postseason collapse in NBA history. They gave up eighty-five points in the second half. Durant had more turnovers (a season-high nine) than shots attempted (eight). The team looked lost. Curry tried to explain what went wrong: "Our aggressiveness, definitely. Our togetherness, definitely."

The lingering effects of the Durant-Green rift seemed the

obvious culprit. But as complex systems, teams face a myriad of disruptions large and small that threaten their success. Every year since their first championship in 2015, Kerr and his players had managed to beat back these threats, including the most insidious of all: success itself. Had it now caught up with them?

Dynasties are rare for a lot of reasons.

First, winning is exhausting. The Warriors' price for reaching the NBA Finals five years in a row was playing 106 extra games. That's the equivalent of adding an entire 82-game season plus 24 games beyond that. The first three years, fueled not only by the novelty of winning but also by the sheer fun of greatness, were like a dream, Kerr said. But in the fourth and fifth years, the players' bodies inevitably began to show the physical toll of hundreds and hundreds of hours on the court and in the gym. The stretches of weariness tested the players' patience, and tolerance for one another could wear thin. Little annoyances blossomed now and then into big ones.

But the psychological price of winning is steeper and more covert than the physical one.

Success changes people.

I used to wonder why championship teams that return the following year with essentially the same players so often suffer a drop in performance. I learned that it's because they're *not* the same players. Suddenly they're sought after for public appearances and endorsements. They feel adored, special, powerful. They have different expectations of themselves and the people around them. They interact with each other differently, changing the dynamics of the locker room.

"That's the irony, which is that success breeds failure. It knocks out the team chemistry that's so vital," said Dacher Keltner, the UC Berkeley professor who wrote *The Power Paradox: How We Gain and Lose Influence.* I had driven over to Berkeley to learn more.

In his book-lined office on a warm summer morning, Keltner's bike helmet and backpack were dumped on the floor. His cargo shorts and T-shirt, his blond hair and tanned face, were not the usual look of a fifty-something career academic. Keltner is an expert on the science of human emotion, having earned a PhD at Stanford and conducted postdoc research at the UC San Francisco laboratory of facial-coding pioneer Paul Ekman. Keltner was also the scientific consultant on Pixar's animated film about feelings, *Inside/Out,* and has twice met the Dalai Lama. "The ultimate team player," he said.

Keltner has spent twenty years studying why certain people within a group rise to power. He found they are good at reading others' emotions. They listen. They're enthusiastic. They show in their everyday actions that their top priority is the well-being of the group.

Then Keltner noticed another pattern: Highly successful leaders—whether in business, Hollywood, politics, or sports— often lose the very traits that made them leaders in the first place. When we're puffed with power, his research showed, our ability to mimic diminishes. Thus, we're less able to read other people's feelings and intentions. Thus, we're less empathetic and compassionate. We feel exceptional, special. ("A town car? Where's the limo?") Rules and social norms no longer apply to us.[3] Keltner and his team of student researchers did a kind of a loony study on this that turned out to be revealing.[4]

They positioned a student at a clearly marked pedestrian crosswalk on a busy street near campus. California law requires drivers to stop for pedestrians. Nearby, other students recorded which cars stopped and which didn't. They divided the cars into categories from least expensive to most expensive. Among drivers in the most expensive cars, more than fifty percent blew through the crosswalk. Drivers in the cheapest cars? Stopped every time.

Power and privilege predicted who was more likely to do whatever they felt like doing.

"That's the power paradox: As I rise and become a star, I become more selfish," Keltner said, referring to athletes. "I sleep with more women on the road, I want bigger contracts, and I speak offensively to my teammates. So the very experience of power reduces the likelihood you'll have team-oriented people."

The clubhouse dynamic changes. *Just Us* splinters. The erosion of trust and togetherness means more anxious, lower-performing people. "Stress wears you down," Keltner said. "It makes you cautious. It tightens you up. You choke. It costs you physically. So a really stressed-out body is not as strong. The physiology of stress is the antithesis of the physiology of positive emotion."

Some define power as the capacity to alter the state of another person. The philosopher Hannah Arendt defined it as the ability "to stir others to collective action." I think of teams with coach-player duos who had that kind of power: the New England Patriots under Bill Belichick and Tom Brady, the Giants under Bruce Bochy and Buster Posey, the Warriors under Kerr and Curry. Few athletes have insulated a team from the ruinous influence of success as well as Curry. He is the rare superstar who is also a Super-Carrier, someone who, through his grounded, happy, fiercely competitive nature, lifts everyone around him.

When I ran my archetypes by Kerr, he agreed that Curry is all seven: the Kid who plays with joy, the Buddy who hangs out with the second-stringers, the Warrior who intimidates, the Sparkplug who electrifies, and, when necessary, the Enforcer, the Sage, and even the Jester. Like every Super-Carrier, he is an exemplar of selflessness. When Durant joined Curry on the Warriors, people envisioned the two MVPs battling for dominance. Instead, Curry threw open the doors. He passed up open shots to feed his new teammate the ball until Durant finally told him to chill. Don't change how you play, Durant said. Just do you. Curry's welcoming, unselfish behavior put the potential rivalry to rest.

"Of course it's not just the behavior that spreads," Keltner said. "It's the feeling alongside the behavior that you begin to imitate, and that is part of the contagion."

As his players' fame and power grew with each championship, and as they plowed through opponents with relative ease, Kerr worked hard at fending off boredom and complacency. One night in 2018, after nearly a month of unfocused, sloppy play, the coach called a time-out in the first quarter against the hapless Phoenix Suns. Kerr handed his black marker and clipboard to veteran Andre Iguodala and walked away, his hands in his pockets and his head down. Iguodala squatted in front of his teammates and sketched out a play. For the rest of the game, the players coached, taking turns in the huddle and barking out plays from the sideline. The Warriors won, 129–83.

"They're tired of my voice," Kerr explained afterward. "I'm tired of my voice. It's been a long haul these last few years. I wasn't reaching them, and we just figured it was probably a good night to pull a trick out of the hat and do something different. It's their team. They have to take ownership of it."

From his years as a player, Kerr always seemed to recognize the limitations of analytics. Leaders without experience as a player can take a bit longer to learn this.

When twenty-eight-year-old Theo Epstein became the youngest general manager in major-league history, he had never played or coached baseball professionally. What he brought to the Boston Red Sox in 2002 instead was an Ivy League degree and a solid grasp of how to use data to build a cost-efficient, high-performing team. He was so committed to analytics that one of his first hires was Bill James, the analytics guru. Two years later, the Red Sox won their first World Series championship since 1918, and they won a second championship three years after that. In 2011, Epstein moved on to the Chicago Cubs, who, in 2016, won their first championship in 108 years, ending the longest drought in baseball history.

The following year, on a bright Monday afternoon in May, Epstein delivered the commencement address at Yale, his alma mater.

"Early in my career," he said, "I used to think of players as assets, statistics on a spreadsheet which I could use to project future performance and measure precisely how much they were going to impact our team on the field. I used to think of teams as portfolios, diversified collections of player assets, paid to produce up to their projections to ensure the organization's success. My head had been down.

"That narrow approach worked for a while, but it certainly had its limits. I grew, and my team-building philosophy grew as well. The truth, as our team proved in Cleveland [the Cubs' World Series opponent], is that a player's character matters. The heartbeat matters. Fears and aspirations matter. The player's impact on others matters. The tone he sets matters. The willingness to connect matters. Breaking down cliques and overcoming stereotypes matters. Who you are, how you live among others, that all matters."[5]

This shift in thinking isn't about questioning the usefulness of analytics. Analytics are essential. They reveal patterns in individual and team performances that are not apparent simply through observation. They tell us what is actually happening over time, reducing misreads and distortions caused by inevitable human bias. Teams are right to stock their front offices with mathematical wizards who can unearth the weaknesses of rivals and detect their own.

But businesses and organizations that rely *too* heavily on analytics risk undermining the performances they're trying to elevate. Overusing statistics is as problematic as not using them at all.

"Humans are great optimizers. We look at everything around us, whether a cow, a house, or a share portfolio and ask ourselves how we can manage it to get the best return," Australian environmentalists David Salt and Brian Walker explain in their book *Resilience Thinking.*

"Our *modus operandi* is to break the thing we're managing down into its component parts and understand how each part functions and what inputs will yield the greatest outputs.... [But] the more you optimize elements of a complex system of humans and nature for some specific goal, the more you diminish that system's resilience. [It] has the effect of making the total system more vulnerable to shocks and disturbances."[6]

Human beings, as psychiatrist Thomas Lewis put it, do not yield to the reductionist's knife.

Look at a current trend in baseball pitching. The data show that pitchers give up more hits the third time they cycle through an opponent's lineup. The theory is that the hitters have adjusted to the pitchers' speed and movements and thus have increased their likelihood of connecting with a pitch. This has spawned two new strategies. Teams will remove their starting pitchers before the third time through the lineup, usually around the sixth inning, and bring in a relief pitcher. Or they use an "opener," a relief pitcher who faces the top hitters in the first inning (and sometimes second). The regular starter then comes in and can pitch deeper into the game.

A few runs surely are saved here and there, which may result in a win or two. But in the long run, this strategy can fragilize a team. Starters are starters for a reason. They're the rare guys who *want* to carry a team on their back. They live to compete. If pitchers are regularly yanked by the sixth inning, they can start to believe they're not capable of anything more. It's similar to kids who are so coddled they develop what's known as "learned helplessness." Without the experiences of fighting through rough patches, pitchers can begin to lose the warrior mentality that invigorated not just them but their teammates. For home games, starting pitchers commence play by leading the team onto the field like a commander in battle. When a team opts for an opener, the starter watches from the bench as someone else leads the troops. He can't throw a complete game, much less a no-hitter or a perfect game. He is denied the exhilaration of fully exercising his talent and testing his heart. The most extraordinary and heroic part of himself flakes away. In the future, will we still witness stirring moments like Madison Bumgarner striding from the center-field bullpen for the Giants in Game 7 of the 2014 World Series, throwing five innings in relief on just two days' rest, hurling pitch after furious pitch until the final out, defying every algorithm?

Analytics are a tool. Like a wrench or a hammer, they have a specific function, which is to shape strategy. They cannot carry out the strategy. Only humans can do that. This is where analytics-obsessed leaders can lose their way. They produce a game plan so dazzling and innovative, they're blinded to the human side of the equation: Who is *executing* it? If their brilliant minds fail to foster a motivated, committed, collaborative workforce, they doom the success they're working so hard to achieve. They're drowning in information but starving for wisdom, as E. O. Wilson says.

After blowing the 31-point lead to the Clippers, the Warriors survived that round and the next against the Houston Rockets, and they headed to Portland to play the Trail Blazers in the Western Conference Finals. Winning would not be easy: Durant was sidelined indefinitely with a calf strain.

There's an ethos in team sports that players "pick up" a teammate who is injured, in a slump, or has failed in a big moment. They try to boost their own performance to make up for the shortfall in production and thus relieve the teammate's feelings of letting everyone down.

With Durant out, Green pushed his game to the next level. He had dropped twenty-three pounds in March in preparation, and it was paying off. Green was indefatigable, pushing the pace, pumping up tired teammates, scrambling for loose balls, hauling down rebounds. But the change in him was more than physical. He wasn't carrying on as he usually did. Almost no screaming at the refs. Hardly any kicks or punches to his opponents' nether regions. One night in Portland, Green had twenty points, thirteen rebounds, and twelve assists—a stat line known in basketball as a triple-double. It was his third of the postseason after notching zero in the regular season. Nearly as impressive, he committed just three fouls, two turnovers, and no technicals. Green apparently felt confident enough in his newfound discipline to allow ESPN to wire him with a microphone that night. At one point, he made a perfect pass to a young teammate named Jordan Bell, who flubbed the breakaway dunk. Moments later, Green appeared to be yelling at Bell. But thanks to ESPN's mic, we know what he actually said: "It's OK. You missed a shot. All of us have. Nobody's perfect."

Green had rarely, if ever, performed better. "He's playing with discipline. He's playing under control. He's not letting anything bother him: officiating, bad shots, turnovers," Kerr said after the game. "He's just moving on to the next play." Klay Thompson called Green's stat line "ridiculous." Curry marveled that "it's like he's got eight eyeballs. He sees everything."

Then, in the midst of this, Green did something remarkable, though few beyond the Warriors faithful probably took any notice. But it was a raw, honest glimpse into one of the hidden strengths of this championship team: the transformative power of its relationships.

On one of the best nights of his career, Green chose to revisit one of his worst. In front of television cameras and the national press, he laid bare his sins and his regrets about his early-season attack on Durant.

"I realized I got to a point where I was doing more crying than playing," Green admitted. "I'm sure it was disgusting to watch, because I felt disgusting playing that way." He had reviewed clips of himself pouting and blowing up at referees. "I was like, 'Wow, that's embarrassing.'"

He said his fiancé, mother, and even his young son influenced him to take a hard look at his behavior. But his self-examination began at a table in Dallas over a bottle of Spanish wine.

"It's funny because when the stuff happened with Kevin this year," Green said, "everyone just laughed like, 'Oh, that's just Draymond. He's emotional.' Kevin said to me, 'You're not emotional, I've seen you locked in and not say a word to the referees. So I'm not giving you that pass.' That stuck with me."

It would not have been unprecedented in the world of elite team sports for Green and Durant to have nurtured their righteous anger for the rest of the season. Such is the privilege of star athletes. Indeed, the trend among offended NBA stars is to demand, and be granted, a trade to a franchise of their choosing. Durant and Green talked instead. To make this choice, both had to care more about each other and the team than their own wounded feelings. Only in a trusting relationship could Durant have spoken so honestly and could Green have come away wanting to be a better teammate. This was the essence of chemistry: one person elevating another.

Green stayed on fire in the postseason, helping the Warriors sweep the Trail Blazers to reach their fifth NBA Finals. But they fell behind, three games to one, to the Toronto Raptors. Durant hadn't played in thirty-three days. And now his team was one game from losing the championship. After consulting with various doctors and testing himself in practice, Durant decided to play in Game 5.

He looked fresh and smooth, scoring eleven points in twelve minutes and making all three of his three-point attempts.

Then, on what looked like an ordinary crossover move, he suddenly grabbed his right calf and slowly sank to the floor. He had ruptured his Achilles tendon. The Warriors eked out a 106–105 win to stave off elimination. But in Game 6 Klay Thompson tore his ACL. Two cataclysmic injuries to top scorers in two days. "Just brutal," Kerr said. The Raptors returned to Toronto with the championship.

The Warriors' loss was a reminder that just as analytics have their limitations, so does chemistry. Chemistry amplifies talent; it doesn't create it. With Durant absent for all but twelve minutes of the deciding series, and Thompson injured in Game 6, the Warriors simply didn't have enough talent on the floor to win.

Within days of the loss, Durant signed with the Brooklyn Nets, with whom two of his closest friends, Kyrie Irving and DeAndre Jordan, would also sign. Soon afterward, Andre Iguodala was traded, and Shaun Livingston was waived. In quick succession, three key contributors to the team's championships were gone.

Those exuberant photos in the Warriors' lobby, which told the story of a franchise flourishing just months earlier, suddenly had the whiff of nostalgia. Alex Ferguson, Manchester United's longtime coach, believed the life span of a successful team is about four years, which suggests that if success and other disruptions don't tear a team apart, time always will. Because team chemistry is a largely physiological phenomenon, it can't last. People change over time, so our impact on others changes, too. We lose energy, or show up with a different type of energy. Our bodies start to betray us, and we no longer perform as we did. Our minds go to dark places. Teammates or workmates drift apart, weary of their roles.

Kerr knew, of course, as I sat with him at the practice facility in Oakland months before Durant, Iguodala, and Livingston were gone, that he would have a less talented team the following season. He would be coaching a team made up mostly of players aged twenty-five and under, a new experience for him. He would have to recalibrate game strategies to fit their talents and experience, and be the mixologist of a new chemistry. He would build it around Curry, Green, and Thompson, whom Kerr identified as the Super-Carrier, the Sparkplug/Enforcer, and the Jester, respectively.* They are masters at weaving invisible threads through the team and, day by day, tugging them tighter. The chemistry will be different. Over time, as the players come to know each other and care about each other, the locker room will be awash in a new brew of hormones and neuropeptides, a new interplay of voices and faces and demeanors that will lift or demoralize, energize or deflate. Maybe Green will emerge as the Sage, taking over Iguodala's role. Perhaps players who aren't yet in a Golden State uniform

---

* Kerr said of Thompson, who is a seemingly unlikely choice as Jester: "He's so quiet with the media but has this great, subtle sense of humor. Everyone loves Klay. He keeps everybody laughing."

will fill Livingston's shoes as the Buddy and Durant's as the Warrior. If the web of relationships becomes strong enough, the team will produce what it needs.

"Basketball is a great metaphor for anything," Kerr said. "Five guys all doing slightly different things. If you had five guys who do the same things it wouldn't work that well. And the reason our team works well is the puzzle fits, the pieces of the puzzle fit. Different talents, different skill levels, different skill sets—they all complement one another.

"To me that's the beauty of team sports. The energy that's generated by playing for each other is much more gratifying than playing for yourself."

When Kerr excused himself for his daily meeting with the press, and I rose to leave, the second-stringers were still on the practice court, fooling around now, taking ridiculous shots. I looked over at the bench. Steph Curry was still there, laughing and needling the guys, stomping his feet in delight as they needled him back, making no move to leave.

WHAT I KNOW NOW

I began this project nearly a decade ago with three questions: Does team chemistry exist? If it exists, what is it? And how does it affect performance? I answer these questions throughout the book, of course, but I revisit them here to offer a straightforward and distilled version.

Does team chemistry exist?

Some have answered this question by quantifying chemistry. Professors Kate Bezrukova and Chester Spell, you might remember, tried to crack the code by looking at "fault lines" between demographic groups. Teams with lots of overlap between different groups (veterans/rookies or American/foreign players, for example) performed better than groups with little or no overlap. According to their algorithm, good chemistry on a major-league baseball team is worth four wins over the course of 162 games. *ESPN The Magazine* invited the professors before the 2014 season to predict the World Series champion. Their answer: Tampa Bay over St. Louis in six games. Instead, San Francisco beat Kansas City in seven. Despite smart hypotheses and careful calculations, reliable results were doomed from the start. The study focused only on sociological factors, with data collected mostly from media reports. We now know that chemistry is the interplay of biological, psychological, and sociological forces, and data has to come from real people in real time, a near-impossible undertaking.

In another stab at quantifying, UC Berkeley researchers tried to predict the performance of NBA teams based on how often players touched each other (high fives, hugs, fist bumps, etc.). Touch is an indicator of bonding, and bonding has been shown to improve group performance. The researchers counted and coded touches from one game of every team early in the 2007–2008 NBA season. They predicted that high-touch teams would be more successful. By season's end, the numbers showed that high-touch teams were 2.3 times more likely to win their division than low-touch teams, controlling for injuries and other variables.[1] Like the fault-line study, the data here is unavoidably limited: the researchers could only code touches visible on the TV screen, and only for one game, thus missing interactions in the locker room, on the team plane, or on the practice court.

To overcome at least some of these limitations, another UC Berkeley researcher tried a different tactic. For several games during the 2017 baseball season, Hooria Jazaieri lashed two tiny GoPro cameras to the corners of the dugout roof at San Jose Municipal Stadium, home of the Giants' single-A team. She positioned a third camera atop the visiting team's dugout, pointed at the home dugout. This allowed her to see all the players during the entire game. For games she didn't attend, she recorded them off MiLB.TV, Minor League Baseball's streaming service. Then she enlisted fellow grad students to tackle the Herculean task of coding the thousands of interactions among the players.

The live GoPro recordings were just one part of Jazaieri's attempt to quantify chemistry's impact on performance. She sent emails to all two thousand writers and broadcasters listed in Major League Baseball's 2017 annual media guide; she wanted their picks for best and worst team-chemistry players. More than a few responded that team chemistry wasn't real and she was wasting everybody's time. Forty-seven gave answers, which resulted in a list of 101 major-league players, of whom only 67 made opening-day rosters. Jazaieri used opening-day television footage of all 67 players and coded their behavior on the field and in the dugout. It takes three hours to code one player in one game, whether from the GoPro cameras or television broadcasts. And each player must be coded by three different coders in order to minimize bias. So for the 67 major-league players, that's 201 separate coding sessions (67x3) for a total of 603 (201x3) work hours. Oh, and she also interviewed the minor-league players and collected surveys during the season.

"This is why nobody does this," Jazaieri joked one day when I met up with her at the San Jose ballpark.

And after all that work? Now a postdoctoral research fellow at the Kellogg School of Management at Northwestern University, she decided there wasn't enough data to draw a meaningful conclusion. She has put the project aside for the moment. "Without another team or another season," she said, "there's no basis for comparison."

I made my own feeble attempts to measure chemistry's effect on performance. With the help of a bright, young Harvard grad who loves analytics and had briefly worked at a major-league team, we attacked the puzzle from a variety of angles. We looked at how many players had career years when they played on good-chemistry teams (controlling for injury and age) and tried to calculate how many wins those performances produced. We charted winning and losing streaks to see if good chemistry extends winning streaks and limits losing streaks, thus resulting in more overall wins. We looked at teams whose win-loss records exceeded their preseason projected records to see if, after controlling for variables, the remaining difference could be attributed to chemistry. We couldn't be sure.

After many months, we recognized it was a fool's errand to measure chemistry the way sabermetricians measure performance. The difference between the two is the difference between measuring speed and measuring love. It is time to end the argument that chemistry isn't real because it can't be quantified. Quantification has nothing to do with what is real. Was light less real before astronomers could measure its waves and calculate its speed? Of course not. Maybe someday we will have the tools to measure chemistry. But measurement won't make chemistry real, only measurable.

So let's move on to how we know team chemistry *is* real.

One, team chemistry lines up with already established knowledge. Humans are open-loop creatures, truly interdependent beings. We are made whole from the outside in. We influence each other's breathing, hormones, heart rate, metabolism, energy, emotions, sleep, productivity—everything. Our oversized, social brains are brilliant at interpreting the tiniest shift in tone of voice, the most fleeting twitch of a facial muscle. We recalibrate our own voices and facial muscles in return, triggering feelings of anxiety or calm, suspicion or trust, disgust or happiness. Virtually everything about us is contagious, from how we mirror the furrowing of a friend's eyebrows to how we're lifted by a coworker's passion and spark. Short of solitary confinement, there is no escaping the profound influence of other people on every aspect of our lives.

Two, we know chemistry exists because we have experienced it ourselves—with our families, among our closest friends, at our jobs, churches, temples, and mosques. We feel it perhaps most acutely in adulthood when we watch sports in a packed stadium. The bond we feel with the team and our fellow fans "lifts us out of ourselves in a collective euphoria," as E. O. Wilson said.[2] The experience taps into our longing for tribe, for something larger than ourselves. We literally feel we're part of the team, so much so that we wear the same jerseys the players wear—and with *their* names on the backs, not our own.

A third reason we know chemistry exists is the testimony of coaches and players, the ones witnessing and experiencing the phenomenon. If enough experts in a particular industry arrive at the same conclusion about a topic related to *their* industry, maybe we ought to believe them. As the nineteenth-century biologist Thomas Huxley said, "Science is simply common sense at its best."

What is team chemistry?

To arrive at a definition, I first needed to be clear about team chemistry's function.

At first I thought chemistry's function was to increase effort. Over time I realized this isn't always true. Sometimes effort is driven by stress and fear. I remember watching a star player try to snap himself out of a batting slump by taking hundreds of swings in the batting cage before every game. The slump deepened. He was exhausted when the game began. So, while he gave Herculean effort in the cage and on the field, his body was spent and his mind gripped by doubt and anxiety.

So effort, on its own, was not chemistry's function.

Maybe chemistry's function is to bring together *all* the elements of winning, including effort. But really: *all* the elements? Analytics and talent are important elements of winning, and they have nothing to do with chemistry.

Chemistry's function needed to be more precise, like the

function of a knife or a chair or a relief pitcher. I looked back on descriptions I had collected during my research:

> "Chemistry is everybody doing their job and taking pride in their job and holding each other accountable."—former player and Washington Nationals manager Matt Williams
>
> "The best way I heard it described—it's a pretty corny concept—but it's basically trust and caring among teammates."—Hall of Fame manager Tony La Russa
>
> "[It is] an eagerness to sacrifice personal glory for the welfare of the group as a whole.... It is not necessary for everyone to particularly like each other to play well together, but they must respect each other and subordinate selfishness to the welfare of the team."—UCLA basketball coach John Wooden, describing "team spirit"

More than a few people, stumped to find the right words, simply said, "You know it when you have it."

Maybe chemistry's function, then, is to deepen trust and selflessness. But this is a bit like saying a knife's function is to be sharp. Sharpness is an attribute of a knife; its function is to cut. That is its only function. Trust and selflessness are attributes of chemistry. What is chemistry's only function, its purpose for existing?

The answer was suddenly obvious.

The function of team chemistry is to elevate performance. That's it.

No matter how much fun the players have together, how many secret handshakes and inside jokes, if performance does not improve, the team does not have chemistry. In sports, chemistry is often used interchangeably with camaraderie. In business, it's often referred to as cohesion. Both are wrong. Camaraderie describes a group's fellowship. Cohesion describes a state of being.

Both are static. Chemistry is active. It produces a change in the work product. To be clear: *There is no team chemistry if there is no improvement in the work product.*

Once I identified chemistry's function, I could formulate a definition.

I went through dozens of iterations and arrived here:

Team chemistry is an interplay of physiological, social, and emotional forces that elevates performance.

Note that team chemistry does not produce *high* performance, but rather *elevated* performance. High performance requires a certain amount of talent. Chemistry cannot manufacture talent, but it ignites the talent the team *does* have, getting the most from every player and boosting performance.

This definition surely will evolve as we learn more about the workings of the brain. We might find that emotions, like light, travel on invisible waves of energy. Or that, as with ants, they travel on pheromones embedded with complex social information honed during millennia of evolution. Maybe someday we'll discover how to "see" and quantify these interactions. Writer Roger Rosenblatt pointed out in the *New York Times* a couple of years ago how the most profound influences on our lives are rarely visible: "Magnetic fields, electric currents, the force of gravity all work unseen, as do our interior arbiters of thoughts, inclinations, passions, psyches, tastes, moods, morals, and—if one believes in them—souls. The invisible world governs the visible like a hidden nation-state."[3]

How does team chemistry affect performance?

It would be so simple if skill alone determined performance. We could devise tests and hire people with the top scores. If this approach worked in any occupation, it would be sports. Every athlete's performance is quantified and recorded. You should be able to fill a team roster without knowing anything about an athlete beyond his or her stat sheet and medical report. In fact, many teams *have* taken this route, particularly in choosing Olympic and world-championship squads, with mixed results.

Russia's Olympic hockey coach loaded his 2014 team with the highest-scoring players in the country, the most dominant players he could find. They lost in a shocker to the less talented but more cohesive Finns. America's 2004 men's Olympic basketball "Dream Team," with LeBron James, Carmelo Anthony, Tim Duncan, Dwyane Wade, and Allen Iverson, lost to Puerto Rico by nineteen points in their opening game. "Humiliated by minnows," one headline blared. The Dream Team lost twice more, to Lithuania and Argentina, and ended up with the bronze medal.

"You just had to shake your head," Wade told reporters later. "Everybody on that team was a good individual player, but when you tried to put it together, it didn't work. It was like a bad mix of food.... We were fighting against each other because everybody wanted to play."

There's a 2014 study out of Columbia called "The Too-Much-Talent Effect."[4] The researchers found that talent increases performance only up to a point, especially in heavily interdependent sports like basketball and soccer. Then the benefit of talent decreases, and the effect eventually turns negative. Dominant players jockey for status, much like chickens in a coop. Poultry scientists have found that too many high-egg-producing chickens leads to increased fighting over food and space, driving egg production down. The phenomenon has been observed on Wall Street, too. A 2011 Harvard study found that too many high-status equity research analysts in a single office disrupts cooperation and hurts the group's overall performance.[5]

Obviously, teams with lots of talent win regularly. Every American basketball "Dream Team" since the 1992 Olympics has won the gold except that one in 2004. Still, it's worth noting how US Olympic hockey coach Herb Brooks chose the 1980 "Miracle on Ice" team. Instead of loading up on All-Stars, he chose units of players who knew each other well: one group from his own team at the University of Minnesota and another from Boston University. He wanted forward lines that trusted and understood each other. He also rode them hard. He believed if players disliked him more than they disliked each other, they would develop tighter bonds and, he hoped, a kind of chemistry that summons greatness.

No entity has studied the impact of bonding and trust on performance more than the military. The research supports what soldiers have contended for hundreds of years: Teams whose members trust and feel connected to each other perform better. "Without this trust," General Stanley McChrystal has said, "SEAL teams would just be a collection of fit soldiers."

We know that in a trusting, accepting culture, scrap-heap players like Aubrey Huff and Pat Burrell can flourish, as they did on the 2010 Giants. Though hardly a scrap-heap player, Teresa Edwards played some of the best basketball of her career on the 1996 Olympic basketball team. Once she and coach Tara VanDerveer fully accepted and trusted each other, the veteran player became the beating heart of the greatest women's basketball team in history. In the squad's gold-medal game against Brazil, Edwards and her teammates achieved near perfection. In an individual athlete, this is called a "flow state."[6] Self-confidence, focus, and an utter absence of fear combine for a feeling of complete physical and mental ease. When this flow state encompasses an entire team, it's a fair description of chemistry.

The players on such teams respond to stressful situations as challenges instead of threats. As I know now, their brains release hormones that cause their blood vessels to open up, delivering the extra blood into their brains and muscles, priming them for battle. They feel emboldened to take risks that push their performance to the next level; they know, even if they fail, their tribe will stand with them.

When we're surrounded by people who believe in us, we almost can't help but believe in ourselves. Our bodies deliver on what our minds believe. If we believe that a Super-Carrier like Jonny Gomes elevates the entire team, performance can actually improve, as the 2013 Boston Red Sox will tell you.

We know, for example, that a teacher's expectations of a student's ability affect how the student performs. A surgeon's mood impacts the quality of his work. We know that social conversation with coworkers, as at that Bank of America call center, has a greater impact on productivity than all other factors—individual intelligence, personality, skill, and the substance of discussions—combined.

I know now that teams, like individuals, are complex organisms. Their components do not interact with each other in a precise, prescribed manner. Behavior that ruins chemistry and hurts performance on one team might have little effect on another. That's why we sometimes see openly hostile teams still perform well enough to win championships. They have awful social chemistry but spectacular task chemistry. They completely trust each other to compete hard on the field.

No team wins without task chemistry. But almost all championship teams also have social chemistry—the bonding, trust, and caring. This is what players carry into the batter's box and onto the free-throw line. They know they're not alone. Their teammates are there, summoning something deeper and stronger that they couldn't summon for themselves, as Jake Peavy put it.

Human nature plays out in infinitely varied and unpredictable ways, and so must the dynamics of team chemistry. Each team is its own superorganism. Chemistry in football and basketball, soccer and hockey, will play out differently from chemistry in baseball because of the nature of the sport and the number of players. Same for workplaces. Chemistry on male teams and female teams plays out somewhat differently because of cultural norms and gender-specific biochemistry, though the differences are not profound.

The influence of the seven archetype characters will vary in every good-chemistry group because they're shaped by what that particular team needs. Thus, people cannot be hired to "fit" an archetype. They emerge, quite literally, from the chemical reaction of a team's unique makeup. In other words, archetypes cannot be inserted into a group to *create* the chemistry. Their emergence is both evidence of chemistry and a fortifier of it, deepening trust and infusing energy.

Serendipity plays a role, too, in gathering enough right people at the right time with the right leader. Their unique brew of hormones, personalities, emotions, and experiences lifts their performance to another level. And this brew is constantly changing as members come and go, as moods shift and disruptions hit. "One year you're capable of finishing each other's sentences and the next it all unwinds," said Doug Smith, a founder of start-up tech company Anaplan. "People show up differently. They step out of their roles. You change one element, and there's a good chance a lot of other things will change with it." That goes both ways, of course. You change one element, and suddenly things change for the better. Jonny Gomes happens to walk through the door—or Sue Bird or Mike Krukow—and you have a different team.

Day in and day out, on the field or in the workplace, we count on other people to stir our emotions, boost our energy, give us something to fight for. I know now that on great team-chemistry teams, meaning and purpose evolve beyond winning gold medals or even making history. Your teammates become the meaning and purpose. You feel the joy and exhilaration of being part of a truly connected, focused, driven group. There is a sense of completeness, of being the perfect you in this moment, with these exact people, in this exact quest.

ACKNOWLEDGMENTS

I dedicate this book to Mike Krukow, because during those long days when I'd lose my way in the mounds of research, I'd picture him. He embodies everything I hoped to capture on these pages. We forged a friendship almost from the day I met him in the Candlestick Park clubhouse in 1985. Lucky, lucky me.

My acknowledgments are many. I've tried to include everyone whose work or ideas helped to shape this book. To anyone I failed to credit, I apologize and ask you to contact me (joan@joanry anink.com) so I can include your contribution in the paperback edition.

I am extremely grateful to my longtime agent, Betsy Lerner, whose tenacity and belief in the book (and me) never flagged, and whose wise counsel and soothing voice pulled me from the brink more than once. Thank you to Glenn Schwarz, who helped conceive and guide the book, and to Ken Conner and Robert Rosenthal, who regularly read drafts and kept reminding me I was onto something.

Thank you to other early readers: Jeff Appleman, Roy Eisenhardt, Suzanne Engelberg, Jennie MacDonald, Elise Magers, Ray Ratto, Doug Smith, and Lorna Stevens-Smith.

Thanks to my tribe of friends and family, especially my son, Ryan, and stepdaughters Andi and Lainie. You all always have my back. You know how much I love you.

ACKNOWLEDGMENTS

Thanks to editor Phil Marino and the team at Little, Brown, particularly Ira Boudah, Sabrina Callahan, Alyssa Persons, Craig Young, and Betsy Uhrig.

Thanks also to the San Francisco Giants, especially Staci Slaughter, for giving me time when I needed it.

And one special acknowledgment to my genius friend Brandon Belt for coming up with *Intangibles* as the title.

As always, thank you to my husband, Barry, because nothing works without you, and because my best days start by talking with you over coffee and end by talking with you over cocktails. In our thirty-five-year (and counting) conversation, we have yet to run out of material.

I am deeply indebted to the many, many people who lit my path, sharing their experiences and expertise, interpreting complex studies, and helping me puzzle through some theory or another:

Jeremy Affeldt, Sandy Alderson, Mike Aldrete, Craig Anderson, Melanie Arenson, Jennifer Azzi, Larry Baer, Andrew Baggarly, Dusty Baker, Harry Barker-Fost, Dylan Barr, Erin Becker, McKenna Becker, Rob Becker, Brandon Belt, Corinne Bendersky, Marvin Bernard, Katrina Bezrukova, Kevin Bickart, Bud Black, Bruce Bochy, Ruthie Bolton, MaeOla Bolton, Barry Bonds, Scott Brave, Bob Brenly, Ellis Burks, Brett Butler, Andrew Butters, Matt Cain, Carol Callan, Kathleen Casto, Mick Chantler, Will Clark, Ned Colletti, Stan Conte, Roger Craig, Brandon Crawford, Johnny Damon, Hugh Delahenty, Anson Dorrance, Kelly Downs, Dave Dravecky, Shawon Dunston, Bobby Evans, Gail Evenari, Mark Eys, Leland Faust, Gary Alan Fine, Rollie Fingers, Kevin Frandsen, Laura Fraser, Micky Freeman, Mike Gallego, Mark Gardner, Phil Garner, Scott Garrelts, Conor Gillaspie, Yeshayah Goldfarb, Jonny Gomes, Pedro Gomez, Hank Greenwald, Stewart Hauser, Geoff Head, Keith Hernandez, Rich Hill, Matt Hovde, Aubrey Huff,

ACKNOWLEDGMENTS

Clint Hurdle, Bruce Jenkins, Jill Kantola, Luke Kantola, Steve Kantola, Jeff Kent, Steve Kerr, Pam Kerwin, Ann Killion, Steve Kline, George Kontos, Mark Kraus, Tim Kurkjian, Mike LaCoss, Norma LaRosa, Tony La Russa, Craig Lefferts, Jeff Leonard, Mark Letendre, Bret Levine, Thomas Lewis, Jim Leyland, Greg Litton, Javier Lopez, Bob Lurie, Joe Maddon, Charlie Manuel, Kirt Manwaring, Jan McAdoo, Brandon McCarthy, General Stanley McChrystal, Bob Melvin, Jordan Miller, Kevin Mitchell, Bengie Molina, Jeff Moorad, Michael Morse, Brandon Moss, Mike Murphy, Phil Nevin, Ken Oberkfell, Jarrett Parker, John Parsley, Alex Pavlovic, Jake Peavy, Hunter Pence, Dave Perron, Piero Procaccini, Dave Roberts, Kevin Roberts, Don Robinson, Jimmy Rollins, Al Rosen, Cody Ross, Justin Ruggiano, Brian Sabean, Henry Schulman, Mike Scioscia, Corey Seager, Second City Improv, Michael Shapiro, John Shea, Jeremy Shelley, Chris Speier, Chester Spell, Dave Stewart, Mark Sutton, Bob Tewksbury, Justin Turner, Tara VanDerveer, Ryan Vogelsong, Jayson Werth, Matt Williams, Randy Winn, Josh Woolley, Ron Wotus, and Paul Zak.

NOTES

Introduction

1. Dacher Keltner, *Born to Be Good: The Science of a Meaningful Life* (New York: W.W. Norton, 2009).
2. Rene A. Spitz, "Hospitalism: An Inquiry into the Genesis of Psychiatric Conditions in Early Childhood," *The Psychoanalytic Study of the Child* 1, no. 1 (1945): 53–74; Rene A. Spitz and Katherine M. Wolf, "Anaclitic Depression: An Inquiry into the Genesis of Psychiatric Conditions in Early Childhood, II," *The Psychoanalytic Study of the Child* 2, no. 1 (1946): 313–42.
3. H. F. Harlow, R. O. Dodsworth, and M. K. Harlow, "Total Social Isolation in Monkeys," *PNAS* 54, no. 1 (1965): 90–97.
4. Giuseppe di Pellegrino et al., "Understanding Motor Events: A Neurophysiological Study," *Experimental Brain Research* 91, no. 1 (1992): 176–80; Vittorio Gallese et al., "Action Recognition in the Premotor Cortex," *Brain* 119, no. 2 (1996): 593–609.
5. Christian Keysers et al., "A Touching Sight: SII/PV Activation During the Observation and Experience of Touch," *Neuron* 42, no. 2 (2004): 335–46.

Chapter One: You Complete Me

1. Robin Dunbar, "The Social Role of Touch in Humans and Primates: Behavioural Function and Neurobiological Mechanisms," *Neuroscience & Biobehavioral Reviews* 34, no. 2 (2010): 260–68.

Chapter Two: The Arrowleaf

1. Scott S. Wiltermuth and Chip Heath, "Synchrony and Cooperation," *Psychological Science* 20, no. 1 (2009): 1–5.
2. Dora L. Costa and Matthew E. Kahn, "Health, Wartime Stress, and Unit Cohesion: Evidence from Union Army Veterans," *Demography* 47, no. 1 (2010): 45–66.
3. Adam Bernacchio, "The Pat Burrell Era Ends In Tampa Bay," *Bleacher Report*, May 17, 2010, https://bleacherreport.com/articles/393131-the-pat-burrell-era-ends-in-tampa-bay.

4. Jean-Claude Dreher et al., "Testosterone Causes Both Prosocial and Antisocial Status-Enhancing Behaviors in Human Males," *PNAS* 113, no. 41 (2016): 11633–38.

5. Pranjal Mehta and Robert A. Josephs, "Testosterone and Cortisol Jointly Regulate Dominance: Evidence for a Dual-Hormone Hypothesis," *Hormones and Behavior* 58, no. 5 (2010): 898–906.

6. Kathleen V. Casto, David K. Hamilton, and David A Edwards, "Testosterone and Cortisol Interact to Predict Within-Team Social Status Hierarchy among Olympic-Level Women Athletes," *Adaptive Human Behavior and Physiology* 5, no. 3 (2019): 237–50.

7. Gary Alan Fine and Michaela de Soucey, "Joking Cultures: Humor Themes as Social Regulation in Group Life," *International Journal of Humor Research* 18, no. 1 (2005): 122.

Chapter Three: Super-Carriers, or the Curious Case of Jonny Gomes

1. Sam Walker, "The Art of Winning Everywhere," *Wall Street Journal*, September 8, 2018.

2. John Wooden and Jack Tobin, *They Call Me Coach* (New York: McGraw-Hill, 2004).

Chapter Four: Super-Disruptors, or the Curiouser Case of Barry Bonds

1. *Simple Sabotage Field Manual: Strategic Services (Provisional)*, prepared by the US Office of Strategic Services (Washington, DC, 1944), https://www.cia.gov/news-information/featured-story-archive/2012-featured-story-archive/CleanedUOSSSimpleSabotage_sm.pdf.

2. Roy F. Baumeister et al., "Bad Is Stronger Than Good," *Review of General Psychology* 5, no. 4 (2001): 323–70.

3. Dacher Keltner, *Born to Be Good: The Science of a Meaningful Life* (New York: W.W. Norton, 2009).

4. Jay Jaffe, "Prospectus Hit and Run: Overachieving Yet Again," *Baseball Prospectus*, September 15, 2009, https://www.baseballprospectus.com/news/article/9529/prospectus-hit-and-run-overachieving-yet-again/.

5. Katerina Bezrukova et al., "The Effects of Alignments: Examining Group Faultlines, Organizational Cultures, and Performance," *Journal of Applied Psychology* 97, no. 1 (2012): 77–92; Katerina Bezrukova and Chester Spell, "Cracking Under Pressure: A Context-Centered Attention-Based Perspective on Faultlines," *International Association for Conflict Management*, Leiden, Netherlands (2014).

6. Thomas J. DeLong and Vineeta Vijayaraghavan, "Cirque du Soleil," Harvard Business School Case 403-006 (2002).

7. David Grann, "Baseball Without Metaphor," *New York Times Magazine*, September 1, 2002.

8. *The Lost Interview of the Great Ted Williams,* hosted by Bob Lobel (Las Vegas: DK Productions, 2009), DVD.

9. Richard Hoffer, "It's Time to Play the Feud!" *Sports Illustrated,* July 2, 2007.

10. Joan S. Ingalls, "Mental Training: Building Team Cohesion," *Rowing News* 5, no. 16 (1998): 23.

11. Hans Lenk, "Top Performance Despite Internal Conflict: An Antithesis to a Functionalistic Proposition," in *Sport, Culture, and Society: A Reader on the Sociology of Sports,* eds. John W. Loy and Gerald S. Kenyon (Toronto: Collier-Macmillan, 1969), pp. 393–96.

12. Anita Elberse, "Ferguson's Formula," *Harvard Business Review,* October 2013, https://hbr.org/2013/10/fergusons-formula/ar/1.

13. Amy Langfield, "How California Can Save Water and Beat the Drought: Psychology," *MoneyWatch,* May 18, 2015; Paul J. Ferraro and Michael K. Price, "Using Nonpecuniary Strategies to Influence Behavior: Evidence from a Large-Scale Field Experiment," *Review of Economics and Statistics* 95, no. 1 (2013): 64–73.

Chapter Five: The Seven Archetypes

1. Theo Epstein, "Class Day Remarks" (speech, Yale University, New Haven, CT, May 21, 2017), https://news.yale.edu/sites/default/files/d6_files/imce/Yale%20Class%20Day.pdf.

2. Shanti Fader, "A Fool's Hope," *Parabola Magazine* 26, no. 3 (2001): 48–52.

3. Dacher Keltner, *Born to Be Good: The Science of a Meaningful Life* (New York: W.W. Norton, 2009)

4. Robin Dunbar, "The Social Role of Touch in Humans and Primates: Behavioural Function and Neurobiological Mechanisms," *Neuroscience & Biobehavioral Reviews* 34, no. 2 (2010): 260–68.

5. Cassandra J. Cope et al., "Informal Roles on Sport Teams," *International Journal of Sport and Exercise Psychology* 9, no. 1 (2011): 19–30.

Chapter Six: Just Us

1. Adam M. Grant, "Employees Without a Cause: The Motivational Effects of Prosocial Impact in Public Service," *International Public Management Journal* 11, no. 1 (2008): 48–66.

2. Barry Schwartz, "Rethinking Work," *New York Times,* August 28, 2015, https://www.nytimes.com/2015/08/30/opinion/sunday/rethinking-work.html.

3. Stanley McChrystal, *Team of Teams* (New York: Portfolio / Penguin, 2015), 96.

4. Joachim Hüffmeier and Guido Hertel, "When the Whole Is More Than the Sum of Its Parts: Motivation Gains in the Wild," *Journal of Experimental Social Psychology* 47, no. 2 (2011): 455–59.

5. Emma E. A. Cohen et al., "Rowers' High: Behavioural Synchrony Is Correlated with Elevated Pain Thresholds," *Biology Letters* 6, no. 1 (2010): 106–8.

6. R. H. Roy, "The Canadian Military Tradition," in *The Canadian Military: A Profile,* ed. Hector J. Massey (Toronto: Copp Clark, 1972), pp. 51–65.

7. Sebastian Junger, *War* (New York: Hachette, 2010).

8. Sara Corbett, *Venus to the Hoop* (New York: Anchor Books, 1998).

9. Ibid.

10. Ad Vingerhoets, *Why Only Humans Weep: Unravelling the Mysteries of Tears* (Oxford: Oxford University Press, 2013).

11. Melissa Dahl, "Why Do Women Cry More Than Men?" *New York Magazine,* January 7, 2015, https://www.thecut.com/2015/01/why-do-women-cry-more-than-men.html.

12. Pat Summitt and Sally Jenkins, *Raise the Roof* (New York: Three Rivers Press, 1998).

13. Corbett, *Venus to the Hoop.*

Chapter Seven: Humm-Baby, Kruke, and the Pygmalion Effect

1. Steve Kroner, "20th Anniversary: Brad Gulden / The Original Humm-Baby," *San Francisco Chronicle,* April 9, 2006, https://www.sfgate.com/sports/article/20TH-ANNIVERSARY-Brad-Gulden-The-orginal-The-2537623.php.

2. Robert Rosenthal and Kermit L. Fode, "The Effect of Experimenter Bias on the Performance of the Albino Rat," *Behavioral Science* 8, no. 3 (1963): 183–89.

3. Robert Rosenthal and Lenore Jacobson, "Teachers' Expectancies: Determinants of Pupils' IQ Gains," *Psychological Reports* 19, no. 1 (1966): 115–18.

4. Christine M. Rubie-Davies et al., "A Teacher Expectation Intervention: Modelling the Practices of High Expectation Teachers," *Contemporary Educational Psychology* 40, no. 1 (2015): 72–85.

5. Robert Rosenthal and Elisha Y. Babad, "Pygmalion in the Gymnasium," *Educational Leadership* 43, no. 1 (1985): 36–39, http://www.ascd.org/ASCD/pdf/journals/ed_lead/el_198509_rosenthal.pdf.

6. Stanley McChrystal, *Team of Teams* (New York: Portfolio / Penguin, 2015).

7. Edward N. Lorenz, "Deterministic Nonperiodic Flow," *Journal of the Atmospheric Sciences* 20, no. 2: 130–41.

8. Alex "Sandy" Pentland, "The New Science of Building Great Teams," *Harvard Business Review,* April 2012.

9. Matt Johanson, *Game of My Life: San Francisco Giants* (Champaign, IL: Sports Publishing, 2007).

Chapter Eight: Synthesis

1. Tim Kawakami, "Kawakami: Where Do the Warriors Go from Here? Sketching out the Next (Final?) Chapters of This Novel," *The Athletic,*

November 20, 2018, https://theathletic.com/664495/2018/11/20/kawakami-so-where-do-the-warriors-go-from-here-sketching-out-the-next-and-final-chapters-of-this-mystery-novel/.

2. Marcus Thompson, "Thompson: The Draymond Green/Kevin Durant Reconciliation Took Time and, More Importantly, Maturity and Thoughtfulness," *The Athletic,* January 21, 2019, https://theathletic.com/777906/2019/01/21/thompson-the-draymond-green-kevin-durant-reconciliation-took-time-and-more-importantly-maturity-and-thoughtfulness/.

3. Dacher Keltner, Deborah H. Gruenfeld, and Cameron Anderson, "Power, Approach, and Inhibition," *Psychological Review* 110, no. 2 (2003): 265–84; Michael W. Kraus et al., "Social Class, Solipsism, and Contextualism: How the Rich Are Different from the Poor," *Psychological Review* 119, no. 3 (2012): 546–72.

4. Paul K. Piff et al., "Higher Social Class Predicts Increased Unethical Behavior," *PNAS* 109, no. 11 (2012): 4086–91, https://doi.org/10.1073/pnas.1118373109.

5. Theo Epstein, "Class Day Remarks" (speech, Yale University, New Haven, CT, May 21, 2017), https://news.yale.edu/sites/default/files/d6_files/imce/Yale%20Class%20Day.pdf.

6. Brain Walker and David Salt, *Resilience Thinking* (Washington, DC: Island Press, 2006).

Conclusion: What I Know Now

1. Michael W. Kraus, Cassy Huang, and Dacher Keltner, "Tactile Communication, Cooperation, and Performance: An Ethological Study of the NBA," *Emotion* 10, no. 5 (2010): 745–49.

2. *E. O. Wilson: Of Ants and Men,* directed by Shelley Schulze (PBS / Shining Red Productions, Inc., 2015), DVD.

3. Roger Rosenblatt, "Seen and Unseen," *New York Times Book Review,* August 27, 2017.

4. Roderick I. Swaab et al., "The Too-Much-Talent Effect: Team Interdependence Determines When More Talent Is Too Much or Not Enough," *Psychological Science* 25, no. 8 (2014): 1581–691.

5. Boris Groysberg, Jeffrey T. Polzer, and Hillary Anger Elfenbein, "Too Many Cooks Spoil the Broth: How High-Status Individuals Decrease Group Effectiveness," *Organization Science* 22, no. 3 (2011): 722–37.

6. Paul J. McCarthy, "Positive Emotion in Sport Performance: Current Status and Future Directions," *International Review of Sport and Exercise Psychology* 4, no. 1 (2011): 50–69.

BIBLIOGRAPHY

Baggarly, Andrew. *A Band of Misfits: Tales of the 2010 San Francisco Giants.* Chicago: Triumph, 2011.

Banks, Amy, and Leigh Ann Hirschman. *Wired to Connect: The Surprising Link Between Brain Science and Strong, Healthy Relationships.* New York: Penguin Random House, 2015.

Barondes, Samuel. *Making Sense of People: Decoding the Mysteries of Personality.* Upper Saddle River, New Jersey: FT Press, 2012.

Beilock, Sian. *Choke: What the Secrets of the Brain Reveal About Getting It Right When You Have To.* New York: Free Press, 2010.

Bennis, Warren, and Patricia Ward Biederman. *Organizing Genius: The Secrets of Creative Collaboration.* New York: Perseus, 2007.

Berri, David J., and Martin B. Schmidt. *Stumbling on Wins: Two Economists Expose the Pitfalls on the Road to Victory in Professional Sports.* Upper Saddle River, New Jersey: FT Press, 2010.

Berri, David J., et al. *The Wages of Wins: Taking Measure of the Many Myths in Modern Sport.* Stanford, California: Stanford University Press, 2007.

Bochy, Bruce, et al. *One Common Goal: The Official Inside Story of the Incredible World Champion San Francisco Giants.* Santa Rosa, California: Skybox Press, 2013.

Bolton, Ruthie. *The Ride of a Lifetime: The Making of Mighty Ruthie.* Sacramento, California: Pathworks Publishing, 2012.

Bolton, Ruthie, and Terri Morgan. *From Pain to Power: Surviving & Thriving After an Abusive Marriage.* Sacramento, California: Blanket Marketing Group, 2017.

Brizendine, Louann. *The Male Brain.* New York: Penguin Random House, 2010.

Bronson, Po, and Ashley Merryman. *Top Dog: The Science of Winning and Losing.* New York: Twelve, 2013.

Carroll, Pete, et al. *Win Forever: Live, Work, and Play Like a Champion.* New York: Portfolio / Penguin, 2011.

Catmull, Ed, and Amy Wallace. *Creativity, Inc.: Overcoming the Unseen Forces That Stand in the Way of True Inspiration.* New York: Random House, 2014.

Collins, Jim. *Good to Great: Why Some Companies Make the Leap...and Others Don't*. New York: Harper Business, 2001.

Corbett, Sara. *Venus to the Hoop: A Gold-Medal Year in Women's Basketball*. New York: Anchor Books, 1998.

Cozolino, Louis. *The Neuroscience of Human Relationships: Attachment and the Developing Social Brain*. 2nd ed. New York: W.W. Norton & Company, 2014.

Crothers, Tim. *The Man Watching: Anson Dorrance and the University of North Carolina Women's Soccer Dynasty*. New York: St. Martin's Press, 2010.

Dweck, Carol S. *Mindset: The New Psychology of Success*. New York: Random House, 2008.

Eibl-Eibesfeldt, Irenäus. *Human Ethology*. Piscataway, New Jersey: Transaction Publishers, 1989.

Fainaru-Wada, Mark, and Lance Williams. *Game of Shadows: Barry Bonds, BALCO, and the Steroids Scandal That Rocked Professional Sports*. New York: Penguin, 2007.

Fine, Gary Alan. *With the Boys: Little League Baseball and Preadolescent Culture*. Chicago: University of Chicago Press, 1987.

Frank, Robert H. *Passions Within Reason: The Strategic Role of the Emotions*. New York: W.W. Norton & Company, 1988.

Gewertz, Bruce L., and Dave C. Logan. *The Best Medicine: A Physician's Guide to Effective Leadership*. New York: Springer, 2015.

Goleman, Daniel. *Social Intelligence: The New Science of Human Relationships*. New York: Bantam Books, 2006.

Gordon, John, and Mike Smith. *You Win in the Locker Room First: The 7 C's to Build a Winning Team in Business, Sports, and Life*. Hoboken, New Jersey: John Wiley & Sons, 2015.

Haft, Chris. *If These Walls Could Talk: San Francisco Giants: Stories from the San Francisco Giants Dugout, Locker Room, and Press Box*. Chicago: Triumph, 2017.

Halberstam, David. *The Teammates: A Portrait of a Friendship*. New York: Hyperion, 2003.

Huff, Aubrey, and Stephen Cassar. *Baseball Junkie: The Rise, Fall, and Redemption of a World Series Champion*. DreamGrinder Press, 2017.

Iacoboni, Marco. *Mirroring People: The Science of Empathy and How We Connect with Others*. New York: Picador, 2009.

Jackson, Phil, and Hugh Delahanty. *Eleven Rings: The Soul of Success*. New York: Penguin, 2014.

——. *Sacred Hoops: Spiritual Lessons of a Hardwood Warrior*. New York: Hyperion, 2006.

James, Bill. *The New Bill James Historical Baseball Abstract*. New York: Free Press, 2003.

Junger, Sebastian. *Tribe: On Homecoming and Belonging*. London: HarperCollins, 2016.

——. *War.* New York: Twelve, 2011.

Kaplan, David. *The Plan: Epstein, Maddon, and the Audacious Blueprint for a Cubs Dynasty.* Chicago: Triumph, 2017.

Keltner, Dacher. *Born to Be Good: The Science of a Meaningful Life.* New York: W.W. Norton & Company, 2009.

Kerr, James. *Legacy: What the All Blacks Can Teach Us About the Business of Life.* London: Hachette, 2015.

Lehrer, Jonah. *Proust Was a Neuroscientist.* New York: Houghton Mifflin Harcourt, 2007.

Lencioni, Patrick. *The Five Dysfunctions of a Team: A Leadership Fable.* San Francisco: Jossey-Bass, 2002.

Leonard, Kelly, and Tom Yorton. *Yes, And: How Improvisation Reverses "No, But" Thinking and Improves Creativity and Collaboration.* New York: HarperCollins, 2015.

Lewis, Michael. *Moneyball: The Art of Winning an Unfair Game.* New York: W.W. Norton & Company, 2003.

——. *The Undoing Project: A Friendship That Changed Our Minds.* New York: W.W. Norton & Company, 2017.

Lewis, Thomas, et al. *A General Theory of Love.* New York: Random House, 2001.

Lindbergh, Ben, and Sam Miller. *The Only Rule Is It Has to Work: Our Wild Experiment Building a New Kind of Baseball Team.* New York: Henry Holt and Company, 2016.

Logan, Dave, et al. *Tribal Leadership: Leveraging Natural Groups to Build a Thriving Organization.* New York: HarperCollins, 2011.

Mavraedis, Chris. *Falling in Love with Baseball: A Collection of E-mails and Memories.* Edited by Bob Sockolov. San Francisco: Chronicle Books, 2017.

McChrystal, Stanley, et al. *Leaders: Myth and Reality.* New York: Portfolio / Penguin, 2018.

——. *Team of Teams: New Rules of Engagement for a Complex World.* New York: Portfolio / Penguin, 2015.

McDougall, Christopher. *Born to Run: A Hidden Tribe, Superathletes, and the Greatest Race the World Has Never Seen.* New York: Vintage Books, 2011.

Murphy, Brian. *Worth the Wait.* Santa Rosa, California: Skybox Press, 2011.

Neyer, Rob. *Rob Neyer's Big Book of Baseball Blunders: A Complete Guide to the Worst Decisions and Stupidest Moments in Baseball History.* New York: Simon & Schuster, 2006.

Peta, Joe. *Trading Bases: How a Wall Street Trader Made a Fortune Betting on Baseball.* New York: Penguin Random House, 2013.

Ross, David, and Don Yaeger. *Teammate: My Journey in Baseball and a World Series for the Ages.* New York: Hachette, 2017.

Sherman, Erik. *Kings of Queens: Life Beyond Baseball with the '86 Mets.* New York: Penguin Random House, 2016.

BIBLIOGRAPHY

Summitt, Pat, and Sally Jenkins. *Raise the Roof: The Inspiring Inside Story of the Tennessee Lady Vols' Undefeated 1997–98 Season.* New York: Bantam Doubleday Dell, 1998.

Svrluga, Barry. *The Grind: Inside Baseball's Endless Season.* New York: Penguin Random House, 2015.

Tannen, Deborah. *You Just Don't Understand: Women and Men in Conversation.* New York: HarperCollins, 2007.

Turbow, Jason. *Dynastic, Bombastic, Fantastic: Reggie, Rollie, Catfish, and Charlie Finley's Swingin' A's.* New York: Houghton Mifflin Harcourt, 2017.

VanDerveer, Tara, and Joan Ryan. *Shooting from the Outside: How a Coach and Her Olympic Team Transformed Women's Basketball.* New York: Avon, 1998.

Verducci, Tom. *The Cubs Way: The Zen of Building the Best Team in Baseball.* New York: Penguin Random House, 2017.

Walker, Sam. *The Captain Class: The Hidden Force That Creates the World's Greatest Teams.* New York: Penguin Random House, 2017.

Wertheim, L. Jon, and Sam Sommers. *This Is Your Brain on Sports: The Science of Underdogs, the Value of Rivalry, and What We Can Learn from the T-Shirt Cannon.* New York: Penguin Random House, 2016.

Wilson, Edward O. *Consilience: The Unity of Knowledge.* New York: Random House, 1999.

———. *The Social Conquest of Earth.* New York: Liveright Publishing Corporation, 2013.

Wooden, John, and Jack Tobin. *They Call Me Coach.* New York: McGraw-Hill, 2004.

Zak, Paul J. *The Moral Molecule: How Trust Works.* New York: Penguin Random House, 2013.

———. *Trust Factor: The Science of Creating High-Performance Companies.* New York: American Management Association, 2017.

INDEX

ABOUT THE AUTHOR

JOAN RYAN is an award-winning journalist and the author of five books. Her groundbreaking book *Little Girls in Pretty Boxes* was named one of the Top 100 Sports Books of All Time by *Sports Illustrated* and one of the Top 50 Sports Books of All Time by *The Guardian*. Throughout her career, Ryan has been awarded thirteen Associated Press Sports Editors awards, the National Headliner Award, the Women's Sports Foundation's Journalism Award, and the Edgar A. Poe Memorial Award for journalistic excellence from the White House Correspondents Association. She is a founding trustee of Coaching Corps in Oakland, California, and the Association of Women in Sports Media. Since 2008, she has been a media consultant with the San Francisco Giants.